DIANA'S BOYS

DIANA'S BOYS

*William and Harry
and the Mother They Loved*

CHRISTOPHER ANDERSEN

WHEELER
PUBLISHING, INC.
ROCKLAND, MA

★ AN AMERICAN COMPANY ★

Published in Large Print by arrangement with William Morrow, an imprint of HarperCollins Publishers Inc., in the United States and Canada.

Wheeler Large Print Book Series.

Set in 16 pt Plantin.

Grateful acknowledgment is made to the following for permission to reprint the photographs in this book.

Alpha/Globe Photos: 37, 38, 44, 47, 50, 51, 52, 55, 57, 58, 59, 61, 63, 67
AP/Wide World: 35, 36, 53, 64, 68
Corbis: 4, 43
Corbis-Sygma: 26, 27, 33
Patrick Demarchelier/Camera Press/Retna: 1
Tim Graham/Corbis-Sygma: 40, 42
Tim Graham/Sygma: 2, 7, 8
Globe Photos: 5, 14, 20, 22, 25, 28, 30
Jones/FSP.Liaison Agency: 34
Liaison Agency: 70
Retna: 9, 11, 18, 19, 31, 32, 45, 56, 60, 66
Rex: 3, 6, 10, 12, 13, 16, 17, 21, 23, 24, 29, 41, 46, 48, 62, 65, 69
Sipa Press: 15, 39, 49, 54

Library of Congress Cataloging-in-Publication Data

Andersen , Christopher P.
   Diana's boys: William and Harry and the mother they loved / Christopher Andersen.
        p. (large print) cm.(Wheeler large print book series)
   ISBN 1-58724-151-X (hardcover)
   1. William, Prince, grandson of Elizabeth II, Queen of Great Britain, 1982-. 2. Henry, Prince, grandson of Elizabeth II, Queen of Great Britain, 1984-. 3. Diana, Princess of Wales, 1961-1997—Family. 4. Princesses—Great Britain—Biography. 5. Princes—Great Britain—Biography. 6. Mothers and sons—Great Britain. 7. Large type books. I. Title. II. Series.

[DA591.A45 W5526 2001b]
941.085'0922—dc21   2001057015
[B]   CIP

For my mother, Jeanette Andersen

William and Harry are my one splendid achievement.

—Diana

Preface

The countless millions of Americans who dragged themselves out of bed at 5 A.M. to share the joy of Diana's storybook wedding to Prince Charles on television now rose somberly at the same early morning hour to mourn with the rest of humanity at the sight of her flag-draped casket in Westminster Abbey. No single image was more poignant than the bouquet of white rosebuds on the coffin. With the bouquet was Harry's handwritten note that read, simply, MUMMY.

—The Day Diana Died

That the beautiful, complicated Princess of Wales—arguably the most celebrated woman of the twentieth century—died so violently, so senselessly, and so young at age thirty-six was tragic. That she was a single mom leaving behind two emotionally vulnerable sons made Diana's death all the more heartbreaking.

Four years after Diana sped into a Paris tunnel with Dodi Fayed at her side and a drunk driver at the wheel, Prince William and his brother Prince Harry—"the heir and the spare," as Fleet Street slyly labeled them—remain the two most talked-about, written-about, and speculated-about young men on the planet. Even more important, people on both sides of the Atlantic feel an intense affection for "Wills" and Harry—and wonder if, absent their mother's loving influence, they will wither or flourish in the House of Windsor.

Our abiding interest in the fate of these two boys is rooted in America's endless fascination with the long-running soap opera that is and has always been the British Royal Family. From the six wives of Henry VIII to the Victorian Age to Edward VIII's abdication for "the woman I love," we have been riveted by the power and pomp, the valor and duplicity, the romance, the scandal, and the spectacle that have to one extent or another shaped much of Western civilization.

Notwithstanding the inexorable transoceanic pull of history and tradition, Elizabeth II's reign had always seemed duller than most. With the exception of her younger sister, Princess Margaret (whose own messy love life would be a precursor of things to come), and her son Prince Andrew's headline-making affair with soft-porn actress Koo Stark, the Windsors were by and large a tame and uninspiring lot.

Then came Diana. Over a seventeen-year period, the world watched her metamorphose from "Shy Di," the apple-cheeked English kindergarten aide with bowed head and bashful smile, into a dazzlingly glamorous, defiantly self-assured young woman determined to break down the barriers between the royals and their subjects.

Along the way, she made the perilous decision to go public with the sordid details of her disastrous marriage, as well as her depression, her suicide attempts, and her bulimia. Such unprecedented candor earned Diana the admiration and respect of millions who faced similar crises in their own lives. Even when it was revealed that she had responded to her husband's infidelity with extramarital affairs of her own, there was only sympathy for her plight.

Diana was the first member of the Royal Family to actually make a human connection with the suffering. She shook the hands of lepers, whispered soothing words to those in the final stages of cancer, cuddled crack babies, championed the cause of those horribly maimed by land mines, consoled battered wives, and embraced AIDS patients when others kept their distance.

Beauty, charm, a disarming mischievous streak, and an air of vulnerability—all contributed to the Princess of Wales's unrivaled appeal. So, too, did her sons. For all but her first year in the spotlight, Diana was a mother—a new breed of royal parent who did not hesitate to scoop her children up in her arms after returning home from a trip abroad or scream with exhilaration on an amusement park ride. Just as she was the first Windsor to make a human connection with the suffering, Diana was the first to connect with her own children.

From the beginning Diana, whose own mother walked out on her family when Diana was only five, vowed to raise her children on her own terms—and to form the sort of unbreakable mother-and-child bond heretofore virtually unknown in the royal household. It would not be easy. Not only did she face opposition from the infamous "men in gray"— Her Majesty's advisers at Buckingham Palace— but when it came to child-rearing issues she often found herself at odds with the Queen herself.

Still, the sight of William and Harry scampering across the lawn at the family's country estate or playfully sticking their tongues out at ever-present cameramen was somehow reassuring. Even as Charles and Diana lurched from one scandalous revelation to another, we took comfort in the fact that the boys at least appeared to be growing up happy and strong and, for the most part, unaffected by the chaos that swirled about them.

Unlike the royal children who went before them, William and Harry were not shielded from public view. So much of what we saw we recognized in our own children and, for that matter, in children everywhere. Parents sympathized when two-year-old William tried to flush his father's shoe down the toilet and when his brother's antics earned him the sobriquet "Harry the Horrible." As they gradually evolved from hellions into seemingly well-adjusted adolescents even as their parents waged open warfare on each other, we were relieved. For the British people, William represented far more—nothing less than the future of the monarchy.

The stage was set, then, for the next act in the saga of Diana's boys—though no one could have remotely imagined how stunning a turn the story would take. On that Sunday morning in August of 1997, millions awoke to the horrible news of Diana's death, and people around the world shared in the sense that they had lost a friend. No sooner did the initial shock set in than we realized that the two most famous boys in the world had lost their mother—and that, in the process, this senseless tragedy had forever altered the course of their lives.

From that moment on, mothers everywhere began to worry about Diana's sons. Any child who loses a parent—even if that child is the future king of England—feels powerless, particularly when it is the parent around whom that child's world revolved. The inevitable feelings of despair can have disastrous effects, ranging from depression, anxiety, and aggression to crippling fears of abandonment that can make it virtually impossible to sustain relationships with members of the opposite sex.

Over the past four years, the British press has scrupulously honored a request by the Royal Family that William and Harry be left alone to come to terms with their mother's death.

But the questions remain: Have they in fact healed? Are the boys, absent Diana's loving influence, simply growing up Windsor—destined like the generations before them to lead aimless lives of privileged self-indulgence, punctuated only by the occasional ribbon cutting or charity ball? Is the bond Diana forged with her sons in life disintegrating in death—severed by the "men in gray" whom she was convinced had conspired against her in life? Or has Diana's singular gift for touching others been inherited by her boys? And if so, how will this future king and his younger brother use the lessons their mother taught them to reshape the monarchy?

At nineteen, William is the mirror image of his mother: tall (six feet two inches), blond, athletic, and soft-spoken, with perpetually downcast Di-blue eyes. The physical resemblance between Diana and her redheaded Harry is less obvious, though he, no less than William, is above all else his mother's son. Indeed, whatever the future holds for the princes, it is unlikely that anyone—not even Charles—will ever exert a more profound influence on their lives and destinies than the woman they affectionately called "Mummy."

Beautiful, sensitive, headstrong, determined, *caring*—many of the same adjectives used to describe Diana are already being used to describe her sons. Yet for all their spirit and proven resilience, the daunting fact remains that the princes are up against the same powerful forces their mother could ultimately vanquish only in death.

Two months before the fatal crash in Paris, Diana confided to friends that she hoped William would ultimately handle the media with the same grace and ease as John F. Kennedy Jr. On hearing this, JFK Jr., whose own life would be cut tragically short in another senseless accident, insisted that the situations were not really comparable. The pressures on the boys, young Kennedy believed, were far greater and more relentless than any he had been forced to suffer through.

But parallels do, in fact, exist. We care about the William and Harry who marched through the streets of London behind their mother's casket for many of the same reasons we cared for the little American boy who bravely saluted his father's flag-draped coffin nearly forty years ago. John and Caroline Kennedy were, after all, America's answer to Britain's Royal Family—the Crown Prince and Princess of Camelot. For the Kennedys and Windsors alike, we hope they will not only survive their incomprehensible personal loss, but succeed in fulfilling their formidable legacy.

To be sure, Diana was a mind-spinning tangle of contradictions: brave yet riddled with doubt, worldly yet naive; shrewdly manipulative yet vulnerable, adored by millions yet sadly alone. She was, in a word, *human*—and never more so than when she was with William and Harry. The undeniable magic that was Diana lives on in the young princes, and that is why the world that mourned her will always care what happens to Diana's boys.

I'm just demented about my children,
and it's mutual.

—Diana

Her world was illuminated by her boys,
and her life revolved around them.

—Lord Palumbo,
Diana's friend

1

Sunday, August 31, 1997
12:21 A.M.

The black Mercedes S280 limousine hurtled through the streets of Paris, down the Rue Cambon and right onto the Rue de Rivoli. Only seconds had passed before it came to a screeching stop at the Rue Royale, but already a pack of photographers in cars and on motorcycles had managed to catch up, and were gunning their engines in anticipation of the chase.

Suddenly, the Mercedes carrying the Princess of Wales and her Egyptian-born lover, Dodi Fayed, jumped the light and swung left on the Place de la Concorde. The mother of the future British sovereign, trying to elude the press that hounded her every waking moment, now passed the spot where the guillotine had brought a bloody end to France's monarchy.

The limousine picked up speed as it paralleled the Seine along the Cours-la-Reine ("Queen's Course"), pressing its occupants against the backs of their plush leather seats. Approaching the Alma Tunnel, Diana could see the chestnut trees strung with twinkling white lights, and looming to the left the brightly illuminated Eiffel Tower, now counting down the number of days to the new millennium in lights forty feet high. Another motorist estimated the Mercedes's speed at 110 miles per hour. "The car was flying as it passed me," taxi driver Michel Lemmonier would later recall. "It was like the hounds of hell. There could be only one ending…"

Hitting a sharp dip at the tunnel entrance, the car was catapulted into the air, then slammed down on the surface of the roadway. Swerving wildly to the left to avoid striking a white Fiat in its path, the Mercedes clipped the compact car's bumper before Fayed's driver lost control. In an instant, the Mercedes plowed headlong into one of the eighteen concrete pillars that divided the thoroughfare. The car then spun 180 degrees counter-clockwise before slamming into the tunnel wall.

Of the four people inside, only one—Fayed's bodyguard Trevor Rees-Jones—was wearing a seat belt. Dodi and his driver, Henri Paul, died instantly. Diana, her earrings torn away by the impact of the crash, lay on the floor behind the front seat.

Henri Paul's body leaned against the horn, sounding a shrill alarm. The tunnel filled with smoke; there was broken glass every-where. Dr. Frédéric Mailliez, a boyish-looking thirty-six-year-old emergency physician, just happened to be driving by on his way home from a friend's birthday party. Mailliez got out of his white Ford Fiesta and rushed to the twisted wreckage of the Mercedes. "Shit!" he thought as he saw the mangled corpses of Dodi and Henri Paul.

While a volunteer fireman comforted the gravely injured Rees-Jones, Mailliez went to help the blond woman slumped in the back. He lifted Diana's head and gave her oxygen using an "Ambu"—a French-manufactured portable oxygen mask—but did not recognize her. "I was too busy," he later explained, "doing my job."

By now more than a dozen photographers were standing nearby, firing off flash after flash—"like machine-gun fire," Officer Lino Gagliardone recalled. Mailliez whispered words of reassurance to Diana, first in French and then—after photographers shouted that the woman was from England—in English. She cried out in pain, and occasionally mumbled something, but the young doctor was too immersed in trying to save her life to stop and decipher precisely what she was saying.

Her sons could not have been far from her mind. Harry would turn thirteen in less than two weeks, and she had wanted to buy a birthday present for him in Paris. But the hordes of press that had descended on the Princess and her new boyfriend made that all but impossible. A virtual prisoner inside her suite at Paris's legendary Ritz Hotel, Diana instead dispatched a hotel staffer to purchase the Sony Playstation Harry had asked for.

Even more fresh in Diana's mind was what she regarded as her most important conversation of the day. William had called just before dinner that evening, concerned about a photo opportunity arranged by Buckingham Palace. William was about to start his third year at Eton, the exclusive prep school, and the Palace had ordered him to pose at the school for photographers from Britain's major news organizations. But he worried that such a staged event might overshadow his younger brother. "I'm just afraid Harry might feel left out," he told his mother, and she agreed. Diana promised William that as soon as she returned to London the next day, she would talk to Prince Charles and they would all come up with a plan that would spare Harry's feelings. "First thing Monday..."

Within six minutes, a rescue unit was on the scene. The mangled bodies of Dodi and Paul were extracted from the wreckage. A bright blue tarpaulin was then placed around the car to shield it from onlookers as firemen with electric chain saws cut away at what remained of the car to free Diana and Rees-Jones.

As the firemen prepared to lift her from the car and place her gently on a waiting stretcher, the Princess of Wales spoke what would be her last intelligible words.

"My God," Diana asked, "what's happened?"

Six hundred miles away at Balmoral, fifteen-year-old William sat bolt upright in his bed. Exhausted from a full day spent fishing the River Dee with his father and his brother, William had buttoned up his tartan plaid pajamas and crawled beneath the covers a little before 11:30 P.M. But over the course of the next few hours, he would fall asleep only to be jolted awake again and again by a sudden, over-powering sense of dread. "I knew something was wrong," William would later say. "I kept waking up all night."

Harry, meanwhile, slept soundly in his room just down the hall. He and his brother loved their summer holidays at Balmoral, reveling in the time spent hunting grouse, riding, and fishing with their father—royal pas-times that appealed to Diana not at all. Now the boys, who had not seen their mother for more than a month, planned to rejoin her at Kensington Palace the next day. Over dinner that evening, they had spoken of how eager they were to see her again. Their belongings had already been packed for the trip to London and were waiting downstairs.

Prince Charles was also sleeping like a baby. Literally. Of all the Windsor men, only Charles, then forty-eight, always went to bed with a stuffed animal—the ragged teddy bear of his childhood that traveled with him every-where, even on state visits. (So devoted was Prince Charles to his teddy bear that when-ever the stuffing began poking out, only his childhood nanny, Mabel Anderson, was per-mitted to make the necessary repairs.)

While William tossed and Harry slept peacefully, the phone at Charles's bedside rang at shortly after 1 A.M. English time. It was Robin Janvrin, the Queen's deputy private secretary, who had just been called by Britain's ambassador to France with the disturbing news.

"I'm sorry to awaken you, sir," Janvrin said, "but I've just received a telephone call from Sir Michael Jay in Paris. It seems there's been an accident. It appears the Princess of Wales has been injured, sir..."

"An accident in Paris?" Charles replied uncomprehendingly. "Diana?"

Janvrin told Charles what little he knew—that the Prince's ex-wife had been injured in a Paris car crash that had killed Dodi and their driver. Charles then called the woman he always turned to—his longtime mistress and Diana's archrival, Camilla Parker Bowles. She reminded him that Diana was in peak physical condition and always wore a seat belt. Camilla reassured her lover that his ex-wife was probably going to be just fine.

Charles then asked the Balmoral switchboard operator, whose thick brogue Diana had so wickedly mimicked, to put him through to the Queen's bedroom. For now, the Queen and Charles agreed, there was no reason to upset the boys. There would be more details about their mother's condition in the morning, and at the moment nothing would be gained by robbing them of a decent night's rest. With that, Her Majesty hung up the phone and went back to sleep.

Charles, unaware that William was still wide awake upstairs, got dressed, went into the private sitting room adjacent to his bedroom, and switched on the radio. He was soon joined by the Queen's private secretary, Sir Robert Fellowes, who also happened to be Diana's brother-in-law. At 3:30 A.M. local time, Charles was listening to Peter Allen of Britain's Radio 5 report that Diana had suffered a concussion and a broken arm, when Fellowes decided to call the Paris hospital where she was being treated for an update on her condition.

Fellowes was totally unprepared for what he was about to hear. Diana, a British Embassy official at the hospital told him in a voice choked with emotion, had died on the operating table.

It was then that Charles's lingering depth of feeling for the mother of his children became stunningly evident to those in the room. "Who would ever believe me if I described the Prince's reaction?" said one witness. "He uttered a cry of pain that was spontaneous and came from the heart, before breaking into uncontrollable sobs." Charles's anguished cries brought other members of the royal household running.

Not William and Harry, however, who remained oblivious to the commotion downstairs. Charles sat weeping with his head in his hands, too distraught to speak. Fellowes then told the Queen, whom he described as "clearly very upset" at hearing the news. In truth,

17

others at the castle would later describe the Queen's demeanor as "cold" and "detached." While even those Palace loyalists who detested Diana made no effort to conceal red-rimmed eyes, the Queen and her husband, Prince Philip, showed an astonishing lack of emotion.

Not that Charles was surprised at his parents' chilly response. For words of solace, the Prince of Wales would have to turn once again to Camilla. He called her a second time and told her that Diana had died of her injuries. "Oh, those poor, poor children!" Camilla said of William and Harry. She had never actually met them, but Charles had confided in her about virtually every detail of their lives.

Camilla, overcome with emotion despite her highly publicized rivalry with Diana for Charles's affections, broke down. She knew Diana's death would almost certainly turn the public against her in ever greater numbers, but insisted nonetheless that Charles focus on ways to help his sons cope with the shock of losing their mother. "Forget about me and concentrate on the boys," Camilla told Charles. "They need you."

Even as Charles and Camilla sobbed on the phone (a scene that no doubt would have confounded Diana), Father Yves Clochard-Bossuet was in a second-floor room at Paris's Pitié-Salpêtrière Hospital administering Last Rites to the Princess of Wales. Father Clochard-Bossuet felt he might collapse as he closed Diana's eyes, anointed her forehead and palms with holy oil, and prayed beside her. "All I could think of," he later said, "was the sadness of this young woman dying when she had everything to live for. I prayed for her sons, William and Harry."

Back at Balmoral, Charles's first instinct was to do what Diana would have done—wake up their sons, then hold and console them in their moment of grief. But before Charles could act on this most human of impulses, his mother summoned him to her sitting room. The Queen still saw no reason to wake the boys. Their mother was gone and there was nothing they could do about it now. Let them have this one last night of innocence.

Charles surrendered on this point. He would break it to them first thing in the morning, though he could not imagine how he would find the strength to do it. "I was paralyzed, terrified at the thought of putting them through such pain," he later told a confidant. "I kept thinking, 'I cannot do this. I cannot do this.' But of course I had to be the one."

But Charles would soon find himself distracted by other issues—notably how the Royal Family would react to the news of Diana's death and what role her ex-husband would play in the mourning process. It was quickly decided that Diana's sisters, Lady Jane Fellowes and Lady Sarah McCorquodale, would fly to Paris and accompany her body back to RAF Northolt, the royal air base northwest of London. After talking it over with their mother, Frances Shand Kydd, and their brother, Charles Spencer, it was agreed that the funeral would be a private Spencer family affair.

The Prince of Wales called Lady Sarah and Lady Jane and told them that he would accompany them to Paris and escort his ex-wife's body home to England. The Queen, however, objected strenuously. She told her son that it would be inappropriate for him even to be at RAF Northolt to meet the plane when it returned, much less fly to Paris to claim Diana's body.

For the first time in his life, Charles defied his mother. Backed by Prime Minister Tony Blair ("This is going to bring public grief on a scale that is hard to imagine," he warned Charles), the Prince of Wales argued forcefully that there would be a public backlash if no member of the Royal Family made the trip to Paris. Grudgingly, Her Majesty acquiesced and gave Charles permission to make the trip.

For the next two hours, Charles paced the floor alone in his sitting room while William and Harry slept. Shortly before dawn, he pulled on a sweater and went out for a solitary walk along the moors. A member of the household staff at Balmoral would later say Prince Charles's eyes were "red and swollen from weeping" when he returned to the castle.

William was already awake when he heard a gentle knock on his door shortly after 7 A.M. As soon as he saw his father, the young prince knew there was a reason he had been tossing and turning all night. Charles sat on the edge of William's bed and told him what had happened that morning in Paris. Then father and son, eschewing Britain's stiff-upper-lip tradition, did something unthinkable to past generations of royals—they held each other and cried.

Now William, who had told his mother during their last conversation that he worried a photo opportunity might hurt his brother's feelings, asked his father how they were going to tell Harry. But there was no easy way. Harry was sound asleep in an adjoining bedroom when his protective older brother led the way into his room and, sitting on the edge of his bed, gently woke the younger prince. Together, Charles and William told him that there had been a terrible accident in Paris, that his mother had been taken to the hospital with severe injuries, and that doctors worked for hours to save her. But they couldn't... Then the three Windsor men wept unashamedly, their sobs audible to household staff and aides standing in the hallway.

William and Harry embraced their father and listened as he sputtered words of comfort. While the public knew that the boys had a warm and loving relationship with their mother, few realized that Charles also lavished affection on them. Nowhere did the family ties seem stronger than when all three princes were at Balmoral, hunting, fishing, and riding together. Evenings were spent reading Kipling or watching videos, and the fact that the boys were now both teenagers did not prevent Charles from continuing to kiss his sons good night.

William and Harry took their father's hand, and the three princes walked to a sitting room where the Queen and Prince Philip were waiting. Seated on a couch on either side of their father, the boys wiped away tears as Charles offered what few details he could.

"Granny," as the princes called the Queen, did not hug them. There was not a moment when she lost her composure. This was to be expected. As fond as she was of William and Harry—and they of her—there was never any physical contact beyond a formal handshake. Still, over the usual 9 A.M. breakfast, both the Queen and Prince Philip went so far as to tell the boys how "terribly sorry" they were that their mother had been killed.

The Queen did not mention what other things she had on her mind. Even before she sat down with her grandsons at the breakfast table that morning and offered her few words of comfort, Her Majesty had been in contact with the British Embassy asking questions of her own. She wanted to know if the Princess of Wales had in her possession any royal jewels at the time of her death. If so, these were the property of the Crown and, the Queen insisted, were to be turned over to the proper British authorities without delay.

At Pitié-Salpêtrière Hospital, the message

would be delivered to the staff in no uncertain terms. One official of the British Embassy rushed into the blue-walled room where Diana lay naked under a sheet and, seemingly unmindful of the body, shouted at nurse Béatrice Humbert, "Madame, the Queen is worried about the jewelry. We must find the jewelry, quickly! *The Queen wants to know, 'Where are the jewels?'* "

As the world began to wake up to the grim news, Charles thought it best that the boys be allowed to grieve in private. But again, the Queen, spurred on by her advisers, thought differently. A believer in both the healing power of mindless routine and the importance of maintaining appearances, Her Majesty saw no reason for any alteration in the daily schedule of the Royal Family. She wanted everyone—including the boys—to attend church as usual that morning.

"At the time, the Queen had no idea of the *people's* deep affection for Diana—how much they truly loved her," said the Princess's close friend and confidante Lady Elsa Bowker. "But I think the Queen did appreciate that it would be very difficult for Diana's boys. She did want them spared any 'unpleasantness,' as she would say." Toward that end, newspapers were temporarily banned from Balmoral and orders were given to disconnect all televisions and radios inside the castle.

The Queen had also instructed the switchboard at Balmoral to hold all calls for the boys. One was from model Cindy Crawford, who at William's urging had been invited to tea at Kensington Palace. ("He's just like me," Diana told Crawford after the Prince and the supermodel met. "When he runs out of things to say, he just blushes.") In the weeks before the accident, Crawford had been talking to Diana about surprising the boys with a holiday in Switzerland. Crawford, who now considered herself a friend of William's, was calling to console him.

"He will be in pieces," Crawford said of William. "He adored his mother. He considered her to be his best friend."

The news blackout at Balmoral notwithstanding, Charles had already told the boys that their mother was being pursued at high speed by paparazzi at the time of the crash. Paris police fueled speculation that the press had caused the fatal accident when they arrested six photographers at the scene.

Diana's younger brother, Charles, now Earl Spencer, having inherited their father's title, had moved to South Africa in part to escape from the same British tabloid press. Only hours after learning of his sister's death, Earl Spencer would read a scathing statement to reporters gathered outside the gates of his Cape Town compound. "I had always believed," he told them, "that the press would kill her in the end. But not even I could imagine that they would take such a direct hand in her death as seems to be the case. It would appear that every publication that has paid for intrusive and exploitative photographs of her, encouraging greedy and ruthless individuals to risk everything in pursuit of Diana's image, has blood on their hands today. Finally, the one consolation is that Diana is now in a place where no human being can ever touch her again. I pray that she rest in peace."

In recent years William and Harry, the darlings of Fleet Street, had become increasingly suspicious of the press. After all, their parents, perhaps more than any other married couple in modern times, had seen every sordid detail of their private lives splashed across the front pages of tabloids throughout the world. If the initial stories were true and the press was proven guilty of chasing Diana to her death, then there was the very real possibility that William and Harry might shrink from their public duties.

For that reason alone Queen Elizabeth, ever mindful of what effect this might all have on the future of the monarchy, swept aside her son's objections and insisted that her grandsons prepare for church. Meantime, she issued a terse statement to the public that would stand in sharp contrast to the eloquent expressions of bereavement being offered by heads of state around the world. "The Queen and Prince of Wales," read the fifteen-word press release, "are deeply shocked and distressed by this terrible news."

William and Harry, immersed in their own shock and grief, were understandably confused by their grandmother's demands. But they were accustomed, as were all royals with the exception of their mother, to follow those commands blindly.

Shortly after 11 A.M., three black Rolls-Royce limousines pulled up to Crathie Church, just across the River Dee from Balmoral. The Queen Mother, ninety-seven, arrived in the first car. She was accompanied by the boys' uncle Prince Andrew and their cousin Peter Phillips, son of Princess Anne.

William and Harry sat in the back of the second limousine, seated on either side of their father. The boys looked, said one church-goer, "shocked and pale, but calm." Another onlooker along the walkway to the small stone church was impressed with the way Charles, his face clearly etched with grief, focused on his sons. "His attention was on William and Harry. They kept staring at the ground and never looked up. Harry looked saddest of all."

William and Harry were greeted by the Reverend Robert Sloan, who was "struck by the way they seemed to be bearing up. It was clear they had gone through great grief and trauma."

Sloan did not deliver the sermon that morning, but turned over the proceedings to a visiting minister, the Reverend Adrian Varwell from Benbecula in the Outer Hebrides. Varwell went ahead with the lighthearted sermon he originally intended to deliver. As was the case every Sunday, prayers were said for the Royal Family. The Queen, the Prince of Wales, and the princes William and Harry were mentioned by name. But not Diana, whom the Queen had stripped of her royal status at the time she divorced Charles. Moreover, the Queen had decreed after the split that she did not want Diana's name spoken in her presence.

This morning when the world was talking about only one thing, the two most important people in Diana's life sat waiting in vain for some mention of their mother. It would never come. Diana's death was being ignored, explained the Reverend Sloan, "to protect the boys. The children had been awakened just a few hours earlier to be told of the death of their mother and we did not wish to disturb them further."

"What could her boys have been thinking?" asked another churchgoer. "I wouldn't have been surprised if they both jumped up and screamed, 'What is going on?' I know I felt like doing that."

At one point during the service, Harry turned to his father and whispered, "Are you sure Mummy is dead?"

Back at Balmoral, Diana's boys lit up when they saw who was waiting for them. The down-to-earth, fun-loving Tiggy Legge-Bourke had been their nanny until Diana, complaining that Tiggy had grown too close to her sons, maneuvered her out of the picture.

Jealousy aside, Tiggy had always been more of a tomboyish older sister to the boys; without informing Diana, Charles had invited her to spend the last two weeks of August hunting, fishing, riding, and generally cavorting with the boys. She had planned to fly home to Wales that weekend, but now, at Charles's request, Tiggy agreed to remain with William and Harry "as long as they need me."

That afternoon, Charles faced the grim task of flying to Paris with his sisters-in-law and bringing Diana home. "I want to come with you," William told his father. "I should be there."

"No," replied Charles. "You must stay here with Harry."

"We'll both come with you," William insisted.

Charles shook his head. Not only would the Queen never allow it, but he did not yet want to subject either of his sons to the heart-breaking ordeal of actually seeing their mother's coffin. "William, Harry can't be left alone. He needs for one of us to be here..." It was all Charles needed to say to convince the devoted elder brother to remain behind.

Judging by Charles's own reaction when confronted with the reality of Diana's death, he was wise to leave the children at home. On first seeing Diana's lifeless body lying in an open casket at Pitié-Salpêtrière Hospital, the Prince "recoiled," recalled nurse Béatrice Humbert. "He drew back his head in one involuntary motion, as though he had actually been stricken. As though he simply couldn't take it in. He couldn't believe it. You could feel his immense sorrow."

Arriving back at Northolt air base at 6:51

that evening, a visibly shaken Charles, Lady Jane and Lady Sarah, Tony Blair, and other dignitaries stood as Diana's coffin, still draped in the lions and harps of the royal standard, was carried off the plane by an RAF honor guard.

An international audience of hundreds of millions watched the moving scene on television, but not Diana's own sons. Back in Scotland, William and Harry remained virtually cut off from the outside world.

Still, they were aware of the tension brewing between the Prince of Wales and the Queen over their mother's funeral. The Prime Minister had told Charles it would be a "fatal mistake" for the monarchy if plans went forward for a small private funeral. "The people," Blair warned, "simply will not stand for it."

But the Queen was adamant in her opposition to any special treatment for Diana. A full state funeral was intended only for kings and queens, though by order of the monarchy and a vote in Parliament this could be extended to such beloved leaders as Winston Churchill. This was out of the question in Diana's case, though there was precedent for a private royal funeral attended only by members of the extended Royal Family. But this would only leave the public feeling, in Blair's words, "cheated."

While William and Harry sat down to dinner with the rest of the Royal Family at Balmoral, their mother's body was taken to a private mortuary, where it was autopsied by the Fulham coroner. Then Diana was clothed in a simple, long-sleeved black coatdress and gently placed in the coffin. A snapshot of her beloved father and the rosary given to her by Mother Teresa were placed in Diana's folded hands—along with the photograph of William and Harry that she had carried with her wherever she went.

From the mortuary, Diana was then moved to the Chapel Royal at St. James's Palace in London. Ironically, she would lie in state in the palace she most despised because it housed the offices of her ex-husband and his hostile staff.

It had been scarcely twelve hours since William and Harry were told of their mother's death, yet no mention was made of the tragedy over dinner at Balmoral. In a genuine if misguided effort to buoy her grandsons' spirits, the Queen steered the conversation toward the stag hunt scheduled for that week. On his return to Balmoral later that evening, Charles was appalled to learn that the Queen intended for life to go on at Balmoral as if nothing had happened.

Shortly before 10 P.M., the boys, still numb from the day's events, spent an hour consoling each other in Harry's room before going to bed. The next day, they awoke to news relayed to them by their father that much of London was engulfed in a tide of flowers. In addition to bouquets left at palace gates and monuments, blossoms were tied to lampposts, trash bins, park benches, and even tree branches.

Over the next few days, the mountains of

flowers around the palaces seemed to grow exponentially. Buckingham Palace, where guards at first refused to allow mourners to leave flowers at the gates, quickly became a focal point of growing resentment toward the royals. The public was demanding to know why, when virtually every other flag in the country was flying at half-mast, the flag over Buckingham Palace was not.

They also wanted to know why the Queen, whose subjects were clearly in pain over the death of the "People's Princess," remained sequestered 550 miles away in a Scottish castle. SHOW US YOU CARE, pleaded the normally ultra-loyal *Express*. The *Mirror* blared, SPEAK TO US MA'AM—YOUR PEOPLE ARE SUFFERING, while the *Sun* asked, WHERE IS OUR QUEEN? WHERE IS HER FLAG?

As much as he cherished the seclusion of Balmoral, William shared in his countrymen's bewilderment. "Why are we here," he asked his father, "when Mummy's in London?"

Already polls showed that two out of three Britons believed Diana's death would bring down the monarchy. There were calls for Charles to step aside in favor of Diana's elder son.

To be sure, William had his mother's knack for reading the mood of the people—an ability not shared by the other royals. "Charles knows the Royal Family must change," one senior Labour MP said. "The only trouble is that, unlike Diana, he does not instinctively understand how that should happen."

William did—so much so that in recent years Diana had come to rely on his advice. The hugely successful auction of her gowns, which raised $3.26 million for charity in June of 1997, had been William's idea. He had also urged her to go ahead with her anti-land-mine campaign despite criticism that such weighty issues were really not her affair.

Now Charles, confronted with the fact that his mother had dangerously underestimated the depth of her people's fondness for Diana, turned to William for advice. Every afternoon the three princes walked for several hours around the Balmoral grounds, with the Prince of Wales's Jack Russell terrier Tigger in tow. Away from his mother's loyal courtiers, Charles briefed William and Harry on the details of the funeral. He also voiced his concerns and asked for their input.

Harry still struggled with his loss. But William "wanted to know," as one Balmoral staff member recalled. "William wanted to know about the telegrams, who has written and what they are saying. He is not shying away from what he sees as his responsibility."

Nor was William shy about voicing his own opinions. Again, he wanted to know why the Royal Family gave the appearance of hiding in Scotland, and why the Queen had remained silent; not a syllable had been uttered since that first fifteen-word statement issued by the Palace the day of the tragedy. William also wanted to know why royal protocol—which dictates that the Union Jack fly over Buckingham

Palace only when the sovereign is in residence—had not been bent so that the flag could be flown at half-mast in honor of his mother.

Granny would not be budged. Even if she were to decide to return to Buckingham Palace, the Queen would not allow the flag to be flown at half-mast, something that historically had only been done to signify the death of the monarch. It had not been done for Winston Churchill, and the Queen was not about to do it for her problematic former daughter-in-law.

As plans for the funeral procession through the streets of London began to take shape, William insisted on one thing above all else: no matter what the length of the route or the conditions, he and Harry would march behind their mother's coffin. The Queen, worried that a two-mile march in the summer heat would be too taxing for her grandsons, at first vetoed the idea. But William had made it clear that this demand was, in Charles's word, "non-negotiable."

While Papa tried to convince Granny to return to London, William spent most of his time explaining what it all meant to his little brother. "It is touching how William and Prince Harry have pulled together when their world is falling apart," a royal insider told veteran British journalist Robert Jobson. "Diana would have been very proud. They are very, very brave."

"It is just too sad for words," concurred one

of the Queen's own advisers. "But everyone is struck by Prince William's strength of character. He really is a remarkable young man who has shown he has great courage."

Enough courage to urge his father to stand up to the Queen. Backed by Prime Minister Tony Blair, Charles convinced his mother to agree to a televised public service at Westminster Abbey—neither a state funeral nor a royal funeral, but something unique befitting the lady herself. The Prince of Wales also pressured Her Majesty into extending the funeral procession an extra mile to accommodate the hundreds of thousands of people who were flooding into London to pay their respects to the young woman they were now calling their "Queen of Hearts." Appropriately, the cortege would begin in front of Kensington Palace, where Diana had lived with her two young sons.

Despite these concessions, Charles cautioned his mother that she might be jeered at at the funeral. Scotland Yard officials, aware of mounting resentment toward the Crown, now worried that the monarch might actually be attacked.

Charles delivered an ultimatum to his mother: The Queen must address her people, and she must command that the flag be flown at half-mast over Buckingham Palace. If she refused, Charles himself would publicly apologize for the Crown's seemingly callous disregard for the citizenry's suffering.

The Queen, stung by the realization that she

had indeed misjudged the depth of affection her people had for Diana, agreed. On Thursday the young princes, wearing suits and black ties, ventured outside with their father to greet well-wishers at the entrance to Balmoral. Oddly, Charles chose to don kilts and pink knee socks for the occasion. The Queen, dressed in more appropriate mourning black, joined them.

William, brushing a lock of blond hair from his face and shyly averting his eyes from the crowd, bent down and examined the bouquets and notes left at the castle gates. Harry, still visibly shaken, held tight to his father's hand as he knelt down to carefully read the notes. "William and Harry, live your lives in her spirit," read one. Another praised Diana as "a truly remarkable, vibrant young woman. As sons of this courageous, compassionate sister of mercy," it continued, "I hope they will stand strong and proud as befitting our young princes."

As they looked over the notes and flowers, the Queen made a special point of chatting with her grandchildren. Prince Philip, who also wore kilts, pointed a particular note out to William. It read, "William and Harry, I hope God gives you the strength to get through the rest of your lives. Your mum will always watch over you both."

The next day, the Royal Family departed Balmoral for London. Outside Buckingham Palace, the Queen and her husband once again surveyed more of the bouquets, stuffed animals, and heartfelt notes left in honor of Diana. Later, with thousands of mourners clearly visible from the palace balcony behind her, the Queen looked squarely into the television camera and addressed her people. "What I say to you now as your Queen and as a grandmother," she said, "I say from my heart. First, I want to pay tribute to Diana myself. She was an exceptional and gifted human being. In good times and bad, she never lost her capacity to smile and laugh, to inspire others with her warmth and kindness. I admired and respected her for her energy and commitment to others, especially for her devotion to her two boys." The Royal Family had remained at Balmoral, she explained, for no other reason than to help William and Harry cope with the "devastating loss" of their mother.

Across London at Kensington Palace, where Diana had lived with her sons, the appearance of William and Harry triggered a sudden outpouring of emotion. As the shyly handsome William expressed his gratitude to the crowd, women reached out merely to touch him. Others, overcome with emotion, broke down after kissing his hand. "Thank you for coming," William said, managing a wan smile. "Thank you."

Anti-land-mine activist Jerry White, who had accompanied Diana on her recent trip to Bosnia, was introduced to William for the first time that day at Kensington Palace. "His sweetness and mannerisms are like Diana's,"

White said. "He had a kind spirit and a kind smile. It was déjà vu. His mother was in him."

Diana had known it too. "When you discover you can give joy to people, there is nothing quite like it," she had said only weeks before her death. "William has begun to understand that, too. And I am hoping it will grow in him." Observed her friend Richard Greene, "Diana felt in many ways that William was a male version of her."

That night, the princes joined their father at St. James's Palace. Over the past five days, more than one million people had waited for up to twelve hours to sign condolence books outside the Chapel Royal where her body lay in state.

Each night butler Paul Burrell, the man Diana called "my rock," sat by the coffin reading aloud from her favorite books, telling her the stories and the jokes that had made her sob with laughter. "I just don't want her to be alone," Burrell told Diana's hairdresser Natalie Symonds.

Now, on the eve of her funeral, Diana's boys would be with her. Charles led William and Harry into the Chapel Royal and up to Diana's coffin, still covered with the red, gold, blue, and white flag bearing the royal coat of arms.

Tentatively, the boys stepped up to the bier. An aide to the Prince of Wales pulled back the flag, and the coffin lid was carefully lifted to reveal Diana, serenely beautiful, the photos of her sons and her father and the rosary from Mother Teresa clasped in her alabaster hands. Tears streamed down William's face at the sight of his mother; Harry, trembling, refused to look.

After only a few fleeting seconds, the coffin lid was gently closed. William then carefully arranged a spray of white tulips at the head of the coffin, while Harry placed a wreath of white roses he had chosen at the opposite end. Atop the wreath was the square white card on which Harry had simply and boldly written MUMMY.

The next morning at nine, William and Harry stood in the late-summer sun outside St. James's Palace, waiting for their mother's coffin to come into view so they could begin what would be the longest walk of their young lives. They were flanked by their father, their grandfather Prince Philip, and their uncle Earl Spencer. Prince Charles whispered a few words of encouragement to his sons, but stopped when he heard the muffled hoof-beats of approaching horses.

Across the globe, an audience of more than 2.5 billion tuned in to watch the solemn progress of Diana's cortege through the eerily silent streets of London and the funeral service at Westminster Abbey. No single event in history was ever witnessed by so many people simultaneously.

William hitched up his pants, and with the other five men walked slowly and deliberately toward the cortege. Even though London seemed to have been engulfed in a tsunami of flowers, only a single red rose lay in the road as the Windsor men and Diana's brother began their interminable journey.

It seemed at times that all 1.5 million mourners who lined the route were weeping. But William and Harry walked resolutely alone, oblivious to the sobs as they passed by. "As the boys appeared," one mourner observed, "everybody who was near them averted their eyes. If you had thought about Diana's sons for six days, to look at them now was impossible. People stared at the road, waiting for the coffin to pass."

William, who quickly fell into lockstep with the Welsh Guards in front of him, looked numb, his eyes riveted to the ground, shielded by his trademark blond fringe. Even twelve-year-old Harry, dwarfed by the men around him, cast a giant shadow in the slanting late-summer sunlight. But Harry, trying hard to keep pace, also fought hard to keep from breaking down. For the entire length of the procession, the youngest prince walked with his arms stiffly at his sides, his small hands clenched into tight fists. So tight, in fact, that even spectators could see from the roadside that his fingernails were digging into his palms.

The cortege moved down the mall past St. James's Park toward the government offices at Whitehall—epicenter of the British Establishment that had resisted the Princess of Wales's immense popularity. Harry's mounting anxiety did not go unnoticed by the other princes and his uncle. But, not wanting to embarrass the little prince in public, they made no effort to comfort him until the cortege was temporarily out of view as it passed under Horse Guards Arch. Then, Charles leaned over and whispered a few tender words to Harry as Earl Spencer reached over and put his arm around the boy's shoulder.

Then they stepped out from under the arch and back into the sunlight. Harry, bolstered by his father's words and the pat on the back from his uncle, managed to look composed as the procession moved past Downing Street and the Houses of Parliament. But as Westminster Abbey loomed ahead, its bells tolling mournfully, Harry's bottom lip began to tremble. His nails, digging in even harder, had begun to draw blood.

As they stepped into the abbey, a strange calm seemed to come over Harry as he stared straight at the coffin. In addition to the white tulips and white roses the boys had placed on the lid, there were now thirty-six white lilies—one for each year of Diana's life. William, who like Harry now stood with his hands clasped in front of him, could not bring himself to look; he continued to stare straight down, reaching up once with his right hand to brush away a tear.

Inside, the more than two thousand mourners covered the spectrum from music, fashion, and film superstars to land-mine victims, cancer survivors, world leaders, and battered wives. The coffin was brought to the center of the nave, and all eyes were on the boys as they joined their father in laying a wreath at the foot of the catafalque. As the princes took their seats with the rest of the royals, Harry looked to his right where his then-ninety-seven-year-old great-grandmother was sitting. The Queen Mother smiled back reassuringly.

No sooner had the Reverend Wesley Carr, Dean of Westminster, begun the service than the strains of "I Vow to Thee My Country" filled the cathedral, said one guest, "like thunder." William had insisted it be the first hymn sung; it had been a favorite of his mother's since she was a schoolgirl.

The Palace had objected to a rock star performing in Westminster Abbey, but when Diana's friend Elton John sat down at the piano to play his tribute to the Princess, "Candle in the Wind 1997," no one was unmoved. (The song, originally an homage to Marilyn Monroe, had been revised for Diana and would fast become the top-selling single of all time.)

John could only keep from breaking down by playing with his eyes closed. When he reached the line "Your candle burned out long before your legend ever will," Harry buried his face in his hands and wept. Next to him, William sat with his head bowed, crying freely.

By the time Diana's brother stood up to deliver his stirring and pointedly provocative eulogy, the level of emotional tension was, said one mourner, "unbearable." Earl Spencer renewed his attack on the press and then, within a few yards of the Queen, leveled an attack on the House of Windsor itself.

William and Harry looked on as Spencer described their mother as "someone with a natural nobility" who proved "that she needed no royal title to continue to generate her particular brand of magic."

Then he turned his attention to the boys. Blaming Diana's death on an avaricious press, Spencer claimed that "she would want us today to pledge ourselves to protecting her beloved boys William and Harry from a similar fate and I do this here. Diana, on your behalf, we will not allow them to suffer the anguish that used regularly to drive you to tearful despair. And beyond that, on behalf of your mother and sisters, I pledge that we, your blood family, will do all we can to continue the imaginative way in which you were steering these two exceptional young men so that their souls are not simply immersed by duty and tradition but can sing openly as you planned.

"We fully respect the heritage into which they have both been born and will always respect and encourage them in their royal role. But we, like you, recognize the need for them to experience as many different aspects of life as possible to arm them spiritually and emotionally for the years ahead. I know you would have expected nothing less from us."

Then, looking directly at the boys, he continued, "William and Harry, we all care desperately for you today. We are all chewed up at the sadness of the loss of a woman who was not even our mother. How great your suffering is, we cannot even imagine..."

Spencer's voice began to crack with emotion as he thanked God "for the small mercies he has shown us at this dreadful time. For taking Diana at her most beautiful and radiant and when she had joy in her private life. Above all we give thanks for the life of...the unique, the complex, the extraordinary and irreplaceable Diana—whose beauty, both internal and external, will never be extinguished from our minds." Outside the cathedral, hundreds of thousands of people watching the service on jumbo television screens burst into applause. While the Queen and her immediate family sat in stony silence, those inside the abbey—including William and Harry—joined in the applause.

Nine days later, on the morning of September 15, a car carrying Lady Sarah McCorquodale pulled up to the gates of Ludgrove, the elite prep school Prince Harry attended in Berkshire. She was there to keep a promise.

Moments later, Lady Sarah hugged her redheaded nephew and handed him a brightly wrapped package along with an envelope. Inside the package was the Sony Playstation he had wanted for his thirteenth birthday. Harry opened the card slowly. It read, simply:

HAPPY BIRTHDAY, HARRY.
LOVE, MUMMY.

I hug my children to death.
I get into bed with them at night and hug
them and say who loves them most in
the whole world, and they always say,
"Mummy."

—*Diana*

I do love having children around me. It gives life to a house.

—*Diana*

He needs to be treated differently because he is different. It's no good Diana pretending he can have a normal life, because he can't.

—*Barbara Barnes, William's first nanny*

2

I will do it, Charles," Diana sobbed from the top of the main staircase at Sandringham, the Windsors' twenty-thousand-acre country estate. "I will throw myself down these stairs!"

Her husband, dressed in his riding clothes, was halfway down the staircase on his way out the door. Bulimia, morning sickness, and searing jealousy over her husband's affair with Camilla Parker Bowles had pushed Diana, now three months pregnant, to the brink. Now the heated argument that had begun in their private suite spilled into the entrance hall. "I am so desperate, Charles," she cried. "Please listen to me!"

But the Prince of Wales kept walking; he had heard all this before. "You're crying wolf," Charles told her. "I'm not going to listen. You're always doing this to me. I'm going riding now."

Suddenly, Diana lurched forward, then screamed as she tumbled down the stairs. The Queen quickly appeared, "absolutely horrified," Diana later recalled, at the sight of her pregnant daughter-in-law sprawled on the floor. Physically shaking ("She was so frightened," Diana said), the Queen summoned a local doctor as well as Diana's gynecologist from London. Princess Margaret, meanwhile, helped Diana off the floor and comforted her until the doctor arrived.

The Prince of Wales remained unimpressed. While his distraught mother trembled at the thought that Diana might lose her baby and his aunt held Diana's hand, Charles continued on his way out the door. When he returned from riding, the expectant father was told that, while his wife's abdomen was severely bruised, tests revealed there was no harm to the fetus.

Besides the nausea ("Sick the whole time. So sick, sick, sick, sick, sick") and the tensions in her marriage, the media "baby watch"—at one time the pregnant Diana was photographed on the beach in a bikini—had reached a fever pitch. By the summer of 1982, Diana could bear it no longer. She instructed her doctors to induce labor.

They chose the date so that it would not conflict with the Prince of Wales's busy polo schedule. "I am, after all, the father, and I suppose I started this whole business," said Charles, who along with his wife took natural childbirth courses. "So I intend to be there when everything happens."

That was not the only thing that would set this apart from all royal births that had gone before. Diana had overruled the Queen, who wanted to follow tradition and have the future monarch's birth take place within palace walls. Instead Diana wanted immediate access to state-of-the-art neonatal technology in the event anything went wrong. The birth would take place in a twelve-by-twelve-foot, $218-a-day room in the Lindo Wing of London's St. Mary's Hospital.

There would be no surprises as far as the sex of the baby was concerned. Although they repeatedly told the press they had no idea if their firstborn was to be male or female, Charles and Diana in fact knew what to expect from sonograms taken in the third trimester. Regardless of the baby's gender, Diana was also determined to do something else that was anathema to most royal mothers: breast-feed her child.

The baby did not come easily; the labor would turn out to be as difficult as the pregnancy. At one point, the princess's temperature soared to such a point that her doctors considered an emergency cesarean. But after sixteen grueling hours and with relief from an epidural, Diana at last gave birth to a blue-eyed, seven-pound, one-and-a-half-ounce baby boy at 9:03 P.M. on June 21.

Charles was at his wife's side throughout the delivery—"a very adult thing to do," he told a friend. At the moment his son appeared, Charles whispered to his wife, "Fantastic, beautiful. You are a darling." By contrast, his own father, Prince Philip, had been playing squash with an equerry while Charles was being born.

Still, there were many things Charles and Diana could not agree on—including a name for the newborn. He wanted to call the boy Arthur or Albert (after Queen Victoria's husband), and she preferred the trendier Oliver or Sebastian. Eventually, a compromise of sorts was reached: William Arthur Philip Louis Windsor. For the first full week of his life, however, the infant was simply known as "Baby Wales." (It had also taken one week for the Spencers to name their daughter Diana.)

A crudely lettered cardboard sign was posted on the hospital gates: IT'S A BOY. Church bells pealed, cannons boomed, and throughout the length and breadth of the kingdom toasts were made welcoming the future king. Outside Buckingham Palace, a crier in full regalia rang a bell as he shouted the news of the princeling's arrival. A crowd that had gathered outside the hospital spontaneously burst into renditions of "For He's a Jolly Good Fellow" and "Rule Britannia!"

Charles was uncharacteristically emotional. Emerging from the hospital two hours later with lipstick on his cheek, he shook the hands of jubilant well-wishers. "Nice one, Charlie!" shouted one loyal subject. "Give us another!"

"Bloody hell," Charles replied. "Give us a chance!"

One reporter asked, "Is he like you, sir?"

"Fortunately, no," Charles replied. "He has a wisp of fair hair, blondish, with blue eyes."

The next day, Diana's mother-in-law, clutching her ever-present pocketbook, visited the hospital. "Thank goodness, he doesn't have ears like his father's," the Queen said pointedly.

Only twenty-one hours after the difficult birth, Diana walked out of the hospital with a beaming Charles, who cradled Baby Wales in a lace shawl. To the cheers of the throng, they paused for photographers, then got into a waiting limousine and sped off for their new home.

Only five weeks earlier, the couple had moved from their cold, impersonal rooms at Buckingham Palace into spacious new quarters at Kensington Palace. Diana was delighted with the new arrangement. Not only was Kensington Palace far from her in-laws and Camilla, who lived not far from Charles's country home in Highgrove, but it was located in the heart of London. "Charles loved the solitude and peace of the countryside," said one friend of the couple, "but that drove Diana crazy. She did not want to feel isolated. She wanted to be in the thick of things. She was definitely a city girl."

In fact "KP," as Diana quickly dubbed it, was originally the country estate of the Earl of Nottingham, who sold it to William III in 1689. Nearly three centuries later, the imposing three-story Georgian brick structure, with its Christopher Wren–designed Orangerie, manicured gardens, ponds, and 274 acres of adjacent parkland, seemed the ideal first home for a future king.

William and his younger brother would

grow up scampering through more than twenty-five rooms filled with antique treasures and art lent to them from the Queen's private collection. The yellow-walled grand reception room boasted a grand piano, an Aubusson rug, and apricot-colored sofas. There was also an oak-paneled library, another drawing room, a dining room featuring a round mahogany table that sat sixteen, and a family room complete with big-screen television and a state-of-the-art stereo system.

A sweeping staircase led to the second floor, where the centerpiece of the master bedroom was an enormous four-poster originally made to accommodate the dimensions of Edward VII. Charles had his own sitting room, where, as the marriage continued to deteriorate, he would often sleep.

Diana's sitting room, where her sons would often come to visit and play games with the Princess, most accurately reflected her personality. Small tables covered in bright blue cloth were heaped with framed photos of family members. There were chairs and sofas upholstered in bright floral chintz, and above the fireplace was a round mirror with a gilt frame. Diana's menagerie of glass and stuffed animals was neatly displayed in two collector's cabinets. In one corner was the writing desk where Diana would sit for hours poring over her mail and composing thank-you notes.

The nursery, with its canopy-covered golden pine crib, stuffed animals, and blue-and-pink gingham linens, was to be the domain of William's nanny—although the new parents battled over just who would get that coveted position.

Charles had wanted Mabel Anderson, a discipline-minded governess who just happened to have been his nanny, brought out of retirement to raise William. But Diana, who did not want anyone else supplanting her in her own child's life, had something more progressive in mind. After a single interview, she overruled her husband and hired Barbara Barnes, the forty-two-year-old daughter of a retired forestry worker.

Barnes was a radical departure from other royal governesses. She had no formal training as a nanny (most had attended either Norland, Princess Christian, or Childton Nursery Training College), adamantly refused to wear a uniform, and declared that her free-form child-rearing style would be dictated by "plenty of fresh air and common sense." Nonetheless, she came highly recommended by Colin Tennant and his wife, Lady Anne, lady-in-waiting to Princess Margaret. For fourteen years, Barnes had taken care of the Tennants' twins, Amy and May.

Convincing Charles to go along with Barnes was, in the end, not that difficult for Diana. Both the Prince and Princess of Wales often spoke of their unhappy childhoods, and of harboring lifelong feelings of abandonment. Like her husband, William's mother grew up in a cocoon of wealth and privilege—all stemming from a fortune built on sheep trading during the fifteenth century. Since then, the

Spencers had always occupied a place at court. William's great-grandmother, Countess Spencer, had served as a lady-in-waiting to the Queen Mother. William's maternal grandfather was equerry to both George VI and Queen Elizabeth II.

None of this mattered to the six-year-old girl whose world was irreparably shattered when her mother walked out on the family, leaving Diana and her brother Charles to be raised by a succession of nannies. A bitter custody battle ensued, but in the end Diana's father prevailed.

Meantime, Diana's treatment at the hands of the nannies hired by her father often verged on the Dickensian. One routinely struck Diana on the head with a wooden spoon, another banged brother Charles's and Diana's heads together when they misbehaved.

Even then, Diana showed a natural maternal instinct. When her three-year-old brother cried for his mummy at night, it was Diana, then six, who made her way down the darkened hallway to comfort him.

"Her own childhood was hell," said Diana's friend Peter Janson. "Her parents hated, despised each other. She grew up under that."

Charles did not fare much better. While Diana's father did dote on his children, relations between the Prince of Wales and his parents were uniformly chilly. Charles would later describe his father as an overbearing, mean-spirited bully, his mother as remote and emotionally repressed.

As a baby, Charles would see his mother twice a day for thirty minutes, once at nine o'clock in the morning and again shortly before dinner. He would later recall being devastated at his mother's long absences while she toured the Commonwealth, and marveled at the fact that, after a months-long separation from her little boy, the most Her Majesty could manage was a formal handshake. This was not, he confided to friends, the sort of childhood he wanted for his son.

Beyond wanting her boys to grow up in a less stifling environment, Diana had another reason for hiring Nanny Barnes. The Princess of Wales was determined to be a hands-on mum, and in Barnes she saw a woman who was more than willing to take a backseat. Even then, Nanny Barnes would not be taking on the job alone. Since the heir to the throne could never be left alone, Barnes was assigned her own assistant, Olga Powell, and a night nurse, Ann Wallace, to help her look after the child.

For the first weeks of William's life, Diana and Charles were "thrilled," Diana said. "Everyone was absolutely high as a kite."

One of Diana's closest friends, Carolyn Bartholomew, visited the young family just three days after the little prince's birth. "She was thrilled with both herself and the baby," Bartholomew recalled. "There was a contentment about her."

To Mummy's surprise, even Prince Charles took unabashed pleasure in the role of proud papa, dropping into the nursery several times a day to check on Baby Wales. And while, contrary to his own public claims, he never came close to actually changing one of William's dirty "nappies," Charles at times seemed overcome with emotion as he rocked the infant in his arms. "He really does look surprisingly appetizing," the Prince of Wales gushed to a friend in a letter, "and he has sausage fingers just like mine."

When Diana stopped breast-feeding William after three weeks, Charles volunteered to give the baby his bottle. "He just loves the whole nursery thing," Diana conceded. As William grew older, Charles actually joined his toddler in the bath, overseeing a small armada of toy boats and a flock of rubber duckies.

As besotted as he was with his son, Charles paid scant attention to his wife. For her twenty-first birthday on July 1—just ten days after giving birth—Charles, by his own account, gave Diana "some flowers and a hug."

It was not long before Diana began a downward spiral into postpartum depression. "It's difficult to explain just how desperate a feeling it is," she told her longtime friend Lady Elsa Bowker. "You know you should be happy, but that only makes it that much worse. You add guilt to the equation. I just kept sinking into this black hole." Diana explained, "It wasn't the baby that produced it. It was the baby that triggered off all else that was going on in my mind. Boy, was I troubled... Tears, panic."

The public, meanwhile, basked in the afterglow of Baby Wales's birth. On a sunny

Wednesday morning in early August, four generations of Windsors gathered in Buckingham Palace's ornate Music Room to mark two occasions: the Queen Mother's eighty-second birthday and the christening of the future king.

In the room where Charles was christened thirty-three years earlier, the forty-five-day-old princeling emitted three faint squeals when Dr. Robert Runcie, the Archbishop of Canterbury, poured baptismal water over his head. While Charles gamely wiped drool from William's chin, Dr. Runcie exhorted the baby's relatives and godparents to "bring up this child to fight against evil and follow Christ."

Hewing to tradition, William wore the 1841 baptismal gown of Honiton lace over Spitalfields satin that had swathed every future monarch since Edward VII. The silver gilt lily font, garlanded in apricot roses and white freesias from the Windsor Castle gardens, was brought from the Tower of London specially for the historic occasion.

Once it was time for Princess Margaret's ex-husband, Lord Snowdon, to take the requisite photos, however, William's mood abruptly changed. As the baby squalled, the Queen proclaimed him "a good speechmaker," and the Queen Mother chimed in, "He certainly has a good pair of lungs." Diana was able to calm him down by giving him a pinkie finger to suck. But when the Queen and the Queen Mother offered the baby their fingers, he rejected them both. William's aunt, Princess

Anne, had no better luck trying to amuse the boy by making clucking sounds.

Diana, blushing with embarrassment and appearing increasingly agitated, tried hushing and cuddling William—but only her finger would do the trick. The baby could sense his mother's unhappiness, she would later explain. "It couldn't have been worse—endless pictures of the Queen, Queen Mother, Charles, and William. I was excluded totally that day," she remembered. "I wasn't very well and I just blubbed my eyes out. William started crying too. Well, he just sensed that I wasn't exactly hunky-dory."

Diana was not being paranoid. In just six weeks, the Princess had lost an alarming forty pounds—the thirty pounds she had gained during pregnancy and an additional ten pounds. In an attempt to conceal her bulimia from the press, the Palace tried to keep Diana out of photographs that would have revealed how emaciated she had become.

Throughout the rest of 1982, Diana's state of mind continued to deteriorate. Resuming her binge-and-purge regimen, Diana was robbing her body of potassium and magnesium, in the process sparking ever-more-hyperbolic mood swings. In addition, the postpartum hormonal imbalance only served to heighten her anxiety over Camilla Parker Bowles. She discovered that Charles placed many of his calls to Camilla from his bathtub. Once, after breast-feeding William, she eavesdropped at the bathroom door. "Whatever happens," she overheard Charles say over the phone, "I will always love you."

Diana's anxiety over her husband's infidelity manifested itself in an obsessive fear that something might happen to William. "Is he all right, then?" Diana would ask Barbara Barnes apprehensively. "Are you sure?" Whenever William suffered even the slightest case of the sniffles, Diana insisted on sleeping next to him on a cot in the nursery.

Shortly after William's christening, Diana sat alone in her sitting room and drank several glasses of Scotch. Then she went to the medicine cabinet, retrieved the tranquilizers Charles had given her and downed half the bottle. Discovered by a bodyguard, she was rushed to the hospital, where her stomach was pumped out.

"I will never do that again," Diana vowed to a friend. "I kept thinking about Wills and how awful it would have been..." As soon as she returned to Kensington Palace, she flushed the remainder of the pills down the toilet.

This pledge not to make a serious effort at suicide notwithstanding, William's mother indulged in an orgy of self-mutilation. At various times, Diana slashed her wrist with a razor, stabbed herself in the chest with a pocketknife, cut herself with the jagged edge of a lemon peeler, and hurled herself against a glass display case, shattering it.

"There is no question in my mind," Diana later said, "that at some level William must have felt the tension even then."

Wills was not yet three months old when Diana felt compelled to make her first solo trip abroad. In September of 1982, Grace of Monaco, the woman who preceded Diana in the role of fairy-tale princess, was killed in a car crash. When Diana had harbored doubts about becoming the Princess of Wales, Princess Grace had been one of the few people she could turn to for advice and encouragement. Now she insisted on representing the Royal Family at Grace's funeral, even if it meant leaving her beloved son behind.

When she returned, Diana had new cause to worry about William. Recent IRA bombings in London had left nine people dead and fifty-one seriously injured, and there were reports of a kidnap plot aimed at the little prince. To hone her survival skills, Diana was taken to a special police driving course in Hereford and taught how to steer away from explosive devices and bullets in the event of a terrorist attack. "Bombs were being thrown at me," she later said. "It was terrifying."

But necessary. In 1974, an armed kidnapper had brazenly tried to snatch William's aunt, Princess Anne, from her car in the center of London, wounding four people in the process. Five years later, the IRA succeeded in assassinating Charles's beloved great-uncle (and William's middle-namesake) Lord Louis Mountbatten. There were other disquieting incidents, such as the time the Queen awakened in Buckingham Palace to find a deranged man sitting at the edge of her bed, and the day someone fired blanks at the Queen as she rode in front of the palace on horseback.

When they first married, Diana had reluctantly agreed to have at least one bodyguard with her at all times. Now it was the Princess of Wales who asked that additional guards be posted at Kensington Palace and Highgrove, Charles's 348-acre estate in the picturesque Cotswolds.

Two days before his first Christmas, six-month-old William posed for photographers with his parents. While Diana dangled his favorite toy—a yellow teething ring—just out of reach, William sat smiling and wriggling in his father's lap. In stark contrast to the inconsolable infant at the christening, William appeared utterly content. Still, Charles cracked as they got up to leave, "Now we'll probably get child specialists in, saying we handled him all wrong."

Charles was joking, but Diana could not shake the feeling that she was "being scrutinized, analyzed, criticized twenty-four hours of every day." She had a point. The bulimia, which had been triggered by a casual comment of Charles's during their engagement ("Oh, a bit chubby here, aren't we?"), was now out of control; Diana's waistline had shrunk from twenty-nine inches to twenty-two inches. A string of psychiatrists was called in to treat her, each with a new set of medications that only seemed to aggravate the situation. Valium was a particular favorite.

In January, Charles insisted that his wife get

away from all the pressures of motherhood and take a holiday by herself. But after a week at the storybook castle of Liechtenstein's Prince Franz Joseph, Diana returned in tears. "I cannot bear," she told her hosts as she cut short her visit, "to be apart from my son."

Nevertheless, when the Palace sought to capitalize on Diana's growing popularity by having her accompany her husband on a six-week royal tour of Australia and New Zealand, Diana was resigned to leaving Wills behind. Then Australian prime minister Malcolm Fraser suggested they bring the boy along—and Diana jumped at the chance. There was never any argument with the Queen, as would later be widely reported. "We never even asked her," Diana said with a shrug. "We just did it."

On March 22, 1983, a small army of reporters was waiting on the tarmac at Alice Springs Airport when Charles, Diana, William, Nanny Barnes, and their entourage of twenty staffers stepped off the plane. The flight had lasted a grueling twenty hours, but William, now just nine months old, looked happy. His parents, conversely, appeared drawn and confused. Nanny Barnes handed Wills over to his mother, and a photographer shouted, "Here's Billy the Kid!" With that, said one of the journalists on the scene, Diana and Charles "just lit up. They were obviously so happy to be there with their little boy. From our standpoint, they seemed like the perfect little family unit."

Moments later, Diana handed William back

to Nanny Barnes, who then took the baby to a waiting plane bound for New South Wales and an isolated four-thousand-acre sheep ranch called Woomargama. Over the next month, while Charles and Diana racked up forty-five thousand miles crisscrossing Australia, Woomargama would serve as home base. Whenever they had a break in their schedule, Mummy and Dad would join Wills for a few days of private time.

Diana was grateful for these stolen hours, but wistful about time spent apart from her son. During a stop in Canberra, a young mother—one of more than a million Australians who came out to see the royal couple during the tour—told Diana she envied the Princess. "Oh, no," William's mother replied. "I envy you. I wish I could stay home with my baby."

Still, Diana took solace that they were at least together in the same corner of the world—"under the same sky."

The last two weeks Down Under were spent in New Zealand, where William and his parents were safely ensconced at Government House in Wellington. There Wills crawled about, Diana recalled, "knocking everything off the tables and causing unbelievable destruction." Their proudest moment came during a press conference, when William stood up on his shaky legs for the first time with some help from Mum and Dad.

The Australian tour was an irrefutable triumph, particularly for Wills's mother. But it also planted the seeds for new conflict in her marriage. The multitudes who showed up in even the most remote corners of the continent were clearly there to see Diana; crowds wildly cheered the Princess of Wales, surging forward to touch her while virtually ignoring her husband. Understandably, he became jealous, and over the next several years that jealousy would fester.

Just three weeks after returning home, William's parents headed off for an official two-week tour of Canada—this time without their son. The trip also meant that Charles and Diana would miss Wills's first birthday. "It's just unfortunate that they will miss the baby's birthday," one of the "men in gray" explained. "But they felt Prince William is too young to notice."

With only his nanny, Barbara Barnes, in attendance, William celebrated his first birthday at Kensington Palace with one thousand cards, one hundred gifts, a sponge cake decorated with Little Bo Peep and Wee Willie Winkie—and a phone call from Mum and Dad. They wished him happy birthday, and, said Charles, William replied with "a few little squeaks." Charles did not divulge what he was giving his son, only that it was "something that he won't be able to break."

Whether he noticed or not, Diana felt guilty about not being there to watch as her firstborn turned one. "I really am missing him," she told a crowd in Ottawa. "He is a beautiful little boy and we are both extremely proud of him."

Nor was Diana about to let Charles's first Father's Day, which happened to fall on the day after William's birthday, pass unnoticed. On William's behalf, she handed her husband a Father's Day card depicting a magician pulling a rabbit out of a hat. "Dad," read the message, "I think you're magic."

They returned home in time to hear William utter his first word—"Yuk," a term Diana often used to express distaste—and watch him play with their new golden retriever, Harvey. Soon, young William would prove himself to be, in Diana's words, "quite a handful."

William was just fifteen months old and safely tucked away in the nursery at Balmoral when a piercing alarm sounded throughout the castle. Suddenly police cars raced to Balmoral while bodyguards and security personnel sealed off the grounds and started searching for intruders. Charles and Diana were attending a function in London at the time, but the Queen, Prince Philip, and the Queen Mother remained holed up in their rooms, convinced Balmoral was under siege. William, it turned out, had found a newly installed "panic button" that alerted authorities to a security breach—and pushed it.

Later, "Willie Wombat" or simply "Wombat," as his father would call him, not only flushed his booties down the toilet but tried to do the same with his father's four-hundred-dollar shoes. He also showed an early talent for smashing objects, from glassware and china to toys. Kensington Palace staffers were routinely calling Harrods to replace shattered knickknacks or books William had taken from Charles's library and chewed on.

"You couldn't keep your eyes off Wills for a second," recalled Kevin Shanley, who came to Kensington Palace every other day to style Diana's hair. "I once had to break off from doing his mum's hair and rescue him from a window ledge." On another occasion, William picked up one of Shanley's brushes and began running around the room with it. "Better get that back or it will end up in the toilet," Diana warned him.

Several times Nanny Barnes fed Wills while Shanley cut his hair. When it was over, Diana would often drop in and ask for a lock of her boy's hair. She would study the floor with a puzzled look and then ask Shanley, "Where is all the hair you chopped off?"

"I didn't like to tell her," he admitted, "that it had fallen onto William's plate and he had eaten most of it."

Around the same time William pushed the panic button in Balmoral, his father was getting into mischief of his own. Since 1975, Charles had been carrying on a sporadic affair with Janet Jenkins, a beautiful blond Canadian resident he had met on a visit to Montreal. Jenkins had even attended Charles and Diana's fairy-tale wedding on July 29, 1981, as a guest of the groom.

"There was one girl who managed to remain very nearly anonymous," Charles's longtime valet Stephen Barry wrote in his book *Royal*

Service. "The Prince saw more of her than anyone realized. Her name was Janet Jenkins, and she was a Welsh girl living in Canada." Barry recalled that he was periodically called upon to sneak Jenkins into his employer's hotel suite.

In October of 1983, Jenkins was visiting friends in England when Charles, unbeknownst to his wife and his mistress Camilla, invited her to Highgrove. "We slipped back into the familiar intimacy that predated the marriage," Jenkins said. Since they had never used birth control before, she said, "neither of us thought of using protection."

Jenkins would claim that she was three months pregnant when she married a well-to-do Canadian businessman in December 1983. On June 13, 1984, nine months after sleeping with Prince Charles, Jenkins would give birth to a blue-eyed boy, naming her husband as the baby's father on the birth certificate. She would call the child Jason.

Although Charles soon knew of Jason's existence, the world was unaware that there was even a remote possibility that William might have a half brother—as the press would suggest but Jenkins ultimately denied. The British public was, however, learning more about the boy who would be king. In December of 1983, Prince William gave his first press conference. Toddling into the walled gardens of Kensington Palace with his parents, he posed for photographs wearing a blue snowsuit with red buttons and the letters ABC embroidered on the front in bright colors. The next day, after Wills's picture appeared on front pages everywhere, there was a run on blue snowsuits throughout Britain.

William's Kensington Palace photo op also gave him an opportunity to show off his expanding vocabulary. At one point, Diana suddenly looked up and pointed skyward. "What's that?" she asked him.

"Helicopter," replied William, whose favorite plaything was, in fact, a toy helicopter.

Charles would spend much of the next year traveling abroad without his wife and son—to Brunei, East Africa, New Guinea, France, Monaco, Italy. While traveling he talked constantly about William, flashing snapshots of the boy at the slightest provocation. And on those increasingly rare occasions when he was home, he doted on "Willie Wombat."

Despite Nanny Barnes's laissez-faire attitude toward discipline, William adhered to a strict schedule at Kensington Palace. Awakened either by Barnes or Olga Powell at 6:30 in the morning, he would climb into his nanny's bed and cuddle for an hour or more before toddling down the hall and into his parents' room, where he would crawl next to his mother.

To give Diana and Charles some extra time together in the morning, Nancy Barnes usually prepared William's distinctly English breakfast: cereal, milk, and a soft-boiled egg with buttered toast sliced into strips to dip into the yolk.

On those mornings when Diana had no appointments, William would play on the floor of her sitting room while she went over her paperwork with her lady-in-waiting and her secretary. Nanny Barnes would then serve lunch in the nursery, and afternoons were devoted to walks around the palace grounds or play dates; Diana broke with tradition and invited the small children of friends to play with her son inside the palace walls. Sometimes Diana, an accomplished swimmer, would drive William to Buckingham Palace for a dip in the palace's indoor pool. As a result, William would learn to swim by the age of three.

If she had no other engagements, Diana was always there when William ate dinner at five, and for the next two hours she would play with him, bathe him, and then tuck him into bed. Charles, whenever it was possible, read to the little boy at bedtime.

Notwithstanding the delight she took in William, Diana, still battling bulimia and chronic depression, later described this year as "total darkness. I can't remember much, I've blotted it out, it was such pain." Curiously, this was also the time that she and Charles, whose affair with Camilla had continued unabated, were trying to have another child—their "breeding program," as Charles called it.

Sometime before Christmas, the Princess of Wales became pregnant a second time—"as if," Diana said cryptically, "by a miracle." Again, she battled morning sickness, though to a far lesser extent than when she was carrying William.

Charles made it clear that he wanted a girl this time, and not just to Diana. At one of his walkabouts in London, the Prince of Wales pointed to the young daughter of one man in the crowd and said, "I think it's time we had one of those."

The fact that his wife was pregnant did not keep Charles from seeing his mistress. Diana could not ignore the signals—furtive phone calls in the middle of the night, letters hastily opened and burned in the fireplace, last-minute changes in his daily schedule that caused Charles to be called away.

William's antics provided some distraction, and Charles, despite his many absences, still enjoyed rolling around in the nursery with his rambunctious young son. By late summer of 1984, Diana sensed that the storm clouds hanging over her marriage were beginning to dissipate. For whatever reason, Diana later said, she and Charles were "very, very close to each other the six weeks before Harry was born, the closest we've ever, ever been and ever will be."

On his second birthday, William again scampered out to meet the press in the Kensington Palace gardens, this time wearing blue overalls and a striped rugby shirt. "Wombat" careened right for the cameras, grabbing one and peering directly into the lens. "He's really interested in cameras," Prince Charles said half apologetically.

Then William pointed to a sound man's boom. "What's that?" he asked.

"It's a microphone," his father answered. "A big sausage that picks up everything you say—and you are starting early!"

To compensate for their being on tour in Canada when he turned one, this time both Charles and Diana set aside the entire day to spend with William. They were on hand at Kensington Palace when the two-year-old's most memorable birthday present arrived— a scaled-down, electric-powered version of the Jaguar XJS Cabriolet sports car, built specially for the tot at the state-owned Jaguar factory in Coventry.

As they approached her September due date, Diana and Charles were, in the Princess's words, "blissfully happy." In part, this was because Charles was convinced Diana was pregnant with the daughter he had always wanted. But Diana knew better. Although Charles refused to look at the sonogram this time, Diana knew that the baby she was expecting was male. "I knew," she later said. "I knew it was a boy and I didn't tell him."

Charles's preference for the gender of his unborn child struck a nerve with Diana. From the very beginning of her life, she had felt unloved and unwanted. After the births of her sisters Lady Jane and Lady Sarah, followed by a badly deformed son who lived only ten hours, the Spencer family was so determined that the baby born on July 1, 1961, be a boy that they did not bother to select any girls'

71

names. It was a week before they settled on Diana Frances. Another three years would pass before Diana's brother, Charles, provided them with the male heir they so desperately craved. Diana was convinced that, had her older brother lived, her parents would have been satisfied and she would never have been born.

No matter that Charles was hoping for a girl; Diana found any expressed preference for one gender over the other "unacceptable." "So what if it is a boy?" she asked a friend. "Does that mean Charles will love him less than if he'd been born a girl? It's simply not fair to the child."

Early on the morning of September 15, 1984, Charles and Diana, wearing a red maternity dress and matching red shoes, returned to the Lindo Wing of St. Mary's Hospital. William remained at Kensington Palace with Nanny Barnes.

At 4:20 in the afternoon, the Princess of Wales gave birth to a six-pound, fourteen-ounce boy. Crestfallen, Charles took one look at the squalling newborn and shook his head. "Oh, God, it's a boy," the Prince said. "And he even has red hair."

Diana stared at her husband in disbelief. At that moment, she later said, "something inside me closed off."

As it had two years before, the British public rejoiced over the birth of its newest prince, Henry Charles Albert David. Actually, putting the name "Henry" down on the birth certificate was a little more than a formality; both

of the child's parents issued a statement pro-
claiming that henceforth William's little
brother would be known by a single nickname: Harry.

He is my mini-tornado.

—Diana on William

Then suddenly as Harry was born, it just went bang, our marriage, the whole thing went down the drain.

—*Diana*

3

Prince Charles held on to William's hand tightly, guiding him up the stairs into St. Mary's Hospital, onto the elevator, then down the hallway toward his mother's room. Diana, concerned about how William would react to the arrival of his new baby brother, decided that the best way to establish a bond was to have them meet as soon as possible. When she heard Charles and William coming down the hallway, Diana lifted Harry out of his bassinet and stood holding him in the doorway. "It's important," she told a nurse, "that the first time William sees his brother I'm holding him in my arms."

"Go on," Charles said, letting go of the toddler's hand, "go and see your baby brother." William ran toward his mother, who bent down so that he could get a good look at the sleeping infant. From that moment on, Diana observed, "Harry was his favorite toy."

More than fifteen hundred well-wishers standing outside the hospital entrance cheered wildly as Diana, cradling Harry in her arms, left the hospital and climbed into the back of Charles's dark blue Jaguar sedan. No sooner did he deposit mother and son at Kensington

Palace than Charles drove off to a polo match at Windsor Castle.

Left behind at Kensington Palace with their day-old son and his older brother, Diana was devastated. Charles had scarcely attempted to conceal his disappointment in the newborn prince, which made Diana more determined than ever to make the infant feel wanted and loved. Though she had breast-fed William for only three weeks, she stretched it to eleven for Harry. "I picked him up and held him every chance I could get—even more than I held William," Diana said. "All children should be spoilt that way, although I don't think it's really spoiling your child to lavish love on them."

At Harry's christening—another extravagant Royal Family affair, this time in St. George's Chapel at Windsor Castle—Charles complained to Diana's mother, Frances Shand Kydd, that Diana had not only given birth to another boy, but one with "rusty" hair.

"You should just be thankful," Shand Kydd scolded her son-in-law, "that you had a child that was normal." Besides, she pointed out, "rusty" hair was a Spencer family trait shared by Diana's brother, her sisters, and—until she began dying her hair blond—Diana herself. From that point on, Charles treated Diana's mother with chilly disdain. "That's what he does," Diana sighed, "when somebody answers back at him."

(Years later, as it became increasingly apparent that Harry bore scant resemblance to any other member of the Royal Family, there would be rampant speculation that Charles's initial concern over the boy's hair color stemmed from nagging doubts about his paternity. There were even published reports that Diana's lover James Hewitt, who did resemble Harry, was actually the young prince's father—and that in one of her love letters to Hewitt, Diana said as much. However, Diana would not even meet Hewitt until 1986—fully two years after Harry's birth.)

Charles was careful to conceal his true feelings once cameras began recording Harry's christening for posterity. Taking the hem of Harry's baptismal gown in his hand, the Prince of Wales whispered to William, "Granny was christened in this, and Great-granny, and I was."

A candid moment was also captured by the cameras as the Queen explained to Princess Anne's children, Peter and Zara Phillips, why she named one of her corgi pups "Dash." Said Her Majesty: "It's a word you use when you're cross. Dash! And it comes out frightfully well as a dog's name, you see."

The Queen was less than amused by William's behavior. Throughout the ceremony, the heir to the throne careened about the room, bumping into people and making bizarre noises. At one point in the proceedings, he began barking like a dog; at another, he ran in circles around the Archbishop of Canterbury. When William was told that he could not hold his baby brother, he exploded into a full-scale tantrum. The Queen tried to reason with William, but to no avail. He simply ignored her.

Still, Harry's birth provided fodder for the Queen's annual televised Christmas message a week later. Suggesting that nations could better coexist if people behaved more like children, the monarch argued that "we could use some of that sturdy confidence and devastating honesty with which children rescue us from self-doubts and self-delusions.

"We could borrow that unstinting trust of the child in its parents for our dealings with each other," she continued. "Above all, we must retain the child's readiness to forgive, with which we are all born and which it is all too easy to lose as we grow older."

No one was in a forgiving mood, however, when Diana's mini-tornado touched down at Birkenhall, the Queen Mother's Scottish residence, shortly after Harry's christening. At one point two-year-old William reeled into the dining room, knocking over goblets, smashing plates, tipping over chairs, destroying a rare portrait of his great-great-great-great-grandmother Queen Victoria, and generally wreaking havoc as the Queen Mother's guests looked on in amazement.

Such anarchy might have been chalked up to boyish exuberance were it not for what happened next. "No!" he shouted at the servants who tried gently to coax him back to his nanny. "I tell *you* what to do. Go away!"

Charles was furious. Mayhem was one

thing. Being rude to Great-granny's loyal servants, several of whom Charles had known since *he* was a toddler, was quite another. Although Diana had fought to get Barnes hired in the first place, she now conceded that William was in desperate need of structure and at least some small degree of discipline.

Papa, as William now called his father, wanted to hire a governess for the express purpose of teaching the boy, preferably inside the walls of Buckingham Palace. But in this as in so many other things, Diana once again insisted on departing from tradition. The former kindergarten aide argued that, in order to become an effective monarch—not to mention a happy, well-adjusted adult—William should attend a preschool and "mix it up" with other children his own age. Otherwise, she told a friend, "I'm afraid he'll grow up to be just another one of these royal robots doing their best to look like real human beings."

Diana's suspicions proved correct when she visited a kindergarten with William and watched him standing on the sidelines. "He walked up to the other children playing games," she later recalled, "and just stood there. William wanted to join in the fun, but he just didn't know how."

When told of the incident, Charles had a change of heart. He remembered that, when he was finally enrolled at a school called Hill House at the age of eight, he felt insecure and shy. "It made me terribly shy," he confessed. "As a result, I never quite felt like I belonged. That's a feeling that never leaves you. I don't want my sons to have to feel that way..."

Diana did her research, asking friends for recommendations and visiting more than a dozen schools before finally deciding on Mrs. Mynor's Nursery School at 11 Chepstow Villas in London. Run by Jane Mynors, the daughter of an Anglican bishop, the school was situated not far from Kensington Palace and boasted three Montessori-trained teachers on its staff.

To try and head off the inevitable frenzy that would accompany his son's first day at school, Charles wrote letters to several newspaper editors imploring them to leave William alone. Diana called the parents of every one of the school's thirty-five other students. Meanwhile, the windows in William's classroom were replaced with bulletproof glass, and a panic button installed next to the teacher's desk. It was also understood that an armed bodyguard would accompany the prince at all times.

On a brisk September morning in 1985, William, wearing a red-blue-and-green-striped sweater, red shorts, and red shoes, arrived at Mrs. Mynor's with his parents for his first day of school. More than a hundred photographers scrambled to get a picture of the young prince, holding on tightly to his mother's hand but otherwise undeterred by the commotion. "He was just so excited by it all," Diana said. "He was so organized that he chose his own shorts and shirt—it's best to let him do that if you want him to smile for the cameras!"

Ostensibly, William was to begin in the school's Cygnets class, then move up to Little Swans, and finally arrive in the Big Swans category. He would soon learn how to finger-paint, make finger puppets, and tie his own shoes.

Just as quickly, he would learn how to terrorize his teachers and his fellow classmates. Aware of his rank, William pulled it—and frequently. He routinely shoved his way to the front of any line, and on the playground quickly established himself as a bully. His bodyguard frequently intervened to break up fights that the young prince invariably started.

"My daddy can beat up your daddy. My daddy is the Prince of Wales" was a frequent refrain. "If you don't do what I want, I'll have you arrested!" was another.

Things were not much better away from school. At home, he was now defying Nanny Barnes as well as his parents and the household staff more or less continually. Wills threw a tantrum every night at bedtime, whined when he didn't get his way, and, rather than picking up after himself, barked orders at maids, butlers, and bodyguards to do his bidding.

At one point when he was left alone in the nursery at Kensington Palace for just a few minutes, Wills picked his little brother up and went to the open window to give him some fresh air. Within minutes, he was dangling Harry by his ankles, thirty feet above the pavement below. A security guard rushed into the nursery and, at the last minute, pulled both boys back from the brink.

None of which boded well for the July 1986 wedding of Prince Andrew and Diana's friend Sarah Ferguson, at which William was to make his public debut as a member of the royal wedding party. By way of a dry run, Diana took William to see his father play polo near Windsor Castle.

No sooner had they arrived at the polo grounds than William began hectoring his mother: "Can I have ice cream? Where are the horses? Where are the polo balls? Where is Papa? I want a drink!" Diana was trying to talk to Fergie about her upcoming nuptials, only to have William pull and tug at her and whine when she didn't respond quickly enough.

Throughout the match, Wills fidgeted and squirmed, leaning so far forward in the royal box that Diana had to pull him to safety by the seat of his pants. Exasperated after only twenty minutes, she scooped Wills up and returned to Windsor Castle.

On another visit to the polo grounds at Windsor, the Princess of Wales watched Wills walk up to a little girl and, for no reason, push her to the ground. Horrified, Diana grabbed the boy, spun him around, and gave him a hard whack with her open hand on the rear end. Too shocked to cry, a chastened William walked up to the little girl and apologized.

Indeed, although Diana gave virtually all of the adults in the boys' lives permission to chastise them for rude or bad behavior, corporal punishment was strictly *verboten*. If any adult had spanked the boy, said Wendy Berry, the Waleses' housekeeper at Highgrove, Diana "would have hit the roof."

When Diana did hit the roof, it was increasingly out of frustration over William's behavior. She decided to bring him along on one of her frequent trips to the gym, and instantly regretted it. As Diana went through her workout with her personal trainer, the prince badgered her nonstop. Finally she had had enough. "Just go away, William," Diana yelled at the heir to the throne. "You're being irritating!"

Being irritating had, in fact, become the boy's specialty. "You couldn't take your eyes off him for a second," recalled Kevin Shanley, Diana's former hairdresser. "He was into everything."

A BBC crew was filming an interview with the Prince and Princess of Wales one afternoon when William awoke from his nap and burst into the room screaming, "What are you doing in Mummy's room?" He ran up to Diana, gave her a karate chop in the knee, and then refused to sit still for the TV cameras. Instead, he went on a rampage, tripping over the cable and knocking over the lights.

Not surprisingly, William stole the show at his uncle Andrew's wedding. While the other page boys and flower girls in the wedding party were models of deportment, William raced ahead and nearly tripped over the bride's seventeen-and-a-half-foot train. Once seated, the prince squirmed in his pew, chattered away to no one in particular, pushed his hat strap up his nose, and stuck out his tongue frequently—at the spectators who lined the streets as well as the bridesmaids in the church. At the moment the future Duke and Duchess of York were exchanging vows, William rolled his wedding program into a trumpet and pretended to play it.

Still, William's mother was pleased with her son's behavior. "Did you see William?" she asked. "I'm glad he behaved himself because he can be a bit of a prankster. It was terribly hot in the abbey, but he did very well considering he is only four."

Apparently no one else in the Royal Family shared that view. What distinguished this embarrassing display from others was that this time William's shenanigans were captured by television cameras and broadcast live throughout the world. Charles, in particular, was mortified. He, too, had had to punish William for his unruly behavior, ordering him back to the nursery whenever he misbehaved. "At times," said one Kensington Palace staffer, "it looked as if the only person who said no to William and really got results was Prince Charles."

But Papa's long absences meant that, for the vast majority of the time, the children were being raised under the more liberal aegis of Diana and Nanny Barnes. Moreover, the

Queen, who had refrained from criticizing her daughter-in-law's parenting skills, now felt compelled to speak out.

During the Royal Family's annual Christmas gathering at Windsor Castle in 1986, both William and Harry behaved outrageously—fighting, running around, whining and crying when they did not get their way. Her Majesty did some investigating of her own and discovered that nursery school teachers and the parents of playmates universally viewed William as a spoiled, incorrigible brat. His grandmother was particularly horrified to learn one of William's favorite lines: "When *I* am king, I'm going to make a new rule that..."

"You really must do something, Charles," the Queen said. "The boys need discipline. Perhaps a new nanny is in order."

For her part, Nanny Barnes—both boys called her "Baba"—had little use for criticism, not even from the Crown. Six months earlier, when the Queen commented that William was "a little out of control," Barnes told another staff member, "His behavior was only natural for a boy in front of his grandmother. What was she expecting, for God's sakes, a mini Prince Charles?"

Barnes was, to a large extent, the only constant in the boys' lives. The demands of their parents' royal schedules were such that both Charles and Diana were often away from home. When that happened, the most anticipated event of the day for the boys arrived around 6:30 P.M., just before bedtime. Wearing their pajamas and squeezing their teddy bears tight, they sat on the edge of the bed waiting for a call from Mummy and Papa. When she had finished talking to the boys, the Princess would debrief Barnes on every moment of their day.

Unlike other members of the staff, Barnes, who took great pride in being the royal nanny, always entered every royal palace through the front door. She could not understand why Diana did not delegate full responsibility to her the way members of the royal family had for generations. "Barbara wanted to run everything in the nursery, and when the Prince and Princess were away she could," Barnes's assistant, Olga Powell, said. But that would all end when Diana returned to reassert her authority.

One way Diana accomplished this was to toss out the customary dark blue royal togs Nanny Barnes had bought for the children and replace them with clothes she had purchased herself—brightly colored T-shirts, sweaters, and shorts from Harrods' children's department. "I want them to look the way children look today," said Diana, "not like sad little adults."

But when her employer was gone, Nanny Barnes could not wait to get the princes out of the clothes their mother had selected. "We'd better be having you out of these things, hadn't we, William?" she'd say before dressing them in the standard-issue uniforms she had picked out. By January of 1987, the boys seemed closer than ever to "Baba"

Barnes; the bond between the nanny and William was particularly strong. The eternally insecure Diana, always wary of being supplanted in the lives of her own children, decided it was time to act. "It almost got to the stage where Diana felt she had to make an appointment to see her sons," deputy nanny Olga Powell remarked, "and she wasn't having any of that."

The announcement of Barnes's departure was timed to coincide with William's first day at Wetherby, a pre-kindergarten located just five minutes from Kensington Palace at Notting Hill Gate. But when five-year-old William was told that his nanny was leaving, he burst into tears. Harry quickly followed suit.

Nor did Barnes's abrupt departure escape the attention of the ever-vigilant British press. "I thought no one would notice," Diana said with a shrug, "but I was wrong, wasn't I?"

"She would have done anything for that child," Olga Powell said of the royal nanny. "The trouble is that Diana obviously feels the same way, and felt her mother's prerogative was being threatened."

For more than a month following Nanny Barnes's departure, Diana took complete charge of the boys. To staff members at Kensington Palace and Highgrove, she never seemed happier as she bathed, dressed, and fed them. With her bodyguard in tow, she drove William to school each morning, and after school played games with William and Harry on the nursery floor.

In February, Ruth Wallace, former nanny to the children of Charles's close friend (and William's godfather) King Constantine of Greece, was hired on to replace Nanny Barnes. "Nanny Roof," as Wallace was soon dubbed by the boys, wasted no time laying down the law and establishing a routine for her charges to follow. Charles had argued that Wallace be given the authority to back up her orders, and for the first time Diana agreed: henceforth, Nanny Roof was given permission to spank Prince William if she felt he deserved it.

He often did. When a small birthday party was thrown for another child at Wetherby, William ran riot, making odd noises and refusing to sit with the other children. Told to behave himself, he began to scream that he hated the food—sandwiches and ice cream—before picking up his plate and hurling it to the floor. Staff members instructed him to clean up the mess, but William just stood there scowling.

"When I'm king," he shouted at the adults, "I'm going to send all my knights around to kill you!"

"Pick it up," one of the teachers stated flatly.

William gritted his teeth and snarled, "Do you know who I am?"

Soon teachers and children alike had a nickname for Prince William. They called him "Basher."

When a footman served him a meat pie for dinner, William flew into a rage. "You've got to get me something else," he shouted at the servant. The prince's fists were clenched tight, and he stamped his feet. "I'm telling you to—so you've got to do it!"

Another time, William walked up to Sir Bob Geldof, the shaggy-maned rock star who was knighted for starting the famine-relief charity Band-Aid. "He's all *dirty*," Prince William declared. "He's got scruffy hair and wet shoes."

"Shut up, you horrible little boy," Geldof shot back. "Your hair is scruffy, too."

"No, it's not," William said indignantly. "My mother brushed it." Then he turned and stormed off.

Not even the Royal Family's sternest taskmaster, Prince Philip, could convince William to shape up. On a family holiday aboard the royal yacht *Britannia*, "Grand-papa" ordered the family on deck for a group photo. Only William, determined to be contrary, stood resolutely with his back to the camera.

By now the tabloid images—of Prince William scowling at reporters, Prince William clenching his fists in anger, Prince William pulling away from his mother or being scolded by his nanny—were all too familiar to the British public. WILLIAM THE TERRIBLE GOES BERSERK, screamed one headline in the *Daily Mail*. THE BASHER STRIKES AGAIN! proclaimed the *Sunday Mirror*. There was a new moniker for the whining heir: William, Prince of Wails.

What the public did not see, however, was

the behind-the-scenes turmoil that fed the boy's anger. "William was by now old enough to be aware of the rows and tensions in his parents' marriage," royal housekeeper Wendy Berry observed. "No amount of playacting can ever fool a child."

By early 1987, Charles had essentially moved out of Kensington Palace and permanently into Highgrove, where he could be close to the woman he had never stopped loving, the still-married Camilla Parker Bowles. Camilla had, in fact, always felt she and the Prince of Wales were fated to be together. She was sixteen months older than Charles, and numbered among her relatives the celebrated Alice Keppel, mistress of Edward VII. On meeting Charles for the first time in 1972, she quipped, "My great-grandmother and your great-great-grandfather were lovers. So how about it?"

At first, the boys stayed with their mother in London during the week. But on weekends, all three joined Papa in the country. There the crowing of roosters and the neighing of horses were accompanied by the sounds of china smashing, doors slamming, and the Princess of Wales sobbing inconsolably in her room.

Frequently, William or Harry would follow the sounds, only to have Diana dash by them in tears on the way to the bathroom. "Why are you crying, Mummy?" soon became one of the boys' most frequently asked questions.

What the children presumably did not hear—and would not have understood if they had—was Diana demanding to know why her husband had refused to sleep with her ever since Harry's birth. "I don't know, dear," he replied facetiously. "I think I might be gay." But of course they both knew the truth: he was still very much in love with Camilla.

Yet most weekends they soldiered on, trying for the children's sake to create the illusion of a happy family. "Boys will be boys—Diana liked to say that about the princes' bad behavior," said her friend Lady Elsa Bowker. "But she was only fooling herself. What are two small boys to think when their mother and father don't get along? Diana would cry for hours, and Charles was obviously miserable. Children sometimes lash out when they are confused about things. But even though Diana and Charles no longer loved each other, they did love their sons—and the boys knew that, too."

Thankfully, Wetherby gradually began to have a civilizing effect on William, and by actively encouraging him to be kind to the servants, Ruth Wallace awakened the little gentleman in him. The future king was now shaking hands with adults, calling people "Sir," and taking singular delight in opening doors for ladies.

Meantime, teachers at Mrs. Mynors's nursery school viewed Harry's arrival there in September 1987 with no small degree of trepidation. "Harry was never quite the handful William was," said one of the younger prince's teachers. "But he did tend to follow his brother's lead. So when William was horrid,

Harry was horrid. And as William came around, so did his brother."

In the beginning, Harry was actually nothing at all like his troublemaking older brother. Shy and withdrawn, he hid from the other children on the playground rather than join in their games. Shunning attention, he was even too embarrassed to hold up his hand to go to the bathroom. "But over time he changed," said one of his teachers. "By the end of the first year he had grown in confidence, and was getting into his share of trouble."

Because of her own tortured childhood, Diana was, unlike the rest of the royals, keenly attuned to the fragile psyches of youngsters. She knew that Harry was destined to grow up in his older brother's shadow, and worried that this would inevitably undermine his confidence and stunt his emotional growth.

Harry's first day at nursery school was a poignant reminder that he was the "spare" half of the "heir and the spare" equation. While cameras recorded the moment and his mother looked on, three-year-old Harry reached up to shake headmistress Mrs. Mynors's hand, only to have her reach over his head and shake the hands of Charles and William.

Undaunted, the littlest prince waved to the photographers, then skipped off to class. Charles and Diana drove off with William in their Jaguar and, just as she did when they were out of sight, Mummy began weeping once they were out of camera range. Two hours later, Diana returned to pick Harry up. "I was upset about leaving Harry," she conceded, "but now I'm going to meet him and I can't wait." Out he bounded with his first school project: a pair of cardboard binoculars.

Like his brother before him, Harry began acting up. Only now Diana had come up with a new kind of ultimatum. "If you're not good," she liked to tell Harry, "I'll exchange you for a girl."

His older brother, meanwhile, seemed to revel in showing off his new manners. Arriving at Highgrove in a red limousine, William took the initiative when he was introduced to the new housekeeper. "Hello, Windy [sic]," he said to Wendy Berry, sticking out his hand. "My name is William. How do you do?" Then he turned to make sure his father had seen him. Charles nodded approvingly, then turned his attention to Harry, who had gotten violently carsick on the ride from London and thrown up all over the Princess of Wales.

William's improved manners aside, both boys kept their mischievous streak. At Highgrove, where the princes were free to run about the grounds without constantly being shadowed by bodyguards, they found plenty of ways to amuse themselves. Visitors would often drive up to a makeshift blockade and suddenly find themselves confronted by two tiny soldiers, each in regulation battle fatigues and brandishing a water pistol. The official regimental uniforms, complete with berets, had been commissioned by Diana's riding instructor—and paramour—Captain James Hewitt.

Pointing his pistol at the driver, William would inform the hapless visitor that, in order to proceed to the main house, a twenty-pence toll would have to be paid. Making a break for it was ill-advised; with only the slightest provocation, Wills and Harry would open fire, squirting the driver and his passengers. "Both boys loved this particular game," recalled Wendy Berry, "and on good days could haul in quite a fortune...it was interesting to see how seriously Harry, in particular, took the game."

Just as often, the princes enjoyed leaping out from behind bushes to startle visitors, brandishing a toy sword in one hand and a squirt gun in the other. Whether it was a footman or a visiting member of Parliament, William and Harry seldom missed their mark.

One unfortunate victim was a new sentry at Highgrove, who, like the guards at Buckingham Palace and Whitehall, always stood at rigid attention in full uniform. William decided to squirt him in the face with his water pistol, and when the sentry did not react, the delighted prince kept shooting until he ran out of water. For the next two hours, the sentry stood at his post, soaked from head to boot.

Diana could hardly keep from laughing when she was told what had happened, but went through the motions of reprimanding her son. Charles, however, was enraged. "They simply cannot do things like that," he told her, "and it makes it so much worse when they see you laughing about it."

In another instance at Balmoral, one considerably more fraught with peril, the boys had taken deadly aim at one figure coming up the walkway and fired before they realized who it was. The Queen, her graying hair covered by a kerchief, stood frozen for a moment. Security was sufficiently tight at Balmoral that members of the Royal Family, Elizabeth included, were permitted to move about the immediate grounds without a guard hovering over them at all times. This particular day, the Queen was enjoying a morning walk with one of her favorite corgis. Now the dog looked up at the bead of water clinging to the tip of the monarch's nose. Her Majesty slowly took a tissue from her pocket, wiped her face, and kept right on walking. "Good shot," she said matter-of-factly.

One of the boys' main partners in crime was Prince Andrew, who, whenever he visited Highgrove, took special pleasure in using their water pistols to drench Fergie and Diana. Andrew also brought his own whoopee cushions to liven up the proceedings, and, when no such props were available, improvised. Uncle Andrew also made ape faces and other grotesque expressions that, Berry remembered, "William in particular thought hilarious."

Princess Anne's daughter, Zara Phillips, was another favorite of the boys. Arriving one afternoon for tea with her cousins, Zara was soon contributing to the mayhem. William began gargling with his Jell-O, and soon Zara and Harry joined in. As usual, Berry said, "there was pandemonium upstairs." At times like these, Princess Diana and the staff knew well, the fastest way to calm down the rambunctious youngsters was a video—preferably something about dinosaurs.

Another frequent visitor to Highgrove during this period was Captain Hewitt. Not surprisingly, Hewitt, whose intense affair with Diana would last nearly six years, appeared only when the boys' father was away. When William was five and Harry three, Hewitt took them to his army barracks. There they clambered over tanks and armored vehicles, pretending to shoot machine guns and generally having a marvelous time.

At Highgrove, Hewitt played games with the boys and read to them from William's favorite book, *Winnie-the-Pooh*. At night, Diana's lover joined in the pillow fights. "I remember accidentally catching William full in the face with a swinging pillow one night," Hewitt said, "and he burst into tears. But soon he recovered and told me not to worry."

Another male figure the boys quickly grew attached to was their personal protection officer, Ken Wharfe. An inveterate opera buff with a penchant for suddenly bursting into song, the extroverted Wharfe also kept Diana and the princes entertained tap-dancing around Kensington Palace—a skill he learned from an aunt.

Wharfe's antics distracted the princes from the bitterness and acrimony that swirled about them. But soon both Charles and Diana fretted that William and Harry were getting too attached to the bluff detective. He was technically reassigned to guard the Princess of Wales, though that meant he was still very much a part of the boys' lives.

Another detective and princely favorite, Sergeant David Sharp, was also told to back off by Prince Charles. When he barred Sharp from attending Harry's fourth birthday party, both boys burst into tears.

No matter how fond William and Harry were of their male minders, Mummy remained their principal source of fun. More than anyone else, it was Diana who encouraged the boys' natural playfulness. At age five, William learned he could get his mother to jump in the air and shriek with laughter merely by sneaking up behind her and pinching her backside. Unfortunately, he soon began pinching other women—the maids at Kensington Palace and Highgrove to start with, then friends who came to visit his mother. Diana did not call a halt to the practice until sports day at Wetherby, when William pinched the bottom of a classmate's unsuspecting mother.

There were limits, even for Diana. One afternoon at Highgrove, William dug up a dead rabbit out of a compost heap. "Look, Mummy," he yelled, swinging it over his head. He then chased Diana around the garden, threatening to throw the carcass at her. Promised the thrashing of his life, William reluctantly put the dead rabbit back where he found it.

Despite his reputation as an aloof father, Charles was, by royal standards, very much a hands-on parent. While Diana and the boys engaged in take-no-prisoners pillow fights at least one or two nights a week, Charles's roughhousing specialty was a game called Big Bad Wolf. The rules were simple enough: Papa stood in the center of the nursery, and the boys tried to get out. As they tried to run past him, Charles would grab the boys and toss them onto the sofa or one of the cushions that had been strewn on the floor. Pandemonium ensued as Big Bad Wolf Papa sent his sons flying through the air, much to their squealing delight.

During the warmer months, Charles also enjoyed tossing his sons into the pool at Highgrove, and was a willing victim whenever one of the boys decided to ambush him. One day at Highgrove, Charles was walking toward the Queen's red helicopter, which was to take him on an official trip, when suddenly Harry, in full camouflage, darted out of the bushes and jumped him from behind.

Charles played along, and then headed back to Her Majesty's waiting helicopter. It was only then that the Prince of Wales's valet pointed out that his Savile Row suit was striped with green and brown. Harry, it seemed, had been tromping around in the sheep barn and was coated with sheep manure. While his valet tried to wipe him off, Charles just shook his head in amazement. "Look at me!" he said. "I'm absolutely covered in sheep shit."

The otherwise fastidious Charles claimed he "never minded the muck" when it came to his young sons' country pursuits. On the contrary, he was delighted that both boys shared his bred-to-the-royal-bone passion for the outdoor life. Only four years old when he went along on his first game shoot at Sandringham, William took aim at the grouse and pheasant with his toy rifle. By the time he was seven, William would be beating the brush to flush the birds into the open. Three years later he had a rifle of his own, and was trained to use it.

The boys were also fond of Tigger, Charles's prized Jack Russell terrier, and Tigger's puppy, Roo. (Charles, who was extremely attached to his dog, told Diana he had given another of Tigger's puppies to a "friend." He neglected to mention the friend's name: Camilla Parker Bowles.)

Although Diana detested what she called "the wretched dogs," she tolerated them for the sake of her sons. Both dogs were fed meals specially prepared by the royal chef, and wherever the Prince of Wales went in England aboard Her Majesty's train, Tigger went along in royal style.

Most important, Tigger and Roo were trained hunting terriers. Whenever William and Harry would go off with their father in pursuit of game at Sandringham or Balmoral, Tigger and Roo led the way—until Roo wandered off one summer at Balmoral, never to be found.

Like his polo-playing father, William also

proved himself to be an accomplished horseman. By the time he was four, he learned to ride his ponies Smokey and Trigger bareback. The following year, William was capable of performing the kind of equestrian stunt generally seen at the circus: he could ride his horse while standing upright on the saddle.

This daredevil streak, which Harry also exhibited to a lesser extent, manifested itself in other ways. "Wills was always getting hurt," a member of the Highgrove staff observed. "He would tumble off fences, scrape his knees and elbows, fall off his bicycle or his skateboards—like any other boy his age, really."

Not exactly like any other boy his age, William managed to walk away unscathed after he wrecked the child-size Jaguar XJS Cabriolet he had been given by the automaker.

William was also a fearless climber who had no trouble scaling to the tops of Highgrove's tallest trees. Unfortunately, he often had no idea how to get down. More than once, he was perched fifty feet above the ground when bodyguards were finally summoned to rescue him.

One of the boys' favorite spots at Highgrove was the woodshed, where they could dive into hundreds of brightly colored plastic balls held in place by netting—the sort of children's play area found at traveling carnivals, country fairs, and amusement parks. The boys would swim through the balls and flail about, shrieking with delight. For household staff members yearning for revenge, tossing the princes headlong into the pool of plastic balls was one way to vent their frustration.

Of course, no one would have a stronger influence on the boys than their mother. While both William and Harry owed their exceptional horsemanship primarily to their father, the grooms at Highgrove, and, to a lesser degree, James Hewitt, Diana could take full credit for turning her sons into excellent swimmers.

A lifelong lover of water sports, Diana swam nearly every day—despite the fact that there was no pool at Kensington Palace—and brought the boys along. At times she took them to the various health clubs she belonged to around London, but just as often she dropped in at Buckingham Palace to use the indoor pool there. "Sometimes William is more like a fish," Diana marveled, "the way he swims and dives— a natural." And like his older brother, Harry would also take to water "as if he had gills."

In London, Diana pulled out the stops to keep her sons entertained. She went with them to see *Joseph and the Amazing Technicolor Dreamcoat* and to watch the finals at Wimbledon from the royal box. She also took the princes to amusement parks, fast-food joints, and go-cart racetracks, throwing herself headlong into each activity with a schoolgirl's enthusiasm.

Her motives were not entirely selfless. In late 1987, housekeeper Berry and Paul Burrell, Diana's trusted butler, began to notice what Berry called "the start of a power play over the boys between the Prince and Princess."

While Charles's happy, rough-and-tumble hours with his sons took place behind the security-camera-ringed walls of Highgrove, Diana's outings with the boys were invariably splashed across the front pages of papers worldwide. Diana often tried to keep William and Harry from their father's polo matches, and even when she did show up, the next day's papers would be filled with photos of the devoted young mother sitting on the grass with her sons—and barely a mention of their father.

Although Diana had little interest in Charles's obsession, the sport of kings, she encouraged the boys' love of horses. Every Sunday morning after their riding lesson at Highgrove, William and Harry would walk into the kitchen to find their mother waiting for them. She handed William, now five, and three-year-old Harry each a knife, and then supervised them as they carefully diced apples and carrots she had put out on the counter. Once finished, they scooped up the chunks of apple and carrot and went out to the cages to feed their pet rabbits and guinea pigs.

Then they returned, grabbed several lumps of sugar, and scampered back to the stables to feed them to the ponies. This kitchen ritual would be played out most Sunday mornings for the next four years.

For the first two months of 1988 it seemed, much to the astonishment of staff and the delight of the boys, that Mummy and Papa were once again enjoying each other's company.

When they called one another "Darling," this time it was devoid of the usual sarcasm. Their tone was, Wendy Berry recalled, "sweeter and more genuine than in previous months."

Wherever she went, Diana took newfound delight in poking harmless fun at the Royal Family and her place in it. On a Virgin Atlantic plane flying directly over Windsor Castle on its approach to Heathrow, Diana went so far as to dress up as a Virgin stewardess. She seized the intercom and said, "If you look out the window to your right now you'll see Granny's place."

Granny took a special interest in William. After all, the future of the monarchy rested on the boy's slender shoulders. At the age of five, William began a ritual that would last until he entered college. Nearly every week he would have tea with his grandmother, usually at Buckingham Palace or Windsor Castle.

Eventually the Queen would use this opportunity to try and educate the future monarch. But for now they both clearly enjoyed chattering away about a subject dear to both their hearts: horses.

Early on, William impressed Her Majesty with his horsemanship. Wills had just finished a riding lesson at Balmoral and was returning his horse Trigger to the stables when he passed the Queen going in the opposite direction. She was riding her favorite horse, a bay called Greenshield.

"Where are you going, Granny?" he asked. "Can I come with you?"

The Queen, an accomplished equestrienne, motioned for William to follow. Soon he was trotting along so fast that, Her Majesty later told guests at a picnic lunch, "I could barely keep up. I thought the bay would pitch me head-first into the road at any minute."

Back at Highgrove, the boys sensed the change for the better in their parents' relationship, and their behavior improved dramatically as a result. But sadly, just as one trip abroad seemed to have resurrected their parents' marriage, another would doom it for good.

On March 8, 1988, Charles, Diana, a pregnant Fergie, and several friends flew to the Swiss ski resort of Klosters. Two days later, while Diana and Fergie relaxed in their chalet, an avalanche came thundering down one of the ski slopes, narrowly missing Prince Charles and killing his friend and equerry, Major Hugh Lindsay.

Strangely, Wendy Berry observed, "it was as if the avalanche had wiped out the newfound goodwill between Diana and her husband." In this time of tragedy and personal crisis, Charles and Diana realized that they could not turn to each other for comfort. Instead, the Princess rushed back to Kensington Palace to be with her boys and Hugh Lindsay's widow, Sarah. Charles, meantime, went to Highgrove, where he could find solace in the arms of Camilla Parker Bowles.

Charles's brush with death had another, unexpected effect. Aunt Sarah, as the boys called the Duchess of York, had introduced Diana to astrologer Penny Thornton in 1986. Over the next few years, Fergie would put her sister-in-law in touch with a wide variety of soothsayers, clairvoyants, tarot card readers, and the like.

One of Diana's spiritual advisers told her that Charles would die before ascending to the throne—and that William would be crowned king. The near miss at Klosters only served to reinforce her belief in the occult. "Diana was absolutely convinced that Charles would never live to be king," Lady Elsa Bowker said. "But she was also convinced she would never be queen. This belief guided her in many of the decisions she made regarding the boys."

Diana's steadfast notion that she would never be queen was rooted in a recurring dream that she began having shortly after bringing Harry home from the hospital. She told her friend Roberto Devorik that, in the dream, she and Charles were in Westminster Abbey and about to be crowned king and queen. The king's crown was brought and placed on Charles's head. A perfect fit. Then the Archbishop of Canterbury placed the crown on Diana, but it slipped down over her eyes and face. She struggled to get it off, but to no avail. Unable to see, she now tried to breathe but couldn't; she was suffocating.

Another astrologer to whom Diana turned for guidance, Betty Palko, cautioned Diana about "deceit and treachery," and pointedly told her what she already knew all too well—that Charles was being unfaithful to her.

In late 1988, Diana was about to throw out the invitation to a fortieth birthday party for Camilla's sister Annabelle Elliot when, she recalled, "a voice inside me said, 'Go for the hell of it.' "

At the party, presumably that same voice told Diana to confront her husband's mistress. "Camilla," she told the startled Parker Bowles. "I just wanted you to know that I know exactly what is going on between you and Charles. I wasn't born yesterday. I'm sorry I'm in the way and it must be hell for both of you but I do know what's going on. Don't treat me like an idiot." Charles and Diana fought in the car on the way home, and that night she "cried like I have never cried before. I cried and cried and cried..."

It was not the only fortieth birthday party at which Diana confronted one of her rivals for Charles's affections. On November 14, 1988, the Queen threw a fortieth birthday party for her son at Buckingham Palace. Among those invited were Janet Jenkins, the Canadian woman with whom Charles had had a long-running affair, and Jenkins's husband.

Jenkins went through the receiving line, but when she came to Diana, the Princess of Wales stared at her coldly and promptly withdrew her hand. "It was an obvious snub," Jenkins recalled. Later, Jenkins looked over to see Diana whispering to the Duchess of York conspiratorially as they glanced in her direction. "Later Fergie gave me the royal snub as well."

Once again, the boys were not oblivious to the friction between Mummy and Papa. While they clearly enjoyed a close and loving relationship with Prince Charles, at this age there was simply nothing more important to them than their mother. Curled up in their pajamas on Mummy's couch, watching the sort of television movie their father frowned upon, the boys seemed utterly content. "It's so frightening," Diana told the housekeeper. "Thank goodness I have my two strong men with me." The boys just smiled.

The effort to create at least a semblance of normal family life resumed when William had an extra three days off from school in May of 1989. Diana and Charles took the boys to the Scilly Isles, off the coast of Cornwall, where the family could ride bikes and stroll along the shore without being hounded by the press.

But the tension between husband and wife was, in the words of one of their entourage, "so thick you could cut it with a knife. They just ignored each other, for the most part. To look at those little boys, trying to get Mummy and Daddy together—it was just so sad, that's all."

Once back in England, Charles and Diana returned to their old habit of assiduously avoiding each other. Previously, she would lock herself away in her room and read or watch videos while Charles spent endless hours working in his beloved garden. The boys would then ricochet from one parent to the other, although it was clear that they preferred snuggling up with Mummy in front of the television to digging in the dirt.

But even this uneasy truce was no longer workable. Now Diana and Charles were unable to coexist under the same roof, even when it meant sleeping in separate bedrooms. From 1989 on, he would usually depart Highgrove just as she was arriving, sometimes within minutes of each other. At times, it took an almost comical turn as their limousines passed each other going in opposite directions. "At least two or three times the boys saw their father go by in his car," said a member of the royal protection squad. "They heard all the arguments. They knew what was going on. They must have just felt totally helpless to do anything about it. It was heartbreaking to watch these boys caught in the middle."

As he approached his seventh birthday in June of 1989, William had for the most part managed to shed his reputation as a royal brat. In sharp contrast to his antics at the wedding of Prince Andrew and Fergie, William took control of the page boys and bridesmaids at the wedding of a Spencer cousin. "Get back!" he ordered the other children. "Get in line!"

William even began cracking down on his brother. When they visited Portland Hospital to see their newborn cousin Beatrice for the first time, Harry borrowed a page from his brother and stuck his tongue out at photographers. "Stop it, Harry," William said, taking his brother aside. "That's very naughty."

Accordingly, Diana came up with another name for her eldest son—Mr. Bossy Boots. But if William's behavior seemed at odds with his mother's diffidence as a child, he began to exhibit another character trait that sounded very much like the young Diana.

"I've often seen him comforting a young child who's clearly unhappy," said a classmate's mother. "He'll talk earnestly to him and make sure he's all right before resuming playing. He really does think of others."

Not surprisingly, William was as protective of his brother as Diana was of hers. When Prince Charles took his sons to play on the giant slide at Windsor Safari Park, William took charge of the other children in general and Harry in particular. "Harry, Harry, take your coat off," he told his brother. "You will go much quicker." William "looked after Harry," said another parent who was present, "and was very gentle."

William was no less concerned when it came to his parents' feelings. After a tense weekend with the boys at Highgrove, Diana and Charles jetted off on an official visit to Kuwait and the United Arab Emirates. When they arrived in the Middle East, Diana opened her suitcase to find an envelope that had apparently been tucked inside at the last minute. Inside the envelope was a note, carefully printed but obviously in a child's hand.

It would be the first letter the future king had ever written to his parents. But William's father was staying in another suite, and he and William's mother were still not talking. So the Princess would read it alone:

Dear Mummy and Papa,
  I hope you have a lovely time on your tour.
But come home soon. I miss you.
                    Lots of love,
                    William
                    XX

Diana sat on the edge of her bed with the letter in her lap and wept.

WILLIAM: When I grow up, I want to be a policeman and look after you, Mummy.

HARRY: Oh no, you can't. You've got to be king!

The day he left I dived into the Kleenex box.

> —*Diana on William's departure for boarding school*

CHARLES: The boys are princes and should be reared as such.

DIANA: They may be princes, but they are children as well. They need to have a normal life or they will end up as hopelessly out of touch as you are.

4

Hurry, Harry," William commanded his brother. "Stand right there. Are you ready?" The two princes were waiting patiently by the front door at Highgrove. Then, as their father passed by on his way out, they snapped to attention and saluted. With the straightest of faces, Prince Charles stopped and returned the salute. "Carry on, men," he said.

The boys had seen soldiers of every service branch salute their father countless times; now, William decided, they would do the same whenever the Prince of Wales was departing. In fact, the boys had widened their scope beyond Papa. "William and Harry," Charles's aide said, "salute anyone they encounter in uniform."

At Balmoral, the Gordon Highlanders returned the favor and for one day made William an honorary member of the regiment. In addition to being outfitted in full camouflage gear, he was taken into the Scottish countryside and allowed to eat with the other soldiers at a field kitchen. When he returned, William regaled his wide-eyed little brother with stories of the military life. "I really love soldiers' food," he told a jealous Harry.

To be sure, Harry idolized his older brother—but there were limits. In an average family, the secondborn child finds himself constantly being compared to the favored firstborn. When that child's older brother is a future king, the pressure to measure up is staggering.

Harry felt this early on. One morning at Mrs. Mynors's nursery school, the children were working with modeling clay when one of the teachers turned to Harry. "Your brother, Prince William, was very good at modeling clay," she told Harry by way of encouragement.

"Well, that did it," recalled another teacher. "Harry threw the clay on the floor and refused to touch it for the rest of the day."

There were still times, of course, when William was anything but a role model. When both boys were at Wetherby in 1989, the heir to the throne decided to relieve himself on a bush next to the school. The next day a tabloid ran two photographs of William caught in the act. The headline: THE ROYAL WEE.

At around the same time, six-year-old William took a page from Henry VIII and proposed to schoolmate Eleanor Newton, five. "If you don't marry me," Prince William told Eleanor, "I'll put you in jail." To another little girl, cast as the princess in a school play, he said matter-of-factly, "You're too ugly. You have to look like my mum to be a princess."

Occasionally, the simple act of disciplining

William would have unexpected ramifications. In June 1989, Diana showed up at Wetherby's sports day to run in the mothers' race, which she won. "This is the first time in my life I've won anything like this," she said excitedly. But when it was time to go home, William simply ignored Mummy and ran off to play with his classmates. The Princess, in turn, sprinted across the field, grabbed William by the arm, and marched him to their car. In the process, paparazzi snapped Diana giving the boy a quick slap on the backside—a picture that then ignited a firestorm of controversy over the merits of spanking and whether Diana's action constituted a mild form of child abuse.

Regardless of whether spanking was justified, Britain's premier child-care expert, Penelope Leach, was among those who defended Diana's attempts to bring her sons into line. "Discipline is vital to a child's self-image: it makes him feel worthwhile," Leach said. "What makes for appalling behavior is the feeling that nobody cares about you, nobody gives a damn how you behave."

One new arrival in the princes' lives gave a damn and said so—frequently. In the summer of 1990, Jessie Webb replaced the retiring Ruth Wallace as the boys' nanny. Webb, a large, outspoken cockney, thought nothing of blasting the princes when they misbehaved. She was no less brutal, however, in her assessment of the boys' parents. "Charles and Diana are both mental, you know," she said. "Those boys

117

are going to need a lot of help if they're not going to end up as barking mad as their mum and dad."

At times, William's defiant streak gave rise to more serious concerns. That August at Balmoral, Diana's "mini-tornado" hopped on his pony and vanished for more than half an hour. "The Queen," said a member of Balmoral's security staff, "was, I think, justifiably upset." From that point on, he was given a tiny electronic homing device to wear on his person at all times.

Eight-year-old William carefully laid his things out on the bed in the nursery—some favorite books, his red-blue-and-yellow felt parrot, a few small toys, the duvet from his bed at Highgrove—and then went to fetch his mother. He would be leaving for boarding school the next day and wanted to show Diana what he was taking. But beneath the brave facade, he was scared.

"I think it's an appalling tradition—singularly British. I simply hate it," said Penelope Leach. "Eight is awfully young for any child to be away from his parents."

Diana, who was still haunted by her own memories of boarding school life, could not have agreed more. But there had been security problems at Wetherby, and now the Princess was being told by the Royal Protection Squad that her son would be safer at a boarding school.

On September 10, 1990, Diana and Charles drove William to Ludgrove, an exclusive school located in Wokingham, Berkshire, about thirty-five miles outside London. There Prince William and 180 other boys would sleep eight to a room in dormitories with bare floorboards and chipped paint on the walls. They would be allowed their toys and games, but no radios or television. Parents could send no more than the equivalent of ten dollars in pocket money per term, and on Sundays each boy would be given his "grub"—a chocolate bar or other candy treat that was his weekly reward for good behavior.

Each Sunday, William and the other boys would also be required to sit down and write a letter home. Communication by phone was forbidden, though students were all allowed to visit home an average of one weekend per month.

From a security standpoint, Ludgrove (annual tuition: $7,050) had a number of advantages—not the least of which was the fact that the school was surrounded by 130 acres and set far enough back from any public roads to discourage the prying cameras of the tabloid press. William's bodyguard at the school, a married veteran of the Royal Protection Squad with the improbable name of Graham Cracker, slept in a room adjoining William's.

All of which was little comfort to the Princess of Wales. While William kept a stiff upper lip that first morning at Ludgrove, Diana dissolved in tears. "She was completely devastated," Lady

Elsa Bowker said. "She felt she was abandoning William the way she was abandoned as a child. To a large extent, she blamed Charles."

Indeed, while Diana sank into a deep depression over William's departure, Charles seemed unaffected. Within days after depositing his son at Ludgrove, the Prince of Wales boarded one of "the Queen's Flight" jets with the royal crown and "ER II" emblazoned on the fuselage and flew to France for a brief holiday. From Paris, he returned for a tryst with Camilla Parker Bowles at Balmoral.

"I can't help it," Diana told anyone who would listen. "I miss William so terribly." When friends commented on how self-assured the boy looked in press photographs taken that first day at Ludgrove, Diana shook her head. "Yes, but he is so young. I can't imagine," she said, "having to go through that stage of my life all over again."

During his first few weeks away, William had a hard time concealing the fact that he was homesick—and that he was consumed with worry over the state of his parents' marriage. Teachers reported that the prince would often wander about the school grounds alone, hands plunged into his pockets, shoulders stooped. "He looked," said the mother of another boarder, "as if he were carrying some heavy burden."

To some teachers and classmates, William came off as aloof, even imperious. "William has much more of an image of himself than Harry," a friend of the Princess's revealed. "And therefore he's more worried about making a fool of himself. He is sensitive, temperamental, and spoiled. He realizes that people defer to him, and even at his age he uses that."

On his first break from school that October, Prince William rushed to his father's study at Highgrove, only to find it empty. Crestfallen, the boy burst into tears. Diana, enraged, called her husband at Balmoral and demanded that he speak to the boy. Instead, Charles faxed him a welcome-home letter.

Several days later, Charles joined the rest of his family at Highgrove. And once again, William found himself caught in the crossfire between his warring parents. Over lunch with William, Charles and Diana managed not to exchange a single word. Instead, they both spoke only with William, who eagerly answered their endless questions about his new life at Ludgrove. Conversely, when William asked his father what he had been doing over the past month, Prince Charles replied that he'd been having a marvelous time hiking and fishing at Balmoral. Diana, realizing all too well that Camilla was also at Balmoral, stormed out of the room.

However awkward such incidents were for William, they were preferable to the screaming matches that had become standard fare when Charles and Diana were together. In the aftermath of one such bitter quarrel at Highgrove, Diana, sobbing, locked herself in a bathroom. William shoved some tissues under the door. "I hate to see you sad," he said.

On yet another occasion, eight-year-old William picked up the phone at Kensington Palace and reserved a table for himself and his mother at her favorite restaurant, San Lorenzo. "Mummy," he told her, "it will be just the thing to cheer you up."

Now that William was away at Ludgrove, Harry was left alone to bear witness to their parents' escalating warfare. Lying alone in the room he had shared with William, he could hear his mother's sobbing and Papa's pleas that she talk to him.

One argument in January 1991 was audible not only to Harry but to much of the staff at Highgrove. "I hate you, Charles," screamed Diana as she stormed off to her room. "I fucking hate you."

"William and Harry had always leaned on each other when their parents fought," said a former maid at Highgrove. "William was always telling Harry that mummies and daddies fought all the time and that it didn't mean they didn't love each other. But now, except for a few school breaks a year, Harry was having to cope with a lot of the mayhem on his own."

There were those on the royal staff who did their best to distract the boy. Jessie launched a one-woman campaign to fatten up the "poor, scrawny little thing" by feeding him scones heaped with clotted cream and English trifle. The police assigned to guard Harry would occasionally take him for a drive, letting him play with the lights and sirens.

Diana's detective Ken Wharfe was particularly good at distracting both boys when it looked as if trouble was brewing. As it became clear that a quarrel between Diana and Charles was starting to spin wildly out of control, Wharfe would put his arms around the boys and offer to share some official police secrets with them outside.

In March of 1991, Diana welcomed another distraction back into the lives of her boys. While Diana battled her husband on the home front in late 1990 and early 1991, her mind was also on the war raging in the Persian Gulf. Specifically, she agonized over the safety of one of the combatants, Captain James Hewitt.

Now that he was back, Diana welcomed Hewitt home much as the wife of any returning soldier would. "It was the most loving and passionate welcome home," he said, "any man could have experienced." Diana went on to tell him that "Harry had been her constant companion during the war, wearing his army uniform, sleeping in her bed so they could follow the Gulf War on television. William had been away at what she referred to as 'prison,' but she was so proud of the way he was turning out."

So proud, in fact, that Diana decided her firstborn was ready for his first official act on March 1, 1991—St. David's Day, the national day of Wales. The future Prince of Wales flew with his father and mother to Cardiff, where William, wearing a daffodil in honor of St. David's Day, gamely worked the crowd of three thousand.

Now and then placing a reassuring hand on the little prince's shoulder, Mummy leaned over at one point and whispered, "Are you all right?" Still smiling broadly, William answered, "How long is it lasting?"

William seemed thrown only once—blushing just like "Shy Di" used to do—when nine-year-old Lucy Willis gave him a bouquet of daffodils. Lucy seemed unimpressed. "I gave him the flowers," she said with a shrug, "because my mum told me to."

Despite the significance of William's first proper walkabout, Papa was nowhere to be seen. After less than an hour, Charles left to visit military wives at a nearby airfield. Pulling William to her side, Mummy bent down and gave him some last-minute pointers before he pulled the cord that unveiled the six-foot-tall plaque promoting Welsh culture. Then, with photographers eagerly snapping away, William signed the guest book—revealing to the world for the first time that he was left-handed.

That spring, the press would take note of how little time Charles seemed to be spending with his children. Only Diana, it was pointed out, had been on hand for Harry's solo at the Wetherby school Christmas concert. During the Easter break, Diana took William and Harry skiing in Austria while Charles entertained Camilla at Sandringham. Royal bodyguard Ken Wharfe, continuing to act as a surrogate father of sorts, was on the slopes to comfort Wills, who, suffering from a debilitating cold and unable to keep up with his little brother, burst into tears of frustration.

Another time, mother and sons were photographed cavorting at an amusement park while Papa went to a horse meet. At the end of May, when Harry had his school break, Papa was again nowhere to be seen when Diana took the boys to visit a safari park and a Royal Air Force base.

In reality, the Prince of Wales still maintained a close and loving relationship with his sons. When the royal helicopter deposited Prince Charles on the lawn at Highgrove, both William and Harry would invariably run up to their father, and he would spin them around in the air until they collapsed laughing on the grass. But scenes like this would be played out away from the television cameras, leaving the public with the general perception of Charles as a cold, aloof figure in his boys' lives.

Just how much of a father Charles was to his boys was put to the test on June 3, 1991. William and several of his classmates were hanging around the putting green at Ludgrove when one of the other boys began swinging a putter wildly over his head. In an instant, the club struck William in the forehead full force, knocking him to the ground. Unconscious, with blood pouring from the gash in his head, William was rushed in a police car to the Royal Berkshire Hospital in nearby Reading.

Diana was having lunch with a friend at

San Lorenzo when her bodyguard took her aside. Ludgrove's headmaster, Gerald Barber, had phoned Kensington Palace within minutes of the accident. Frantic, she rushed from the restaurant, slid behind the wheel of her green Jaguar, and sped the thirty-six miles to the Royal Berkshire Hospital. Called at Highgrove, Charles was, according to housekeeper Berry, "white with shock" at the news. He drove down the gravel drive and on to the hospital in his blue Aston Martin sports car.

Charles and Diana "were walking behind his stretcher, reassuring him," said witness Sarah Prince, as the boy was wheeled in for a CAT scan. The injury was serious enough, doctors told them, to warrant his being taken to a hospital that specialized in such things. Diana rode in the ambulance with William as he was transferred to Great Ormond Street Hospital in London. Charles followed in his car.

At Great Ormond Street, Diana and Charles were told that William's injuries were serious, and that an operation would be necessary to check for bone splinters and fully ascertain the damage. Charles, satisfied that everything was under control, went ahead with plans to attend a performance of *Tosca* at Covent Garden. Entering the royal box after the first act, he told his guests that William's condition was "not too bad." Following the performance, Prince Charles then boarded a night train for an environmental conference in North Yorkshire.

Diana, meanwhile, held William's hand as

he was wheeled into surgery. Seventy-five minutes later, neurosurgeon Richard Hayward emerged to pronounce the operation "a complete success." Moreover, there was no sign that the prince would suffer from the more terrifying complications often arising from such injuries—infection leading to meningitis and epilepsy.

William's distraught mother, grateful for the outcome but still concerned that the injury might have some lingering effects, stayed with her son at the hospital. The next evening, Charles returned from his conference and spent forty-two minutes at William's bedside before leaving for what was officially termed a "private engagement."

Predictably, Charles's failure to comprehend the serious nature of William's injury incensed the public, and he was roundly condemned in the press for not staying by his son's side. "What sort of father of an eight-year-old boy, nearly brained by a golf club, leaves the hospital before knowing the outcome for a night at the opera?" asked Jean Rook of the *Daily Express*. A headline in the *Sun* was equally blunt: WHAT KIND OF DAD ARE YOU? it wanted to know.

Charles was stunned by the public outcry and blamed Diana for making too much of the incident. It was a response she had fully expected. "She wasn't surprised," a friend observed. "It merely confirmed everything she thought about him."

"Her reaction to William's accident was

horror and disbelief," said Diana's friend James Gilbey. "By all accounts it was a narrow escape. She can't understand her husband's behavior, so, as a result, she just blocks it out. Diana thinks: 'I know where my loyalties lie. With my son.'"

After two nights, William was released from the hospital and left with his mother in a chauffeured limousine. Despite his injuries, the young prince looked on with genuine concern as a *London Express* photographer snapped photos of his mother slunk in the backseat, her face etched with worry and fatigue.

By August, William had completely recovered, and Diana asked her husband if the family could go on a "fun holiday" to an amusement park before the boys returned to school. Prince Charles refused—he preferred a tour of the local churches and perhaps a picnic or two—and the inevitable row ensued. Finally they reached a compromise of sorts: Charles agreed to go on a Mediterranean cruise aboard Greek billionaire John Latsis's lavish four-hundred-foot-long yacht *Alexander* (named after Alexander the Great), on the condition that only his friends accompany them. The cruise was billed by the Palace as a "second honeymoon," but in truth Charles spent all his time with his highborn adult companions while a bikini-clad Diana swam and dived with her boys.

As soon as they returned, Charles and Diana once again waged open warfare. Both boys were fully aware of the tensions between their parents, but the situation was taking its greatest toll on William. Nearly every day, William would come upon his mother fleeing down a hallway in tears or crying in her room.

At Highgrove one afternoon, William went searching for Mummy and finally discovered her at the top of the stairs in the servants' quarters.

"What's wrong, Mummy?" William asked.

Convulsed with sobs, Diana struggled to regain control. "I... I'll tell you, darling... when you're older."

It was then that William turned to see his father standing in the hallway. "Come with me to the garden, William," Charles said. "I'd like to speak with you for a moment."

William was trembling with rage. "I hate you, Papa," the boy yelled. "I hate you so much. Why do you make Mummy cry all the time?" William dashed down the stairs, and Papa, clearly shaken, ran after him.

"Now look what you have done, Charles," Diana screamed. "Why upset the children?"

No longer was it possible for Charles and Diana to simply ignore each other and channel all the conversation to the boys. It had reached the point where Mummy and Papa could not even go through the motions of eating with their children. Now, whenever their father was at Highgrove, Harry ate dinner with Nanny Jessie in the nursery, Diana and William dined on trays while watching television in the Princess's bed—and Charles ate alone in the dining room.

"Both William and Harry spent a significant amount of their childhood in Mummy's bed watching television or eating off trays," said a former staff member. "It was a refuge for them—a warm and happy place. Of course Charles was explicitly excluded, and it was very painful for him."

So painful, in fact, that the Prince of Wales sank into a deep depression. He would spend endless hours behind the walls of his garden, on his hands and knees working the soil even in the driving rain. Then he ate alone and would collapse in bed.

Although Diana's suicidal tendencies would soon be fodder for Fleet Street, Charles had hit rock bottom emotionally. "I have nothing to live for," he bluntly told royal lawyer Lord Arnold Goodman. Lord Goodman, along with those closest to Charles, now recognized the classic symptoms of severe depression. In a word, Goodman determined the Prince of Wales to be "suicidal" over the impending breakup of his marriage and the inevitable impact on his sons, the Royal Family, and the institution of the monarchy.

At Highgrove, where most of the confrontations between the Prince and Princess had taken place, there was consensus that violence between Charles and Diana was imminent—such was the depth of their hatred for each other. At one point detectives of the Royal Protection Squad grew concerned that one of the many firearms kept on the premises might be used by either party to commit sui-

cide or kill the other. They also feared that the
children might literally be caught in the crossfire. "We made sure," said a former security
officer, "that any guns—pistols, rifles,
shotguns—on the estate were locked away. Just
so no one was tempted to do something in the
heat of anger."

Once again, the boys had a ringside seat for
their parents' marital dysfunction. Invariably, Mummy would be in tears as the car pulled
away from Highgrove for the ride back to
London. With her protection officer at the
wheel, Diana would sit slumped in the back
between the boys, tears streaming down her
face, before burying her face in her hands. Harry
would simply sit in bewildered silence while
William placed a small, reassuring hand on his
mother's shoulder.

However tempestuous the royal marriage,
William and Harry remained profoundly
attached to both parents. This was never
more obvious than when it came time for
William to return to Ludgrove. As each school
break and vacation neared its end, William
pleaded tearfully with his parents not to make
him go back to boarding school.

Charles sympathized. His own school days
had been miserable, and he remembered
reacting in much the same way as William when
it came time to return. By way of cheering the
boys up, Charles would take them aside and
regale them with hilarious tales of stiff-necked
schoolmasters and loutish bullies. "Everybody feels the same way you do," he would reas-

sure William and Harry. "As soon as you're back with your chums, everything will be fine."

But William, who like the rest of the students at Ludgrove would not even be allowed to speak to his parents on the phone until the next school break, was inconsolable. As Diana waited for him in the car—now she always insisted on driving both boys to school—Charles put his arm around William and whispered more comforting words to the boy. On the hourlong drive to Ludgrove, the Princess tried to lift William's spirits by recalling what fun they'd had on their cruise aboard the *Alexander* and promising similar adventures in the future.

Yet no sooner did she drop her son off than Diana dissolved in tears. "I know how it feels to be all alone at that age. You feel totally abandoned by the people who are supposed to love you the most," she told one of her bodyguards. "Why is Charles making us do the same thing to our children? For God's sake, he knows better than anyone what it's like to be a small boy shipped off like this."

But William did settle back into school life quickly. As a Ludgrove spokesman hastened to explain, the golf club episode "was not a fight, but an accident. He is a very much liked boy here."

With William away at Ludgrove and Harry poised to join him the following year, their mother looked ahead to a bleak future without her sons. One of the few royals who tried to bolster her spirits was Fergie. "You mustn't worry," she told her sister-in-law, "everything is going to be fine."

But things were not going to be fine—least of all for Fergie. Diana watched as criticism of Fergie's weight, her clothes, her spending, her raucous behavior, and her mothering skills gradually eroded her friend's confidence.

In January of 1992, Prince Andrew and the Duchess of York separated after photographs were published in the tabloids showing Fergie romping in the South of France with Texas oil scion Steve Wyatt. That August, there would be even more fireworks when, as the family gathered at Balmoral, photographs were published of a topless Fergie having her toes sucked by yet another American, her so-called financial adviser John Bryan. The Queen summoned the Duchess to her study, flew into a rage, and banished Fergie from the bosom of the Royal Family.

Diana was convinced—with no small degree of justification—that the Palace's "men in gray" saw her as unstable and a threat to the monarchy. As her marriage teetered on the brink, the question of who would have the upper hand in the raising of the princes became preeminent. "I won't let anyone," she said disdainfully of her in-laws, "change my boys into one of *them*."

The war, Diana correctly determined, would be waged in the court of public opinion. The Palace's chief goal would be to discredit the

Princess of Wales in much the same way Fergie discredited herself. By late 1991, Diana had already set in motion a plan to get her side of the story across. "I was at the end of my tether. I was desperate," she later explained of her decision to tell all to journalist Andrew Morton. Over a period of weeks her friend Dr. James Colthurst brought Morton's written questions to her Kensington Palace apartments. Alone in her private sitting room, she poured out her heart into a tape recorder. Colthurst then secretly delivered the tapes to Morton.

William and Harry's mother had approved the final manuscript of Morton's book by the time her father died suddenly on March 29, 1992. At the time, the Waleses were away on a skiing trip to Austria. Charles, well aware of the public relations ramifications, insisted on returning with his wife to London—strictly for the sake of appearances. When Diana refused to go along with the ruse, Charles called his mother. The Queen ordered them both to return to London together. Once there, Charles, who had not spoken a word of comfort to his grieving wife, left for Highgrove.

William and Harry made up for their father's lack of compassion. When William joined his brother and Mummy at Kensington Palace, all three wept over Grandpa's death. "Don't be sad, Mummy," William told her. "Remember, Harry and I are always here for you."

Both Mummy and Papa were on hand when

King Constantine threw a party in the garden of his North London home to celebrate William's tenth birthday. Despite their scorn for each other, this time Charles and Diana managed to look like the picture of marital harmony.

So convincing was this show of togetherness that Smartie Artie, the entertainer for the children's party, refused to believe reports of an impending breakup. "The party had a cowboys-and-Indians theme," Artie said, "and the Princess came in a cowgirl outfit and the Prince wore a Stetson. They joined in all the silly team games with the other parents and children, like running with a glass of water and trying not to spill it... You wouldn't have known anything was amiss."

But within days even Smartie Artie's doubts were dispelled by the publication of Andrew Morton's *Diana: Her True Story*. Not only did the book cause an international furor, it uncorked a series of scandals that would shake the British monarchy to its foundations. Then, in early July, one of Diana's New Age confidants, massage therapist Stephen Twigg, gave an interview to the *Sunday Express* defending his client. Diana's suicide attempts as accurately described in Morton's book could, Twigg argued, "happen to anyone. The idea that she is ill, unstable in some way, emotionally unbalanced, is nonsense." Twigg's interview, though intended to defend his friend, had the effect of fanning the flames of controversy. Diana was livid.

"Are there any friends of yours," Charles asked his wife, "who are *not* talking to the newspapers?" Certainly the Prince's confidants were proving more discreet. While Diana was buffeted by one revelation after another, Charles invited his old friend from Canada, Janet Jenkins, to Highgrove.

Jenkins, whose son Jason was now eight, sat and held the Prince's hand for four straight hours as he talked of the separation that was now imminent. He was also convinced that Diana would press for a divorce. "He was shattered," Jenkins recalled. "He didn't want the divorce."

Foremost in Charles's mind, said Jenkins, was "what impact it would all have on the children. Ever since the marriage began to fall apart, he was consumed with worry over the psychological health of the boys—how all the fighting and bitterness would affect them in later life. He wanted them to grow up remembering that he was not the one doing all the shouting and screaming."

That night, Charles and Jason's mother slept together again. "That was the last time," Jenkins said, "we were sexually intimate." Only later would she learn that Camilla was still very much Charles's mistress. "It's ironic," Jenkins said, "that he was cheating on his mistress with me!" (Jenkins would actually meet Camilla in 1996, when she was again invited to Highgrove. Seated next to Camilla at dinner, Jenkins found her to be "absolutely charming. Either she didn't know that Charles and I had been lovers or she didn't care, because she treated me wonderfully.")

That August, around the same time Fergie's toe-sucking snapshots found their way into the *Daily Mirror,* transcripts of an illegally taped conversation between Diana and her friend James Gilbey were printed in the British tabloids. Gilbey, who called her "Darling" and "Squidgy," listened patiently as she discussed her problems with Charles and the rest of the royals, her anxiety over becoming pregnant again, and even her affection for James Hewitt. "Squidgygate," which revealed Diana to be almost pathetically needy, dealt a serious blow to her already flagging self-esteem. (Five months later, a weird sort of balance would be struck when a similar transcript of a phone conversation between Charles and his mistress was published in the tabloid press. During the passionate exchange, the Prince of Wales expressed the bizarre wish to be turned into one of Camilla's tampons.)

Fortunately Harry, not yet eight years old, seemed largely unaffected by the uproar. And since he was still a day student, Diana felt she could shield the seemingly happy-go-lucky lad from some of the nastier things being said in the media.

William was another matter. At Ludgrove, William quickly used up his allotted number of calls home. When a classmate's mother dropped in to the school, young William begged the woman to use her cell phone "just to call Mummy."

"I'm worried about William," Diana told her friend Carolyn Bartholomew. "He's just like me. He is too sensitive. He feels everything too much." That August of 1992, Diana convinced Charles to send William out of the country so that the boy could escape the insanity—if only for a brief time.

At the E-Bar-L, an exclusive Montana dude ranch set deep in the Rocky Mountains, William quickly impressed even the most grizzled ranch hands. "There were absolutely no airs about him," one cowboy said of the prince, who wore jeans, boots, and a ten-gallon hat during his weeklong stay at the E-Bar-L. "The other kids here loved him. Because he's so good at riding and shooting, he was like the hero. By the end of his stay, he could lasso a steer."

William, who (along with his bodyguard) was accompanied by his best friend Miles Duffy and Miles's businessman father, Simon Duffy, began each day at 7 A.M. with steaming bowls of porridge and tea served in tin mugs. After a schedule packed with shooting, riding, fishing, and swimming in the Black Foot River, William hopped on the back of a wagon with the other children and went on a sunset hayride through the foothills. Then William joined the others around a blazing campfire for a Wild West dinner of steak and beans.

The prince even whooped it up to Texas Tom's Country and Western Band at the Clearwater Inn. Patrons clapped along as the

138

young stranger gamely tried his hand at square dancing and line dancing. "He was two-stepping like a Texan and throwing his hat in the air," one said. "I didn't even know who he was. When someone told me, my admiration for the Royal Family just rocketed. He conducted himself as the perfect little gent."

"We get a lot of celebrities passing through," said Clearwater Inn owner Jim Loran, "but I never thought I'd see the future king of England jigging in my dining room. You could see William didn't want to leave; he was having too much fun."

There were no televisions at the E-Bar-L and only a single telephone that the guests all shared. William got two calls a day—one from Diana and one from Charles. "Harry," he was overheard telling his envious brother, "this is the best holiday *ever*."

William's joy would be short-lived. That September of 1992, as the world's press indulged in an orgy of speculation over the state of their parents' marriage, a gently smiling Harry joined his brother as a student at Ludgrove.

There both boys, staying in separate dormitories, fell into the same unchanging routine: At precisely 7:15 each morning a matron rapped on their dormitory room door, stuck her head in, and shouted, "Good morning!" to the groggy students. The princes then washed up in the bathroom they shared with all the other boys on the floor, and breakfasted in the paneled dining room. Then the boys studied geography, science, history, and

French before heading for the pool or the playing fields for soccer practice.

After dinner at 6 P.M., the boys were allowed to watch television—but only a few preapproved, mostly educational shows—until their 8 P.M. bedtime. The one most frequent infraction at Ludgrove: listening to music after hours. Anyone caught with a Sony Walkman after 8 P.M. was instantly reported to headmaster Gerald Barber.

Barber, who, with his wife, Janet, acted as a surrogate parent to the boys at Ludgrove, took steps to shield William and Harry from the blizzard of tabloid stories about their parents. Staff members were asked not to turn on their television sets when any student was in the vicinity, and told in no uncertain terms not to leave any newspapers lying around.

William circumvented this by stealing into his bodyguard's room next door and turning on the TV or perusing Sergeant Cracker's magazines and newspapers. And even if the other boys weren't reading the scandalous stories about Charles and Diana, their parents certainly were. Soon whatever the princes didn't learn by sneaking into their bodyguard's room filtered back to William and Harry, who reacted in different ways. "Harry just became more and more quiet," said one teacher, "but William seemed visibly upset."

At one point, when another student repeated what he had overheard his parents saying about the Prince and Princess of Wales, William responded by sticking the boy's head in a toilet—and flushing it. Hauled before headmaster Gerald Barber, Prince William promised to never do it again.

For the most part, William did not ask for special treatment. But as his parents' marriage unraveled, he did often ask to phone his mother. Even though there was a general rule against it, an exception was made in the prince's case.

As it turned out, William was not calling to hear comforting words, he was calling to say them. "It'll all be fine, Mummy," he was overheard saying. "Don't worry about us. Harry and I are doing fine..."

In return, Diana indulged her boys without hesitation. On a school break in October, she took them to a racetrack in Kent for a spin in new two-thousand-dollar, 60cc go-carts with their names painted on the front. Diana, clad in leather jacket and jeans, cheered them on as they whipped around the track at fifty miles per hour.

A few weeks later, on November 18, 1992, Charles was eagerly awaiting the arrival of his sons at Sandringham for his annual three-day shooting party when Diana called to cancel. Rather than spending another tense weekend with her in-laws, she would take William and Harry to Highgrove instead.

For Charles, this was the final straw. He was no longer willing to have her dictate the terms of his access to William and Harry. That weekend, he made the decision to ask his wife for a separation. "There was no future in

141

it the way things were going," he later said. "I had no choice."

That Sunday at Highgrove, the boys' go-carts were rolled off the back of a flatbed truck in the middle of a driving rain. Diana checked to make sure Wills and Harry were properly belted in—the Princess always made a point of wearing a seat belt, and drummed this into her children at every opportunity—and then waved a handkerchief to signal the start of their first race. With a slicker-clad Diana again hopping up and down and clapping with glee, the boys careened around the grounds for hours, laughing as they splattered their body-guards and members of the household staff with mud.

Diana, William, and Harry took a short break to share lunch with their loyal help in the staff dining room. This time, the Princess and her princes took obvious pleasure in turning the tables by doing the actual serving. Before she drove the boys back to Ludgrove that evening, the Princess thanked everyone for a perfect weekend at Highgrove—and, as it would turn out, their last there as a family.

Less than a week later, Charles went to Kensington Palace and told Diana he wanted a separation. She was not surprised, though she insisted she had done nothing to intentionally provoke Charles. "I come from a divorced background," she later said. "I didn't want to get into that one again."

While details of a formal separation were being worked out with Buckingham Palace,

Diana was, in her own words, "consumed with worry" over what impact this would have on William and Harry. Earlier, she had revealed some of her own feelings on the subject in a speech to a media seminar marking European Drug Prevention Week. "When I've asked addicts why they become addicted, the most common reason given is anger. Anger at their parents, anger at their schools—at life in general. But why this anger? They feel they were deprived of affection as children and the stability this gives. They are all looking for a firm emotional base," she went on. "A child's stability arises mainly from the affection received from his or her parents. With it, children feel increasingly confident to venture out and face the challenges of the outside world.

"Children are not chores. They are a part of us. If we gave them the love they deserve, they would not try so hard to attract our attention... If the immediate family breaks up, the problems can still be resolved—but only if the children have been brought up from the very start with the feeling that they are wanted, loved, and valued."

On December 3, 1992, Diana drove to Ludgrove to warn William and Harry that news of the separation was about to break. The boys were brought to headmaster Gerald Barber's office, where their mother anxiously waited for them. Ten-year-old William was well aware of the role Camilla played in the breakup. "I put it to William," Diana recalled, "particularly, that if you find someone you love in life, you must hang on to it and look after it and if you were lucky enough to find someone who loved you, then one must protect it. William asked me what had been going on and could I answer his questions, which I did. He said, was that the reason why our marriage had broken up, and I said, 'Well, there were three of us in this marriage, and the pressure of the media was another factor, so the two together were very difficult,' that although I still loved Papa, I couldn't live under the same roof as him, and likewise with him... I put it gently, without resentment or any anger."

William wept, but Harry said nothing. When it was over, William kissed his mother on the cheek. "I hope you'll both be happier now," he said.

It was a tearful moment, but now Diana could breathe a sigh of a relief. "From day one I always knew I'd never be the next queen," she said. "No one ever said that to me. I just knew it... I just had to get out." As for the children: "It's been very hard, but everything will turn out much better for the boys in the end."

The Queen, among others, devoutly hoped this would be the case. She had been worried about what effect all this was having on her grandsons, who more and more seemed to find themselves at ground zero. Michael Shea, the Queen's former press secretary, said of the royal couple that at the end, "the only arguments they had were over the children."

After trying so hard to hold the marriage

together, she now admitted defeat. "I understand it has been very hard on William and Harry," she said. "Perhaps this will make everyone's lives somewhat easier—theirs in particular."

On December 9, 1992, Prime Minister John Major stood up in Parliament to formally announce the separation of the Prince and Princess of Wales. "This decision has been reached amicably," the carefully crafted statement from Buckingham Palace read, "and they will both continue to participate fully in the upbringing of their children. The Queen and the Duke of Edinburgh, though saddened, understand and sympathize with the difficulties that have led to this decision. Her Majesty and His Royal Highness particularly hope the intrusions into the privacy of the Prince and Princess may now cease. They believe that a degree of privacy and understanding is essential if Their Royal Highnesses are to provide a happy and secure upbringing for their children..."

That same year, William and Harry also watched as the marriage of Uncle Andrew and Aunt Sarah came to a nasty end. Then they saw pictures of Granny standing outside in a raincoat and watching as Windsor Castle nearly burned to the ground. For the Royal Family, 1992 had been, in Granny's own words, an *annus horribilis*.

It would not be the last for the young princes. But for now, they grappled with the impending end of their parents' marriage.

145

Diana had tried to prepare William and Harry for the separation announcement, but it nonetheless hit them both hard. William, in particular, seemed moody and distracted. He had already begun shooting up in height, which only made him more awkwardly self-conscious.

"I get this sick feeling in my stomach," he told a friend, "every time I see my mother's picture or my father's picture in the newspapers. I know they're going to say something just terrible. My father calls them 'vultures,' and I think he's right."

From without and within the Royal Family, there was pressure for the boys to take sides. Shortly after their mother came to visit them at Ludgrove, William took Harry aside and they agreed this would never happen. "We mustn't say anything bad about them, or make it seem as if we like one more than the other," William explained to his brother. "Mummy and Papa quarrel, but they both love us equally, so we mustn't hurt either one."

The strain for both boys over the next few months was incalculable, and everyone around them—teachers, bodyguards, maids, valets, the staffs of both the Prince and Princess of Wales—sympathized with the predicament the princelings found themselves in. "Of course it can't help," said Nanny Jessie, "having two parents who are both off their rockers."

Perhaps to compensate for the chaos around him, William tried hard to become the perfect little gentleman. "The press have always written up William as the terror and Harry as a rather quiet second son," said their uncle, Earl Spencer. "In fact William is a very self-possessed, intelligent, and mature boy and quite shy. He is quite formal and stiff, sounding older than his years when he answers the phone."

Diana's friend Carolyn Bartholomew concurred. "Harry is the most affectionate, demonstrative, and huggable little boy," she observed, "while William is intuitive, switched on, and highly perceptive... William is kind-hearted, very much like Diana." Even Diana went out of her way to point out that William was no longer the family hellion. "Harry's the naughty one," Diana said slyly. "Just like me."

Still, William now seemed determined to make up for his days as the marauding "Basher." At church, he could now be counted on to take the Queen Mother's arm and help her down the stairs. Harry, meantime, would lag a few paces behind, holding the church door open for Mummy. By now, William had also begun to master the rules of protocol regarding Granny. He always bowed slightly in the Queen's presence, did not sit in her presence unless she asked him to, tried not to be the first to start a conversation, and never started eating until she began to eat.

Not all lessons in decorum came from the Windsor side. Frances Shand Kydd had drilled into her daughter the importance of responding to every letter with a reply and every gift with a thank-you note. Although William's fan mail, mostly from young girls and their mothers, outnumbered Harry's ten to one, both boys sat down each evening at precisely 6:00 to answer each letter personally.

That first holiday season following the separation announcement, the royal Christmas card spoke volumes. For eleven years, Charles and Diana had sent out a joint Christmas card intended to convey the joy of their loving family unit. They showed the couple with William as an infant, and on a swing, then joined by Harry in a variety of settings. But now that the Waleses were officially separated, they refused to be seen together on the card. Instead, the card was illustrated with a formal portrait of the boys—and only the boys—by Lord Snowdon. In the photograph, William sat in a medieval-looking carved wooden chair, his brother standing behind. Both boys, unsmiling, stared wistfully into the camera. "This really is a heartbreak, isn't it?" Diana said when she saw the card. "A heartbreak."

Beyond the emotional toll, the breakup rocked the institution of the monarchy to its very core. A series of public opinion polls taken immediately after the official announcement of the separation indicated that more and more British subjects wanted William to succeed Queen Elizabeth, bypassing Charles altogether. In a *Sunday Express* poll, 45 percent of those questioned wanted to see Charles crowned the next king, as compared to 49 percent for William. Similarly, polls conducted by the *Sunday Times,* the *Sunday Telegraph,* and the *Mail on Sunday* all showed Charles losing ground to his ten-year-old son.

On Christmas Day, the boys joined their father and the rest of the Royal Family—sans Mummy, of course—at Sandringham. Now that two separate households were being set up to accommodate the boys as they divided their time between Charles and Diana, the Prince of Wales did what he had wanted to do all along: he hired the woman who had been his nanny, sixty-nine-year-old Mabel Anderson, to watch over William and Harry when they were with him.

Anderson was more than just a sentimental choice. While Olga Powell continued to serve as the boys' nanny at Kensington Palace, Charles did not want members of Diana's camp mingling with his. "He won't have any contact between Diana's household and his," said veteran British journalist and royal watcher Ingrid Seward, "because he doesn't want any back-stabbing, gossip, or spying."

With her mercurial daughter-in-law no longer in the picture—at least at family gatherings—the Queen seemed to take special, if characteristically subdued, delight in her grandsons when they arrived at Sandringham that Christmas. "Why, Charles," Granny said as she cast a glance in the direction of Nanny Anderson, "it's like old times."

Perhaps. Granny, Grandpapa, and the royal uncles and aunts did smile and make small talk with the boys. But for the first time William and Harry took serious notice of how much deference was paid to their grandmother—even by their parents. "Diana used to say, 'They are all so cold. They have no heart,' " her friend Lady Bowker said. "William and Harry started to see that it was more than just respect for the Queen that made people bow and scrape. It was fear. Even grown men in uniform, government leaders like the Prime Minister—William and Harry could see them all bowing, everyone afraid to do or say the wrong thing in Her Majesty's presence. Their grandfather Prince Philip having to walk behind their grandmother—for two small boys, it was very intimidating."

The day following Christmas, Boxing Day, the boys joined their mother for a second Christmas celebration at Althorp, the Spencer family's spectacular five-hundred-year-old country estate in Northamptonshire. The separate arrangements made it clear that the hatred Charles and Diana harbored for each other was so intense they could not make an exception even for their sons at Christmas. Nevertheless, Diana was determined not to ruin the holidays for her sons.

In sharp contrast to the dour proceedings at Sandringham, Diana's boisterous, decidedly unstuffy relatives filled Althorp with the sound of raucous laughter. "There were children running around everywhere and the boys just joined right in. They were able to forget all the protocol and just enjoy being children," a Spencer relative recalled. "Diana made sure of that. She loved giving the boys presents and they loved getting them. She just wasn't going to let the separation stand in the way of the boys having a wonderful Christmas." For his part, Spencer allowed the boys to use silver tea trays to toboggan down Althorp's carpeted grand staircase.

Court life had always been the very antithesis of what Diana offered the boys. The rooms at Kensington Palace were nothing less than a shrine to William and Harry. Everywhere there were framed photos of the two men in her life—fishing, riding their bikes and their go-carts, splashing in the pool at Highgrove, clamoring atop tanks, at school, on horseback. The five-foot-tall red leather rhinoceros they reclined on while watching television was propped up next to the fireplace.

It was here, surrounded by needlepoint cushions that read YOU HAVE TO KISS A LOT OF FROGS BEFORE YOU FIND A PRINCE and GOOD GIRLS GO TO HEAVEN, BAD GIRLS GO EVERY-WHERE, that the boys could spend endless hours watching television (*Mr. Bean* videos were a particular favorite) with Mummy, or reduce the Princess of Wales to a giggling heap simply by tickling her. "I tickle back," she said, "but it's two of them and one of me and I am so much more ticklish than they are anyway. It's not fair, but of course that doesn't bother them in the slightest."

What did bother the boys—and their mother—was the unrelenting assault on their privacy by the tabloid press. On a ski trip to Austria in

March of 1993, William and Harry were taking a stroll through the town of Lech with their mother when a pack of paparazzi descended upon them, pushing and shouting until they were rescued by bodyguard Ken Wharfe.

William clearly took such intrusions personally. While his mother and brother managed a few wan smiles for the photographers, William refused to raise his head so they could get a decent shot. "William, William. Head up, please!" they shouted at the boy. At best, the prince would look up and shoot a withering look in the direction of the cameras.

"You should see the way he scowls at them," Diana told a friend. "He hates the press even more than I did when I first got into this family. He sees them as the enemy, but he's going to have to learn that they can be handled." But for the moment, she conceded, "William has every right to be angry. They ruin everything."

As for Harry: The "mischievous imp," as his uncle Earl Spencer described him, was more interested in besting his brother on the go-cart track and the ski slopes than brooding over the loss of his privacy. Still, in the wake of the separation and the frenzied press coverage of one royal scandal after another, William and Harry felt the boundaries of their world shrinking. Where once they could ride their bicycles in Kensington Gardens (albeit with a bodyguard close at hand), now such forays into the open were increasingly rare.

"To not even be able to ride your bicycle or

play with your friends without being attacked by grown men with cameras—do you know what that does to you?" Diana asked. "Do you know how worthless it makes you feel—that people care so little about your feelings? They are just two little boys, just two little boys..."

Unable to venture out without being set upon, the princes drew ever closer to their mother. "Diana was their world," Lady Bowker said, "and they were her world. She was not interested in sharing them with anyone—not Charles, and especially not another woman."

But Charles had other plans. Whenever the boys spent a weekend or holiday with him in the country, they reveled in their time riding, fishing, and shooting together. Nevertheless, Charles told his mother, something was lacking. What the boys needed, it was decided, was a vibrant young woman in their lives other than Diana—a "surrogate mother" who could also be counted on to liven up the proceedings whenever the boys were spending time with Papa.

Charles was still searching for the right "surrogate mother" to help him with his sons when William and Harry arrived in April to spend the Easter holiday with him at Balmoral. Now that William was about to turn eleven, his father decided it was time to take him on his first hunting expedition. Armed with a single-barrel shotgun and backed by two gamekeepers and a valet, William shot six rabbits in the space of two hours.

The next day, newspapers across Britain carried photographs of Wills traipsing through a field with his rifle slung over his shoulder and his valet trailing behind with the day's kill. Harry, too young at age eight to join in the hunt, watched from the sidelines with his father.

Animal rights activists were horrified. "It's a crying shame that yet another generation of the Royal Family is being raised to be degenerate," said John Robbins, head of the group Animal Concern. "I'm sure his mother doesn't approve."

Diana was, in fact, upset—not because she was squeamish about hunting, but because she felt both boys were too young to indulge in such blood sport. "Charles promised me he would wait until William was fourteen before they started killing things," she complained.

A bred-to-the-bone British aristocrat who had been around hunting and hunters all her life, Diana was only thirteen when she shot her first stag. She harbored no illusions about what role hunting was destined to play in her sons' lives. Early in her courtship with Charles, Diana seemed to fit right in with the Royal Family's outdoorsy lifestyle. One of the then–Lady Diana's favorite pastimes was stalking game in the wild. "We went stalking together," recalled Patty Palmer-Tomkinson, a frequent guest at Balmoral. "We got hot, we got tired, and she fell into a bog, she got covered in mud, laughed her head off, hair glued to her forehead because it was pouring with rain... She was sort of a wonderful English schoolgirl who was game for anything."

By the summer of 1993, Diana viewed such pursuits as not only primitive but cruel. Yet her anger over William's rabbit hunt was short-lived, as it became clear that Charles had made yet another serious public relations blunder in their ongoing war to prove who was the better parent. Once again, in comparison to the Princess, Papa Charles looked insensitive and woefully out of touch with the times.

Yet Diana also knew that, given her sons' undeniable love of the outdoors, she could not compete with grouse hunting at Sandringham or fishing along the River Dee at Balmoral. Then, in the spring of 1993, Diana's brother unexpectedly offered her a solution to this problem.

A high-living womanizer of considerable renown, Charles Spencer was only twenty-two when Fleet Street dubbed him "Champagne Charlie." When his father died in 1992, the year the Prince and Princess of Wales separated, Champagne Charlie became Earl Spencer. He also inherited a $122 million estate that included the ancestral home, Althorp.

Now Spencer was offering his sister the four-bedroom Garden House on the grounds of Althorp. There, he suggested, she could start a new life for herself and her sons. The Garden House was in many ways ideally suited for this purpose. For once, the omnipresent armed bodyguard who lived at Kensington Palace could be stationed in another building on the estate grounds. The Garden House also afforded its occupant total privacy; it was not visible from any other building at Althorp. "At long last," Diana said, "I can make a cozy nest of my own."

Three weeks later, Spencer called to tell Diana he was withdrawing the offer. He had gone over the security precautions that would have to be taken, and was told that guards and security cameras would have to be placed all over Althorp, infringing on his family's privacy. He also pointed out that Althorp, like other stately homes of England, was open to the public. With tourists roaming around, Diana would have to virtually lock herself in her little Garden House several hours out of every day for much of the summer and part of the fall.

A crestfallen Diana wrote a letter begging her younger brother to reconsider. She received no reply. Brother and sister did not speak for months.

Diana saw her brother's actions as nothing less than an act of betrayal. It only served to fuel the Princess's conviction that she was routinely being victimized by men, and led her to address a conference on women and mental health on June 1, 1993. She discussed her fears for women "trapped in the private hell of mental turmoil" and mothers thrust into "deeper and darker depression by feelings of powerlessness."

Not long after, she met with her solicitor in Kensington Palace and signed a will stating flatly that, should she die, Charles would not have the sole final word in their children's upbringing. "I express the wish," the will read, "that should I predecease my husband, he will consult with my mother with regard to the upbringing, education, and welfare of our children."

Then, by way of delivering a slap to the face of the Royal Family, Diana insisted that, in the event that both she and Charles died, their sons would be raised by her family, not his. "Should any child of mine be under age at the date of the death of the survivor of myself and my husband, I APPOINT my mother and my brother EARL SPENCER to be the guardians..."

The bulk of the estate, the document stipulated, would be divided equally between William and Harry but held in trust until they turned twenty-five. Signed "Diana" in the Princess's distinctively bold hand, the will was witnessed by Paul Burrell and Diana's private secretary, P. D. Jephson. Its contents, which revealed the depth of Diana's distrust of the Royal Family—and her desire to have William and Harry grow up outside their sphere of influence—would remain secret for the next five years.

Even as she saw William being indoctrinated in the ways of the Windsors, Diana was adamant that neither child be pressured into public appearances. "They have a lifetime of ceremony ahead of them," she told a friend. "I want them to stay children as long as possible." Nevertheless, on July 29, Harry, who like most boys his age was obsessed with playing soldier, enjoyed his first official public engagement accompanying his mother on a visit to the Light Dragoons regiment in Germany.

Diana could take solace in the fact that Charles was not the only male role model for her sons. Their leather-jacketed, shaggy-maned thirty-one-year-old cousin David Linley occasionally dropped by to give the boys rides on the back of his motorcycle. Princess Anne's son, Peter Phillips, who at fifteen was four years older than William and already an accomplished horseman, regularly visited Harry to give him riding tips. And while the Waleses were away—Diana on an official visit to Zimbabwe and Charles at a polo match—Formula 1 racing legend Jackie Stewart took Harry for a spin around the Silverstone track, home of the British Grand Prix.

Mummy, exhausted from her trip to Africa and a seemingly endless series of tree plantings, ribbon cuttings, and walkabouts, tried to spend what little spare time she had with the boys. The stress, William and Harry could not help but notice, was taking its toll on their mother. On August 2, Diana and her sons were photographed as they left a screening of *Jurassic Park*. William and Harry watched in amazement as Diana dashed past stunned ticket holders in London's Leicester Square and shrieked, "You make my life hell!" into the face of the hapless photographer.

It did not help matters that the Princess was

about to turn William and Harry over to their father for an eighteen-day vacation. While the Windsor men went off on a cruise of the Greek isles aboard John Latsis's yacht *Alexander*, Diana hied away to Bali with her pals Rosa Monckton, head of Tiffany's in London, and Lucia Flecha de Lima, wife of Brazil's ambassador to the United States.

While Diana soaked in the sun at two of the world's most exotic resorts, the Amanusa and the Amanwana, her sons stayed belowdecks watching videos aboard the *Alexander*. When they boarded a royal train for Scotland on August 16, William and Harry, dressed in ties, sport coats, and corduroys, looked, in the words of the *Daily Mail*, "pale and glum." Chimed in the *Sun*: "The young princes looked awkward and uncomfortable in stiff, old-fashioned clothes." William and Harry, the paper continued, "walked three paces behind their dad in total silence. They were a far cry from the boisterous boys who giggle happily when they are out with Princess Di."

Most of the world was already convinced that Charles was a somewhat cold, emotionally repressed dad. But this was not enough for Diana. Much of the Princess's time during her South Seas idyll was spent thinking of ways to top her husband when it came to entertaining the boys—and at the same time prove to the world that she was the more devoted parent. In an audacious move certain to capture the attention of the world press, Diana returned to London and on August 24, 1993, swept her children off to Florida for a ten-day holiday at Walt Disney World. Their British Airways flight landed in Orlando at 3 P.M., and two hours later William and Harry were plummeting down Space Mountain as Mummy screamed with delight at their side.

An unmitigated public relations triumph, the trip to Disney World nevertheless only served to fuel criticism from the Palace's old guard. The "men in gray" continued to portray the Princess of Wales as a manipulative, emotionally unstable publicity hound. "Diana is headstrong, but we must show her love and understanding and bend over backwards," a Palace official told the press. "Because if she became bitter and twisted, it would be impossible for the children."

Such patronizing comments aside, Diana returned to England from her Florida sojourn feeling relaxed and refreshed. The feeling vanished in an instant when Diana was told what for her was devastating news: Charles had found the "surrogate mother" he had been looking for.

Diana was furious. Charles had at least been scrupulously careful never to involve Camilla Parker Bowles in their sons' lives; she had never even met William and Harry. But now he had hired a stranger to usurp the role Diana valued above all others—that of mother.

Within days of the boys' return from Disney World, Charles introduced the attractive brunette to William and Harry. She was officially hired as a thirty-two-thousand-dollar-

"Absolutely high as a kite" was the way Diana, not yet twenty-one, described her mood when "Baby Wales" was born on June 21, 1982. He was a week old before his parents finally agreed on a name: William.

2

3

4

In an increasingly rare moment of family togetherness, nine-month-old William posed with his parents in Auckland, New Zealand. A few weeks later, Mummy and Papa embarked on a tour of Canada without their baby, missing Wills's first birthday.

William the Terrible, a.k.a. "the Basher." A page at the wedding of Sarah Ferguson to Prince Andrew in July 1986, four-year-old Wills repeatedly made faces and squirmed in his seat.

5

William is scolded by one of his nannies, Olga Powell, after throwing a tantrum.

6

7

8

9

Wills laughed when Prince Harry, eight months old, tried to play the piano. Later, they shared horsey time in the Kensington Palace nursery. On their way to watch Papa play polo in 1987, the protective older brother helped Harry stay dry.

On vacation with the king and queen of Spain in Majorca, Harry, four, hugged a pup. Then Charles and Wills looked on while Mummy helped "the spare" with his shoe.

10

11

12

"There was an unspoken language between them," a friend said of Diana and William. As his parents' marriage crumbled, the prince took it upon himself to cheer up his mother in 1987.

William takes the wheel of a royal fire engine while Harry gets lost in his helmet at Sandringham in January 1988.

13

Like all members of
the Royal Family,
William was put on
horseback almost
from the time he
could walk. In March
1988, Highgrove
groom Maureen Cox
put William's pony
through its paces.

14

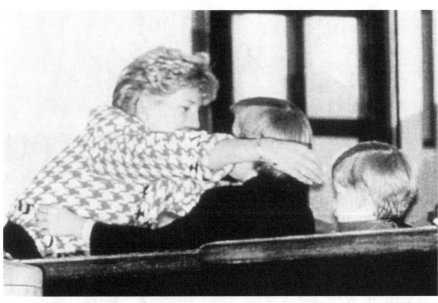

15

"I can't bear to be away from them," Diana often said.
That was evident when William and Harry joined her
in Canada for a holiday aboard the royal yacht
Britannia in October 1991.

In September 1989, a small army of photographers was on hand to record Harry's first day of school at Wetherby, where his brother was already enrolled.

16

17

Vacationing with Mummy on the Caribbean island of Necker in April 1990, William and Harry took a stab at building a sand-castle. A better skier than William, Harry showed off his prowess on the slopes while vacationing with Mummy in Austria.

18

For their first Christmas card following Charles and Diana's December 1992 separation announcement, the boys struck a lonely pose—the first card without their parents. "A heartbreak," Diana said.

19

At the Swiss ski resort of Klosters, the princes posed with two of their favorite cousins— Beatrice and Eugenie, daughters of Prince Andrew and Fergie.

20

Determined that William and Harry experience the joys of childhood, Diana took the boys careening down a water ride at Thorpe Park outside London in 1993.

21

22

23

24

Harry and nanny Tiggy Legge-Bourke enjoyed each other's company at a country fair, roughhousing at Balmoral, and rushing to join Prince Charles at St. James's Palace. Over Diana's objections, Tiggy remained an important figure in the boys' lives.

25   During a trip to Colorado in July 1995,
William and Harry went white-water
rafting with Mummy.

26

With both parents looking over his shoulder, William enrolled at Eton on September 6, 1995. The next day he was on his way to class in tails and striped pants.

27

28

Life with Harry:
Mummy and her
second son
enjoyed a tender
moment while
watching a
tennis tourna-
ment in 1994.
Later, after
lunch at a
London restau-
rant, they
checked to see if
the coast was
clear of
paparazzi.

29

Much to their mother's regret, both William and Harry embraced the Windsors' love of hunting at an early age. In November 1995, Harry and his father shot grouse at Sandringham.

30

How much longer? the princes wonder during VJ Day ceremonies in August 1995. William and Harry were themselves casualties in the ongoing war between their parents, who kept a chilly distance.

31

Looking like any fourteen-year-old boy (albeit one with a bodyguard nearby), William goes virtually unnoticed as he shops in London's West Kensington district.

32

33

While vacationing with Dodi Fayed in the South of France, Diana and Harry took a Jet Ski out for a spin.

34

William watches the wind catch Great-granny's dress on the occasion of her ninety-seventh birthday in August 1997.
She disliked Diana *and* Camilla.

Five days after her death, Diana's boys fought back tears after looking over the mountain of floral tributes left outside Kensington Palace. After the funeral service at Westminster Abbey, William and Harry stood with Earl Spencer and Papa as the hearse carrying Mummy's body pulled away.

35

36

a-year aide to Charles's private secretary, Commander Richard Aylard. But, Charles told his sons, she would in fact be replacing Mabel Anderson as their thoroughly modern nanny. The young woman's name was Alexandra, but she hastened to tell her new charges, "No one calls me that." From now on, the princes were to call her what everyone else called her: Tiggy.

I want them to lead from the heart, not the head.

—*Diana on raising her sons*

There was no emotion in the Royal Family, no feeling for other people. Diana was teaching her boys what it is like to be a real human being.

—*Lady Elsa Bowker, Diana's friend*

I know I shouldn't spoil you boys, but I can't help it. You're irresistible!

—*Diana to William and Harry*

5

Idon't need a substitute father for the boys when they're with me," Diana said. "So why does Charles need a substitute mother when they are with him?"

No one fully appreciated the extent to which Diana resented Tiggy Legge-Bourke, least of all Tiggy herself. "She immediately became an object of curiosity and suspicion to the Princess," said Diana's private secretary, P. D. Jephson, "and of course an innocent target for much of her unhappiness about the rest of the world."

Although Tiggy worked for Charles and therefore had little direct contact with Diana's camp, she did pay a call on Jephson. By way of friendly warning, Jephson cautioned Tiggy that the Prince and Princess of Wales used their children as pawns in their ongoing power struggle, and that it was important she not find herself, as the boys' new nanny, caught in the middle.

"Doesn't bother me," Tiggy replied matter-of-factly. "I'm just the nursery maid, guv."

Tiggy made it clear at the time that she regarded Jephson as "completely paranoid." Still, he knew that Tiggy's "idealism and transparent good nature would be sorely tested. Whatever world of security and happiness she intended to build up around William and Harry, it was inevitably at risk of becoming an exposed position in the no-man's-land between two hostile front lines."

Ironically, in many ways she reminded the boys of their mother—a tall, beautiful, ebullient young woman with an incandescent smile, a rafter-rattling laugh, and a talent for doling out hugs and tickles. There were differences, to be sure. Not remotely as stylish or sophisticated as the Princess of Wales, thirty-year-old Tiggy was a self-avowed fresh-scrubbed country girl who loved to ride, hike, fish, ski, and shoot.

Tiggy's love of the outdoors began in the Welsh mountains, where she grew up the daughter of a merchant banker and a Welsh aristocrat on her family's six-thousand-acre estate, Glanusk Park. As a young girl she attended a convent school run by Ursuline nuns, then went on to the Manor House in Dunford, an exclusive school run by Lady Tryon, mother-in-law of one of Prince Charles's old flames, Lady "Kanga" Tryon. From Manor House, Tiggy enrolled in Heathfield, an elite boarding school for girls in Ascot, a village in Berkshire. Coincidentally, Tiggy then proceeded to the Institut Alpin Videmanette, the same Swiss boarding school Diana had attended.

Tiggy continued to follow Diana's career path. Just as Diana had become a teacher at the Young England kindergarten school in central London, Tiggy attended a Montessori teaching seminar before opening her own nursery school in Battersea, South London, in 1985. She named the school "Mrs. Tiggiwingle," after Beatrix Potter's legendary hedgehog. The name stuck—from then on Legge-Bourke would always be known as Tiggy—though the school did not.

After three years, Mrs. Tiggiwingle folded, and Tiggy went looking for work. She would not have to look for long. The Legge-Bourkes were no strangers to the Windsors; Tiggy's mother had been lady-in-waiting to Princess Anne. Tiggy was only six when she was first introduced to Charles, and over the years impressed the Prince of Wales with her seemingly boundless love for the outdoors. On visits to Balmoral and Sandringham, Tiggy quickly proved that she was a match for any man when it came to fishing and shooting.

Within months, Tiggy had established herself as a sort of big sister to the boys. At Highgrove (which Charles had had redecorated and where not a single photograph of Diana could be found), Sandringham, St. James's Palace, and Balmoral, Tiggy spent endless hours playing with the boys. When William and Harry climbed trees, she climbed right up after them. She was a worthy competitor on the soccer field, and in the pool, Tiggy pushed and dunked and splashed her young charges without hesitation. Since she was always given a room next to the princes, Tiggy could join in their requisite pillow fights well into the night.

"Both boys adored Tiggy, and she was devoted to them," a friend of Legge-Bourke's

167

later said. "She was more like an older sister or a cousin. They teased her and she gave back as good as she got." Tiggy also provided a much-needed respite from the escalating tensions between Mummy and Papa—tensions that were having their effect on William in particular.

While Harry seemed, in his mother's words, to "take everything in stride," William's grades began to slip in the months immediately following the announcement of his parents' separation. At home, he had become anxious and withdrawn. Where once he slipped tissues under the door to his distraught mother, William was now the one locking himself in the bathroom and sobbing quietly.

Tiggy's appearance on the scene boosted William's flagging spirits—and his grades at Ludgrove. "She brought stability to the princes' world, but she also made them laugh," said a member of the household staff at Highgrove. "They needed that, perhaps more than anything."

Nevertheless, Diana fumed. Not only was Charles still putting his polo matches and trysts with Camilla ahead of William and Harry, but now he had a "surrogate mother" to keep her sons entertained. Whenever the boys were not at home with the Princess or in school, Diana would pick up the papers and see photographs of Tiggy taking the boys shopping, playfully teasing the boys as they walked across a muddy polo field, or generally just keeping the young princes entertained. Whenever Charles took the boys on holiday to Klosters or the Mediterranean, Tiggy was always there, making the boys laugh while freeing up time for their father to socialize with his grown-up friends.

Equally upsetting to Diana were the overt signs of affection between Tiggy and the boys. Diana cringed when she saw photos of Harry sitting on Tiggy's lap, or of Tiggy hugging William in public. One series of pictures showed Tiggy joking around with William as they left church one Sunday, playfully throwing an arm around him and mussing his hair before the prince, laughing, managed to break free. Tiggy had even taken to calling William and Harry "my babies"—a degree of familiarity their mother was not about to countenance.

Diana fired off a series of letters to her husband demanding clarification of Legge-Bourke's role and demanding to be involved in deciding what the nature of Tiggy's contact with the boys would be. Charles did respond by telling Tiggy to keep a somewhat lower profile, although the nanny's influence over the young princes continued to grow exponentially.

"Her greatest frustration was her inability to influence the day-to-day direction of Tiggy Legge-Bourke's contact with the boys," Jephson said. "Although this caused her genuine distress, my sympathy was tinged with the thought that the Prince's role as father would have been very hard to discharge *without* Tiggy's assistance, given his other commitments."

"Diana raged that Tiggy always seemed to be having fun with the boys," said Richard Kay, a *Daily Mail* columnist and trusted confidant of the Princess. Jephson noted that it was "hard for the Princess to be content with the reality of her reduced influence over her children's activities." Perhaps, but Diana had never voiced an objection to the hiring of a nanny to help Charles out with the boys. Tiggy was clearly far more than "just the nursery maid, guv," as Legge-Bourke so wryly put it. She was a best friend, big sister, and surrogate mum all rolled into one.

"Tiggy was all the more of a threat," said Andrew Morton, "because she was similar in age and social status to Diana and mixed easily with Prince Charles's friends." Not surprisingly, Diana, knowing full well that Charles had slept with a not inconsiderable number of high-bred young women during his bachelor days, began to speculate about the exact nature of his relationship with the boys' attractive nanny. The Princess, noted her private secretary, "developed an increasingly lurid fantasy picture of Tiggy's private life. No man in the Prince's entourage was safe from her suspicions, including the Prince himself."

Diana's suspicions, however ill founded, were understandable given her embattled position within Britain's First Family. "Everyone in the Royal Family was against her," Lady Bowker said. "*Everyone,* including the Queen and the Queen Mother. They made her life hell." All of which was made more ironic by the fact that the Spencers, who could trace their British ancestry at least as far back as the eleventh century, were infinitely more English than the royals themselves. The Windsors were, in fact, not Windsors at all but Wettins; the Teutonic-sounding name was changed to Windsor at the height of anti-German sentiment during World War I. Diana disdainfully referred to her Windsor in-laws simply as "the Germans." Greek-born Prince Philip, meanwhile, was "Stavros," and Charles variously "the Great White Hope" and "the Boy Wonder." Diana had no nickname for the Queen, although for friends she often performed a dead-on imitation of her.

With Tiggy suddenly thrown into the equation, Diana, already marginalized by the "men in gray," grew desperate over the thought of losing her sons. "What would any mother do under these circumstances?" one of the Princess's closest allies asked. "Tiggy may have been a wonderful girl, but all Diana saw was a young woman hired to replace her in the princes' lives. She was frantic."

Diana told Bowker and other friends that she was sure the Palace was behind the hiring of the young Legge-Bourke. "It's the men in gray," she said during one tearful call. "I know it. They're trying to brainwash my boys so they will forget me. But that won't happen, because I am their mother and I won't let it happen."

For her first few months on the job, Tiggy

took care to personally hand off the boys to their mother and to stay for a few moments at Kensington Palace to chat with the Princess. Paradoxically, according to friends of Legge-Bourke, she harbored no small degree of respect for the Princess of Wales—if for no other reason than that she had played the biggest role in raising William and Harry. "Whatever people say about her," Tiggy remarked, "whatever problems she may or may not have, the Princess has done a brilliant job raising those two boys."

But by the autumn of 1993, Diana was no longer inviting Tiggy inside Kensington Palace. Instead, the Princess insisted that the boys simply be dropped off with their bodyguard at the door.

Whenever William and Harry did return to Kensington Palace after spending time with their father, Diana deftly debriefed the boys on their activities. At first, they eagerly shared the details of their fun times with Tiggy. But even so skilled an actress as Diana could not conceal her simmering jealousy for long; soon William and Harry were volunteering nothing, and, when their mother pressed them for information, played down their affection for Tiggy. "I can't get anything out of them anymore," the Princess complained. "The boys know it upsets me, so they just keep trying to change the subject."

In truth, neither boy could understand why their mother harbored such intense feelings of resentment toward Tiggy. "Diana was a very fragile person, very insecure," said Lady Bowker. "She worried that the boys would be stolen from her. Perhaps she did not realize how much William and Harry both worshiped her. No one could ever take Diana's place in their lives."

Moreover, while Diana seemed to be willing to concede that Harry—the child Charles had initially spurned for not being a girl—had formed a special bond with his father, she also admitted that hers was more than a typical mother-son relationship with William.

"Diana had a mother-and-son relationship and a mother-and-husband relationship with William," said her friend the designer Roberto Devorik. "She told me she had with her son William very private and very profound conversations, and he was an extraordinary moral support."

From an early age, said her friend Rosa Monckton, Diana "told Prince William in particular more things than most mothers would have told their children. But she had no choice. She wanted them to hear the truth from her, about her life, and the people she was seeing, and what they meant to her, rather than read a distorted, exaggerated, and frequently untrue version in the tabloid press."

That meant sitting down and pouring out her heart to her eldest son, sometimes for hours on end. She talked about their father's lasting devotion to Camilla—hardly necessary, since the Prince of Wales now openly kept a photo of his mistress at his bedside. But she also discussed how difficult the Palace was making her life, and how overwhelming the demands of her public schedule had become.

Diana also shared with William what had become an abiding interest in what she called her "spiritual journey." Beginning with Stephen Twigg, who had first turned up at Kensington Palace to treat the Princess's anxiety with deep massage therapy, Diana sought the advice and counsel of a wide range of New Age gurus. Spiritual healer Simone Simmons visited her at Kensington Palace once a week. In 1992, Debbie Frank replaced Betty Palko as Diana's permanent astrologer, and two years later the Princess would begin seeing psychic Rita Rogers, whose work with parents trying to contact their deceased children struck a chord with Diana.

William listened as his mother described what she had learned about homeotherapy, hypnotherapy, aromatherapy, reflexology, and herbal medicine. She told him about the magical powers of crystals; a white crystal (ostensibly conferring on the wearer stability and a clear state of mind) often dangled from her neck. William listened while she explained the ancient science of feng shui and why she hired an expert to arrange her furniture at Kensington Palace to promote harmony in her environment.

Mummy also went to her close confidante Ursula Gately twice monthly for colonic irrigation. The Princess did not share these details with William, but she did take him with her for t'ai chi lessons and to be pierced with acupuncture needles by Irish nurse Oonagh Toffolo.

When Mummy spoke of her intense belief in the healing power of touch, William understood. Time and again he had witnessed the almost mystical connection his mother made with the afflicted. She perched on the beds of children undergoing chemotherapy, held hands with AIDS patients, and embraced women who wept as they told harrowing tales of domestic abuse. "When I cup my hands around the face of someone suffering," she told William, "they are comforting me as much as I am comforting them."

This "special genius for compassion," as Rosa Monckton called it, was never more in evidence to William than in the months following his parents' separation. By way of distracting herself from the tragic disintegration of her own marriage and shoring up her support among the public at large, Diana plunged headlong into her various causes.

In addition to her grueling schedule of public appearances—including an endless number of galas and celebrity fund-raisers as well as ribbon cuttings and hospital visits—there were the countless unpublicized acts of kindness. "I pay attention to people, and I remember them," Diana told William. To prove the depth of her concern, Diana sometimes dropped in on the parents of children she had visited in the hospital to see how they were doing. This way she established friendships that lasted for years without ever being publicized in her lifetime.

By late 1993, Diana was arguably the world's most celebrated humanitarian, next to her friend Mother Teresa. "Her overall effect on charity is probably more significant than any other person's in the twentieth century," said British fund-raising manager Stephen Lee.

Yet Diana herself was emotionally fragile—something William also knew all too well. That very vulnerability made his mother's courage in the face of other people's pain that much more astounding to her son. "She had a huge capacity for unhappiness," Monckton once observed of her friend, "which is why she responded so well to the suffering face of humanity." She had, Monckton went on, "a unique ability to spot the brokenhearted. I shall never forget her face, her touch, her warmth and compassion."

As for her own "spiritual journey," Diana dared not mention any of her offbeat beliefs to her in-laws because, as her friend Vivienne Parry put it, the Palace already had embarked on "a whispering campaign that this woman was a cracked vessel, that she was potty—a danger to the family."

But she knew she could share her innermost thoughts with William. "Both boys were *incredibly* proud of their mother," Simmons said. "They would never make fun of her."

At age eleven, William was Diana's most trusted confidant cum soul mate. The position did not come without a price. "William's role was more that of alternative husband than son," said one friend. "It was a heavy burden for anyone, but especially someone so young." Ironically, the very thing that made him such a compassionate listener—the heightened sensitivity he had inherited from Diana—left him feeling drained.

A recurring theme in their conversations was Diana's growing sense of isolation—and the nagging fear that, in the end, she would be shoved out of her sons' lives altogether. Diana had cause for concern. The Royal Family had closed ranks solidly behind the Prince of Wales. Princess Margaret, whom Diana had regarded as a friend, wrote her a stinging rebuke. Prince Philip penned a similarly damning letter to his daughter-in-law, and refused even to acknowledge her presence at William's eleventh birthday party. The Queen, who had long resented Camilla for conducting an extramarital affair with her son, now wanted to hurt Diana so badly that she invited both Camilla and her husband, Andrew Parker Bowles, to her royal box at Ascot.

Yet as devoted as they were to Mummy, the boys were also close to Papa, and, by extension, to the rest of the Royal Family. As is common in many families, Prince Charles's overbearing father and his cold, distant mother proved to be doting grandparents.

The boys were well aware of how much Diana and Prince Philip detested each other, but that did not stop either from loving their grandfather. At Sandringham and Balmoral,

Philip took his grandsons hunting wildfowl, taking special care to teach them some of the finer points of shooting.

Meantime Granny, who had made a point of seeing William for tea each week at Buckingham Palace, was already an integral part of the boy's life. The Queen would occasionally take care to invite Harry along for tea as well, although she did not try to conceal the fact that her first priority was the heir, not the spare. In the coming years, Granny would strengthen that bond as part of the Palace's overall strategy to reduce Diana's dominion over their lives.

Yet if William and Harry were already showing signs of growing up to be fine young men, then surely Diana deserved the lion's share of the credit. "The future monarch was King William V, and the Princess took none of her responsibilities more seriously than this—to prepare her children for life in the public eye," said P. D. Jephson.

She stepped up the campaign after the separation, when it became clear that she would never be Queen. "She concentrated instead," Jephson said, "on passing on to William the art of being royal." Toward that end, Diana had taught the boys from the very beginning to be considerate to the staff that shared their lives.

The Princess also made sure her sons behaved graciously in their everyday dealings with other people. At McDonald's and at the movies, she made the boys wait in line—albeit with their Personal Protection Officer—like everybody else.

"If someone brought them orange juice when what they really wanted was a Coke," a friend said, "they were instructed to say thank you and drink the orange juice." On one occasion, Harry asked politely for something other than what he'd been served. Diana was not pleased. "She told him it didn't matter what he wanted; he should simply have thanked the person for what he had been given," Rosa Monckton said.

"That's the sort of thing," Diana said as she continued to scold Harry, "that gave the Royal Family a bad name for being difficult."

Behind closed doors, correcting her sons' manners would not always be an easy task. At Kensington Palace one day, Diana passed Harry's room when she noticed he had left a pile of laundry on a chair.

"Oh, Harry, pick up your laundry," Mummy said.

"Don't say, 'Oh, Harry,' " he snapped in reply.

When she walked by fifteen minutes later, the laundry was still on the chair. "Oh, Harry, I told you to pick it up," his mother said.

"It seems to me," he said imperiously, "I asked you not to say, 'Oh, Harry.' " As Diana's eyes widened in anger, the prince quickly swept up the laundry in his arms and departed.

Those few times they accompanied their mother during public appearances, Jephson said, the princes "learned how to conduct a walkabout in streets lined with beseeching, expectant, and adoring faces—a daunting sight for a ten-year-old—with every sign of genuine delight."

"Isn't it funny," Diana would say, "that when everybody is telling their children not to talk to strangers, I'm telling my sons to go out of their way to be warm and friendly to them."

As a result of Diana's civilizing efforts, William's royal bearing was evident early on. At the family's first Christmas party following the separation, William delivered a polished speech to hundreds of guests. "Sometimes he sounds like a thirty-year-old," his mother often observed.

It was no coincidence that Diana's rooms at Kensington Palace were heaped with books about Jacqueline Kennedy Onassis. Beyond seeing the obvious parallels between herself and that other twentieth-century avatar of chic, Diana admired the way she was able to raise two happy, well-adjusted, scrupulously polite, and defiantly normal children in the white-hot glare of global fame. "Jackie has done such a brilliant job raising Caroline and John," she told a visitor to Kensington Palace. "I want to emulate her as a mother."

Like Jackie, Diana was a master manipulator of the media. And like Jackie, Diana found there were times when even she was pushed to the breaking point by the unrelenting intrusiveness of the press. In early November of 1993, the Princess picked up the London *Sunday*

Mirror to see a series of rather unflattering photographs of herself, clad in a leotard and spread-legged on an exercise machine. The pictures had been taken secretly by Bryce Taylor, the owner of the West London gym where she frequently worked out. Taylor, a New Zealand businessman, had been paid a reported $150,000 for the photos.

William and Harry, home at Kensington Palace for the weekend, walked into their mother's sitting room to find her weeping with frustration.

"They have no right," William said as he put his arm around his mother. "Mummy, isn't there something you can do?"

Diana, who would tell P. D. Jephson and others that this flagrant violation of her privacy was akin to being "raped," phoned her solicitors and instructed them to sue Taylor and the Mirror Group Newspapers. Eventually, Diana would prevail, and the paper would agree to pay a significant amount to one of the Princess's favorite charities.

The publication of the secret gym photos was a watershed event for Diana and her boys. Until now, William and Harry had watched as their parents stood by helplessly, unable to combat the rampant stories about their marital woes because, for the most part, those stories were all too painfully true. "It was a small light at the end of the tunnel," said a family friend. "But for the first time William and Harry saw that in some cases they could fight back—and win."

Diana went one step further. She now wanted to drop out of sight for a while, and asked her most trusted adviser what he thought of the idea. William urged her to go ahead with the plan. "He told me that I worked harder than anybody," she said, "and that I should do whatever made me happy."

At a charity luncheon on December 3, 1993, Diana, her voice shaking with emotion, announced her withdrawal from public life. After a dozen years center stage, she now pleaded for more "time and space." When she married the Prince of Wales, she said, she knew the press would pay attention to her private and public lives but had no concept of "how overwhelming that attention would become—nor the extent to which it would affect both my public duties and my personal life, in a manner that has been hard to bear."

Diana went on to say that, in order to focus on rebuilding her private life, she would scale back the number of charities she supported. "My first priority will continue to be our children, William and Harry, who deserve as much love, care, and attention as I am able to give, as well as an appreciation of the tradition into which they were born."

It was a move the Princess might not have made had it not been for the unauthorized workout photos. "Bryce Taylor pushed me into the decision to go," Diana said. "The pictures were horrid, simply horrid."

Now that Diana had slashed her public schedule dramatically, William and Harry were, more than ever, the focus of her life. According to the terms of the separation, she saw them on alternate weekends and divided school holidays evenly with Charles.

On Fridays, Diana would drive to Ludgrove with her bodyguard, pick the boys up, and have them back at Kensington Palace in time for tea. It was important to her that the boys regard Kensington Palace as their base as much as or more than Highgrove. "I want them to know Kensington Palace is their home," she said, "and not a public building."

At 8:30 the next morning, the boys would have breakfast together with their Kensington Palace nanny Olga Powell, then join their mother at her new gym, the exclusive Harbour Club in Chelsea. There they took tennis lessons or swam; to the surprise of other club members, Diana and the boys engaged in furious splash fights, and took obvious delight in dunking one another.

Occasionally, the Princess took them to race go-carts at a track in Berkshire—Harry's favorite diversion—or to local amusement parks. More often than not, they amused themselves riding their BMX bikes or tossing water bombs at each other on the ample grounds of Kensington Palace.

Harry was, at age nine, fast emerging as the feistier, more combative, and more competitive of the two. Always cast in a supporting role, the "spare" was struggling to emerge from his brother's shadow. Although William was already showing signs of becoming a superb athlete,

Harry was already besting him on horseback and as a marksman. He also routinely beat his older brother on the go-cart circuit.

William, humiliated by suffering defeat so many times at the hands of his little brother, reacted by spending more and more time with his own circle of friends. "Prince Harry was ferociously intent on beating his brother, whatever sport or game they were playing," said the mother of a classmate. "You could see it in his face—he would grit his teeth and really make that extra effort. William didn't have the same need to win, but you could tell he was embarrassed."

Diana did not discourage Harry's competitive streak. "Harry was a bit of a rascal, and she loved that about him," Lady Bowker said. "But Diana was always closer to William, and of course everyone was always more interested in the future king, so Diana felt perhaps a bit guilty about that. She knew that Harry sometimes felt ignored, and I think she understood why he wanted to show people that he was as good as his brother."

In London with Mummy, the princes also went to West End musicals such as *Oliver!,* such eateries as the Chicago Rib Shack and Smollensky's Balloon, and Alton Towers amusement park. They also stocked up on fashionably laid-back clothes—the jeans, sneakers, sweatshirts, and bomber jackets that Diana preferred to see them in—and after dinner watched videos or played Nintendo before going to bed.

William and Harry reveled in the time they

spent with their mother. But they also enjoyed the alternate weekends they spent with Papa and Tiggy. Torn between his fondness for his nanny and his concern for his mother, William made a point of praising his mother whenever possible around other members of the Royal Family.

Still, Diana's in-laws would continue in their ongoing campaign to push Diana out of her children's lives. "She had no level of trust in the Royal Family," her friend Richard Greene observed. "She was fully aware of their intentions." On Christmas Eve of 1993, the Princess gamely showed up to spend time with her sons at Sandringham, but the next morning returned alone to Kensington Palace. While Charles, the Queen, and the Windsor relatives celebrated Christmas with Diana's boys, she ate lunch alone in her room and then went for a swim at Buckingham Palace.

The following morning, the Princess flew to Washington to visit Lucia Flecha de Lima. She told her friend how desperately she missed William and Harry. "I cried all the way out and all the way back," Diana said, "I felt so sorry for myself."

But it was the boys she felt sorry for when, on June 29, 1994, their father admitted to a national television audience that he had committed adultery. The interview, designed to pique interest in his forthcoming authorized biography, ignited a firestorm of controversy. NOT FIT TO REIGN, shouted the banner headline in the *Daily Mirror*.

William and Harry had other reasons to be upset. By bizarre coincidence, the same day the controversial taped TV interview aired, Prince Charles was manning the controls of one of the Queen's jets when it ran off the runway on the Scottish island of Islay.

If this was not disconcerting enough for the boys, newspapers the next day also carried photographs of their mother, looking glamorous and happy as she swept into a gala at Hyde Park's Serpentine Gallery. The message was clear: despite her husband's hurtful remarks on television, his estranged wife was having the time of her life.

No one could protect William and Harry from the barrage of revelations, scandals, and headlines that would ensue. Two months after their father's televised confession, it was reported that the boys' mother had made hundreds of harassing phone calls to millionaire art dealer Oliver Hoare, the married father of three.

Then, in October, *Princess in Love* hit the bookstores and made headlines around the world. In it, James Hewitt recounted in lurid detail his six-year-long affair with William and Harry's mother. The book included the dates, times, locations, and circumstances of their trysts.

Diana, concerned about the impact on her sons, would later recall that she "ran to them as fast as I could." The Princess drove straight to Ludgrove, sat down with them both, but, before she could utter a syllable, twelve-year-old William handed her a box of chocolates. "Mummy," he said, "I think you've been hurt. These will make you smile again."

Diana was overcome with emotion, touched by her sons' sensitive gesture but also disturbed that they had obviously read the torrid headlines—this despite the fact that elaborate precautions had been taken to prevent that from ever happening. At Ludgrove, students were not permitted access to television, magazines, or newspapers. And when the boys attended soccer matches away from school, an elaborate route was mapped out in advance to avoid newsstands with oversized billboards trumpeting the latest royal scandal in lurid red headlines.

No matter. According to a former faculty member at Ludgrove, "William and Harry know everything that's going on. The other boys can't resist teasing them about it, and it's impossible to keep them from smuggling the tabloids into the school." And William had long been in the practice of sneaking into the adjoining room of his bodyguard, Graham Cracker.

In May of 1994, while Diana was vacationing in Spain, a paparazzo reportedly snapped the Princess sunbathing topless. When she got home, William called her from Ludgrove. "You didn't do that, did you?" he demanded.

"Of course not," Diana said. A cameraman lurking in the bushes had, apparently, snapped a picture when the Princess's bikini top slipped.

"If he's alerted to that," royal observer Ingrid Seward said of the relatively minor Topless in Spain incident, "he must have been very upset about all the rest."

It would not be long before Diana rushed back to Ludgrove. Just two weeks after the Hewitt revelations, Papa's literary time bomb exploded. In *The Prince of Wales: A Biography,* Charles revealed to author Jonathan Dimbleby that he had been ignored by his mother, bullied by his father, and persecuted by a spoiled and mentally unstable wife. Most significant, the Prince of Wales claimed he had never loved his sons' mother, and that he married her only after Prince Philip ordered him to do so.

"How awful incompatibility is and how dreadfully destructive it can be for the players in this extraordinary drama," Prince Charles whined to Dimbleby. "It has all the ingredients of a Greek tragedy... I never thought it would end up like this. How could I have got it all so wrong?"

William and Harry were devastated by the remarks, and so was their mother. "He did love me," the Princess protested to her astrologer Debbie Frank, "and I loved him." Her own feelings of humiliation aside, Diana was most concerned about the book's impact on their sons. "Imagine being told that your parents never loved each other," she said. "How do you think poor Wills and Harry must feel?"

Yet again, it was Diana who raced to Ludgrove to soften the blow. As before, William spoke before she could utter a word. "Is it true," the prince asked, "that Papa never loved you?"

Diana would later say that the question and the doleful look in both her sons' eyes "pierced my heart like a dagger. I just wanted to cry." But for now, she maintained her composure for the boys' sake. "When we first got married," she told them, "we loved each other as much as we love you today."

The brothers had little choice but to believe their mother and proceed with life as usual. William, however, was not so eager to forgive his father. "Why, Papa?" he demanded when he next saw his father at Highgrove. "Why did you do it?" Before Prince Charles could reply, Wills, fists clenched, turned away and ran to his room.

William and Harry were not the only ones reeling from the revelations in Papa's book. The first excerpts from *The Prince of Wales* had been published on the eve of the Queen's state visit to Moscow, and both Granny and Grandpapa were furious. When they returned, Elizabeth moved to quell rumors that a divorce was imminent. "As was stated quite clearly when their separation was announced," a Palace spokesman said, "the Prince and Princess have no plans to divorce. That remains the position."

Diana, who steered clear of what she called "the D-word," insisted that she had no intention of being the one to initiate divorce proceedings. "I'm not going anywhere," she said with a shrug, "until he tells me to." Yet behind palace walls both camps were in fact immersed in divorce negotiations—secret talks to hammer out the terms of a settlement that would drag on for months.

Although William and Harry remained unaware that their mother had cooperated with Andrew Morton on the writing of the sensational *Diana: Her True Story*—she could still honestly tell the boys she had never talked to Morton—Diana added to their burden with unsavory headlines of her own.

After art dealer Oliver Hoare, she became infatuated with star rugby player Will Carling after they met at the Harbour Club gym. Both William and Harry were rugby-crazed, so Carling, captain of England's national team, arranged for the boys to have a "kickaround" with team members during a practice session. Soon Carling and the Princess were meeting for breakfast. "When Diana fancied him," her hairdresser Natalie Symonds revealed, "she started studying the sports pages of the newspapers."

Carling's wife, Julia, a British television personality, fought back, publicly branding William and Harry's mum a homewrecker. Carling continued to see Diana, however, and in the end Julia Carling would blame the Princess for destroying her marriage.

"It must be quite horrendous for them to have to cope with all this at such a tender age," Marina Mowatt, daughter of Princess Alexandra, said of the boys. "They will have to shoulder the burden of their parents' actions."

Yet to all those who met them, William and Harry appeared remarkably unaffected by the scandal and intrigue that swirled constantly around them. "They are two terribly sweet, well-mannered boys," said Diana's acupuncturist and friend Oonagh Toffolo.

The more outgoing, rambunctious Harry still seemed unfazed by the tumult surrounding his parents' disintegrating marriage. At the prestigious Olympia International Show Jumping Championships in London that December of 1994, photographers snapped ten-year-old Harry clowning in the royal box. Prince Harry made a series of grotesque faces and at one point positioned a pointed party hat on his forehead to resemble a unicorn horn, then lunged at the boy sitting next to him. Witnessing the whole episode from several yards away, Diana pointed at the boy's antics and laughed.

Conversely, William continued to impress everyone with his growing poise and maturity. "I now," one of the Queen's aides said of the twelve-year-old, "treat him as an adult."

Charles and the rest of the Royal Family deserved some of the credit. Coming out of church services at Sandringham and Balmoral, Wills and Harry honed their skills at making small talk with the well-wishers who lined their path.

Diana gave them tips on how to work a crowd, as well. But she also did something that no parent of a future British monarch had done before: she exposed them to the pain and hardship of the real world beyond palace gates. "I want them to experience," the Princess said of her sons, "what most people already know—that they are growing up in a multiracial society in which not everyone is rich, has four holidays a year, speaks standard English, and has a Range Rover."

Mummy took her sons to hospitals, soup kitchens, and shelters for the homeless. "I am only too aware of the temptation of avoiding harsh reality; not just for myself but for my own children too," she conceded before visiting AIDS patients at a London hospital. "Am I doing them a favor if I hide suffering and unpleasantness from them until the last possible minute? The last minutes which I choose for them may be too late. I can only face them with a choice based on what I know. The rest is up to them."

Most important, the Princess later explained, "I want them to have an understanding of people's emotions, people's insecurities, people's distress, and people's hopes and dreams." Diana rightly suspected that the Palace's "men in gray" would object to these fact-finding visits as inappropriate. "The Princess may wish to hold hands with the indigent and the dying," said one, "but should her two small boys be subjected to such things?"

Yes, Diana argued, especially if one was to be king. "I've taken William and Harry to people dying of AIDS, although I told them it was cancer," she said. "I've taken the children to all sorts of areas where I'm not sure anyone of this family has been before, and they have a knowledge. They may never use it, but the seed is there, and I hope it will grow because knowledge is power."

Still convinced that Charles would die young and that their son would ascend to the throne, Diana admitted that this crash course in reality was intended primarily for William. "Through learning what I do, and his father to a certain extent, he has got an insight into what's coming his way," she said. "He's not upstairs hidden with the governess."

Diana was careful to make her intentions clear to her mother-in-law. "I want William and Harry to grow up in the real world outside the 'Big House,' " she told the Queen during a meeting at Buckingham Palace. "I want them to experience not only the everyday life that ordinary people in Britain live, but I want them to understand the impact of that life on those people. And I am talking about all sorts of people here. Britain must not be a foreign country to my boys."

To Diana's delight, it quickly became apparent that both boys—but William in particular—shared her compassionate touch. While the Royal Family and the rest of Britain's aristocracy sipped Dom Pérignon at Ascot, Diana secretly took her sons to Refuge, a homeless shelter in London. While Harry joined in a game of cards, William played chess with an elderly gentleman.

On another secret visit—this time to the Passage day center for the homeless in Central London—they were accompanied by the Catholic Primate of England, Cardinal Basil Hume. "What an extraordinary child," Cardinal Hume told Diana as they watched William chat amiably with grizzled alcoholics, trembling drug addicts, and others simply down on their luck. "He has such dignity at such a young age."

Like his mother, William soon sought out such close encounters with the needy, the suffering, the indigent. "He loves it," Diana said, "and that really rattles people."

William's inherent kindness was also evident at Ludgrove when a group of retarded children were invited to the school Christmas party. The young prince took charge, making sure that no child was excluded from the festivities. "I was so thrilled and proud," said Diana, who watched from the sidelines. "A lot of adults couldn't handle it."

Charles also marveled at both his sons' newfound presence. Hounded by the press at a ski vacation at Klosters, William and Harry trooped Prince Andrew's daughters, six-year-old Beatrice and four-year-old Eugenie, out onto the slopes for a photo shoot. Smiling and cooperative, the boys helped their cousins pose and politely fielded questions. When a reporter asked who was the best skier, William nodded in the direction of the girls and replied gallantly, "These two are improving."

"My sense was that her children were

Diana's revenge," said her friend Richard Greene. "She was grooming them to be *not* like the rest of the Windsors—especially to be free of that shut-down, emotionless quality that she abhorred." When she publicly embraced them, Greene added, Diana was sending a message about the boys to "the world but also to Charles and the Queen. The message was: 'Hey, they're *mine*. They're real human beings, not the cardboard cutouts that you have in your family.' "

Wills was also showing signs of having inherited his mother's media savvy. In November of 1994, animal rights activists again protested when the prince led his first pheasant shoot at Balmoral, bagging fifteen birds in a single morning. Later, when his mother was offered the presidency of the Royal Society for the Prevention of Cruelty to Animals, Wills advised her, "You can't do that—every time I kill anything, they will blame you."

Diana watched as her eldest son matured in other ways, as well. On board a train bound for an Ireland–Wales rugby game in Cardiff, William and a classmate were grinning broadly as they scanned the *Daily Express*'s *This Week* magazine. Then William motioned for his bodyguard to take a look.

Finally, the Princess of Wales leaned forward to see what the boys' found so riveting: steamy photos of the buxom Barbi twins, *Playboy* centerfold models Shane and Sia. Diana grabbed the magazine from her son's hands, and to the surprise of other passengers tore out the raciest page showing the near-nude twins. She then tore the page in two, handing one half to William and one half to his friend—a Barbi for each.

Holding his page and shaking his head, William looked at his mother. "Mummy," he said, "it was only the top halves we wanted." Diana shrieked with laughter.

William was becoming a polished royal performer, but both he and his brother still found one aspect of the job almost unbearable. At Ludgrove, in addition to the omnipresent Sergeant Graham Cracker, they were shadowed by a rotating team of nineteen bodyguards—enough to post one outside each of their classrooms. "Harry was still young enough to just ignore them," said a faculty member. "But William was turning thirteen and really wanted at least some degree of privacy."

On several occasions, William convinced his friends to cover for him while he disappeared on school grounds. Like schoolboys everywhere, he sampled his first cigarette behind an outbuilding while the others stood guard—and promptly threw up. Soon, Wills's vanishing act—his friends managed to conceal his whereabouts from his bodyguards for up to an hour at a time—began causing real concern for his minders.

Eventually, Prince Charles was asked to intervene. He drove to Ludgrove and met with William in headmaster Gerald Barber's office. Charles commiserated with his son, remembering how he wept with frustration as a boy because he never had a moment to himself. But he told William that the bodyguards had a job to do, and that when he disappeared their jobs were put in real jeopardy. William grudgingly agreed not to disappear again. "But," he told his father half jokingly, "that will all change when I'm king."

As close as William and his brother were to Diana, their relationship with their father strengthened as they approached adolescence. Harry had always been especially close to Papa, and now even shared the Prince of Wales's long-standing interest in botany. Both boys read with their father—Kipling was a particular favorite—and watched videos together. While their tastes at Kensington Palace ran to such pop fare as *E.T.*, the *Star Wars* trilogy, and Sylvester Stallone's *Rocky* and *Rambo* series, the boys were exposed to more classic British film fare at Highgrove. Still, Charles noted that the boys were particularly delighted by "the gory bits" in Kenneth Branagh's film version of *Henry V*.

The princes were also at an age when riding, fishing, blood sports, and the weapons that went with them held a special fascination. This was never more true than at Balmoral, the baronial granite mansion built on the banks of Scotland's River Dee by the boys' great-great-great-grandmother Queen Victoria and her husband, Prince Albert. "This dear Paradise," Victoria called it, and with good reason. With its glistening groves of silver birch trees, dark pine forests, and endless purple savannas of heather, Balmoral was as magical a place for the princelings as it had been for their royal forebears.

Nowhere in the realm was wildlife more abundant. The river and its tributaries teemed with pike, salmon, and trout. Peregrine falcons and golden eagles were protected, but just about everything else was fair game: pheasant and grouse, of course, but also deer, rabbits, wildcats, and pine martens.

Traditionally, Balmoral always marked the beginning and ending of the court calendar, despite the fact that the Royal Family was in residence less than three months a year—the longest stretch being from the official start of grouse season on August 12 until October.

For the Queen in particular, Balmoral held special memories. Elizabeth had been seventeen—four years older than Diana—when she shot her first stag there in October of 1942. Elizabeth no longer picked up a rifle, but she was never happier than when she slogged through the muddy fields in her Wellingtons, her beloved corgis in tow.

Now, during grouse season, William and Harry joined the all-male, dawn-till-dusk shooting parties. Invariably led by Grandpapa, these more closely resembled military maneuvers: a small caravan of Land Rovers crisscrossing the moors, meeting up at various points with platoons of "loaders" who made sure they never ran out of ammunition and "beaters" to flush out their quarry.

There were elaborate picnic lunches set up along the way, and the Queen joined them to check up on the progress of her grandsons. Nursing a gin and tonic, she listened attentively to the boys recount their kills and their near misses.

It was a very different scene over tea inside the castle, where pâtés, cakes, and biscuits were served, and the Queen herself refilled the pot from a giant silver kettle. At precisely 8:30, dinner would be served by liveried footmen in red waistcoats—two footmen per guest.

The boys also seemed eager to take part in the royals' social life at Balmoral. The main events of the season were the two Ghillies Balls given by Her Majesty as a way of expressing her gratitude to the locals and her estate workers. All female members of the Royal Family—the Queen, Princess Margaret, Princess Anne, the Queen Mother—wore their glittering diamond tiaras and their Stuart sashes.

William and Harry, meantime, gamely joined Papa and Grandpapa and their uncles Prince Andrew and Prince Edward in donning tartans and kilts for these affairs. Both of Diana's boys happily plunged into the business of learning Scottish steps like the reel and the Highland Fling.

Granny's dance card was also full. To protect the Court, a detachment of soldiers from one of the Scottish regiments was assigned to Balmoral each summer. By way of thanking them, the Queen tried to dance with as many of the servicemen as possible. She also made a point of dancing with Harry and Wills.

"The Queen remembered how Diana used to lock herself in her room at Balmoral and not come out, and she was afraid the boys might hate it too," a courtier remarked. Her Majesty was "relieved that Prince William and Prince Harry shared her love of the place."

Balmoral, where a sign posted at the entrance reads SLOW: BEWARE HORSES, DOGS, AND CHILDREN, had always been the closest thing the royals had to a family setting. And for William and Harry, things were far less Spartan than they had been when Charles was their age. Where their father had been forced by Grandpapa to swim in the icy rivers and brooks, William and Harry were allowed to swim at the local pool (Balmoral itself had none) or go to the local movie house, provided Granny approved of the subject matter.

Diana, who remained behind in London, could only watch as her sons were indoctrinated in the ways of the Windsors. It only aggravated matters when British tabloids ran photographs of a newly svelte Tiggy Legge-Bourke laughing with Diana's sons as they climbed into Land Rovers or hiked through the Dee River valley. Tiggy did fit into life at Balmoral in a way the Princess never could. "She's a country person, which the boys love," said Tiggy's friend Santa Palmer-Tomkinson. "She's one of the only women I know who can skin a rabbit or gut a stag."

Nor could Diana ignore newspaper photos

of Charles planting an affectionate kiss on Tiggy's cheek, or *Daily Mail* columnist Richard Kay's speculation that "Tiggy is slimming down to please Prince Charles." Tiggy had lost weight—not from dieting, but from the effects of celiac disease, a digestive disorder that also causes nausea and severe abdominal pain.

Try as she might to humanize the future king with visits to amusement parks and homeless shelters, Diana worried that he and his brother were growing up in the Windsor mold. For William's thirteenth birthday, Charles "gave" the boy his own valet. To the socially conscious Diana's dismay, her son was, in her words, "totally delighted to have a manservant all his own."

The international furor surrounding his parents' marriage did not prevent William from enjoying his last year at Ludgrove. "Both of the princes have the ability," said one of Harry's teachers, "to push all the unpleasantness out of their minds and live their own lives. For them, this would seem essential for survival."

While Harry struggled with his studies but excelled on the athletic field, William excelled in both departments. A champion soccer player and cricketer, William was also made a prefect—a position that carried with it the right to be one of only a handful of students permitted to have radios in their rooms.

During the 1994 Christmas carol service, William was selected to give the reading before an audience of several hundred students and parents. William's deft delivery did not surprise his father. "You know," Charles volunteered, "he reads poetry beautifully."

William's newfound comfort level at Ludgrove had much to do with his bodyguards' willingness to give the prince more breathing room. In return for William's agreeing not to pull his disappearing act, the prince's security officers kept a discreet distance when he was on school grounds. They literally hid in the shadows and lurked behind buildings and trees, remaining out of sight but still aware of their charge's every move.

Off school grounds, however, it was a different story. On holiday and during trips abroad where they had little or no control over the environment, members of the Royal Protection Squad drew a tight cordon around the future king. William, like all adolescents struggling for some degree of privacy and independence, chafed under the control of his ever-present minders.

Things came to a head on a holiday in Switzerland, as William wound up a day of sledding with friends. It was just after sunset when the prince took off from the top of a steep hill, seemingly unaware that a heavily trafficked road was at the bottom of the slope. Suddenly, one of William's bodyguards leapt out from behind a pine tree and hurled himself onto the sled, knocking William off before the sled slid beneath the wheels of a passing car.

Instead of being grateful, William pulled himself out from under the detective and flew into a purple-veined rage. "Why do I have to be surrounded by policemen all the time?" he screamed. "I knew I was safe. Why won't you let me be a normal person?"

Security would only get tighter that September of 1995, when William enrolled at the most famous and prestigious prep school of all: Eton. Situated on the Thames in Buckinghamshire, Eton bore scant resemblance to Gordonstoun, the Spartan Scottish boarding school Charles had attended. Even on those days when it snowed, Gordonstoun's mostly middle-class students began each day with a shirtless run followed by an icy shower. The other students belittled and bullied Charles, who came to view his time at Gordonstoun as "a prison sentence."

Conversely, Eton's thirteen hundred students strolled about the ivy-covered campus in pinstripe trousers, stiff white collars, and tails. Established by Henry VI to prepare young scholars for another educational institution he founded, King's College, Cambridge, Eton had been preparing the sons of Europe's most influential families for life on the world stage for 558 years. History, as George Orwell observed, was "decided on the playing fields of Eton."

William was apparently still uncertain about precisely what his future role would be. Registering at Eton under the name "William of Wales, H.R.H. Prince," Wills suddenly had trouble filling in one of the blanks. The future titular head of the Church of England turned to his father with a quizzical look and asked, "What religion?"

With its red-brick chimneys, wrought-iron gates, mullioned windows, and Gothic turrets, Eton provided the sort of baronial atmosphere to which William was accustomed. The adjacent town of Eton was equally picturesque, boasting the Hogs Head and Crown and Cushion inns, Lillie Langtry's Restaurant at the Christopher Hotel, the cozy Eton Tea Room, and the 581-year-old Cockpit restaurant. Many of the shops along narrow High Street, like Murrays of Eton and Nutters of Savile Row, catered specifically to the sartorial needs of Etonians.

Prince Charles had been alternately shunned and teased by the other, less highborn boys at Gordonstoun who did not want to be accused of "sucking up" to the future king. But William's classmates at Eton were hardly likely to resent his presence in their midst. He may have been the only "F-tit"—"tit" being Etonese for "squirt" and "F" indicating the school block inhabited by first-year students— who would be referred to by his first name (all other students are called by surname). And he certainly was the only Etonian with a nineteen-member security detail and his own portable transmitter, but he was decidedly one of them. These were the sons of British aristocrats, Arab sheiks, barristers, bankers, and political leaders. "The students there," one member of the class of 1973 observed, "aren't frightened of important people."

In a rare moment of consensus, both Charles and Diana were thrilled that William was now an Eton F-tit. Charles, who had been virtually friendless at Gordonstoun, had heard from Old Etonians that the friends they made at school remained friends for life. It was something he devoutly wanted his son to have. Moreover, at Gordonstoun Charles had grown fond of one young teacher, Eric Anderson, who had gone on to become headmaster of Eton. These factors, coupled with the school's unrivaled reputation for academic excellence, appealed immensely to the Prince of Wales. So much so that the notoriously penurious prince did not hesitate to pay the twenty-thousand-dollar annual tuition. "Charles is absolutely delighted," Camilla told a friend, "that William is going there."

So was Mummy. Diana's father and brother had both gone to Eton, and the school's close proximity to London—a thirty-minute drive from Kensington Palace, even more accessible than Ludgrove—meant that she could see her son whenever the mood struck her.

Like Charles, Diana hoped that Eton would become a second family to their son—an emotional bulwark against the trying times that were to come. William's housemaster at Eton, Dr. Andrew Gailey, would be counted on to lend a sympathetic ear, as would Gailey's wife, Shauna.

This was no accident; the summer before William arrived at Eton, Charles and Diana, who had communicated for months only in terse, angry letters, put aside their differences long enough to invite Andrew and Shauna Gailey to St. James's Palace for drinks. William's parents made it clear to the Gaileys that they were being counted on to perform as the heir's surrogate parents.

"William is very strong, as I am," Diana told the Gaileys. "But he is also very sensitive. He can be hurt easily. He'll really need all the love and support you can possibly give him."

"And friends," Charles chimed in. "He'll have lots of friends he can turn to there, I suppose..."

The Gaileys would share the job of watching over William with housemother Elizabeth Heathcote, "Dame"—or matron—of Manor House. A veteran of thirty years at the school and herself the daughter of an Old Etonian, Heathcote ate lunch and dinner with the younger boys, issued chits for items like stationery and toothpaste, and even served as a nurse, taking temperatures and dispensing every over-the-counter remedy from aspirin to cough syrup. Most important, Dame Elizabeth would soften the transition for the F-tits, offering advice, encouragement, and a compassionate ear.

At the four-story Manor House, where he was one of fifty boys aged fourteen to eighteen, William slept in a ten-by-seven-foot room— granted, the only one with a private bathroom and no nameplate on the door. As at Ludgrove, a royal protection officer slept in an adjacent room.

For William, the adjustment to life at Eton

was remarkably smooth. Unlike his father, William arrived already knowing several of his classmates. Lord "Freddie" Windsor, son of Prince and Princess Michael of Kent, was an upperclassman there. Among his fellow F-tits: Ludgrove rugby teammate Johnny Richards and Andrew Charlton, a banker's son who had gone along with Diana, William, and Harry on their highly publicized trip to Disney World. William would soon count among his closest chums Nicholas Knatchbull, a grandson of the late Lord Mountbatten and a distant cousin of William's.

There was perhaps one person above all others who took special satisfaction in seeing William take his first steps toward becoming a proper Etonian. From wherever he stood at Eton, William could look up and see the medieval stone monolith that loomed atop a hill just across the river—Windsor Castle. Wills's new proximity to "Granny's House" was no accident. As part of the Royal Family's ongoing campaign to indoctrinate him in the ways of the Windsors, the Queen wanted frequent access to her grandson. And she would have it.

All turrets, keeps, granite battlements, Gothic arches, and flying pennants, Windsor Castle has been the chief residence of England's rulers since William the Conqueror. By the time William entered Eton in the fall of 1995, much of the damage incurred during the fire of 1992—the Queen's *annus horribilis*—had been repaired, although it would be another eighteen months before Her Majesty deemed the restoration complete.

Even as artisans and craftsmen toiled to remove all traces of the fire, the grandeur of Windsor was undeniable. From the apricot-walled Grand Vestibule festooned with hundreds of antique firearms to St. George's Chapel, one of the most splendid churches in England and the spot where Knights of the Garter are installed amid much pomp and ceremony, the castle's chambers, anterooms, and great halls are as awe-inspiringly opulent as the exterior is austere.

Windsor also houses one of Europe's great art collections. Six Gobelin tapestries and a six-foot-high malachite urn given to Queen Victoria by Czar Nicholas I decorate the gilt-encrusted Grand Reception Room. Paintings by Rembrandt, Holbein, Rubens, and Van Dyck line the walls of the King's Dressing Room, while scores of works by Hogarth, Gainsborough, Canaletto, Sir Thomas Lawrence, and Sir Joshua Reynolds are scattered among the Crimson Drawing Room, the Octagon Dining Room, the State Dining Room, the Green Drawing Room, the Garter Throne Room, the Queen's Ballroom, the Queen's Audience Chamber, the Queen's Presence Chamber, the Queen's Guard Chamber, the Queen's Drawing Room, and the cavernous Waterloo Chamber, built by George IV to commemorate the Duke of Wellington's defeat of Napoleon.

Even here, harsh twentieth-century reality

intrudes constantly. The cooling tower of a nuclear power plant rises in the distance. And every three minutes any semblance of calm is shattered as another jumbo jet flies at a surprisingly low altitude directly over the castle, heading for a landing at Heathrow.

But there were other things the Queen could see as she peered from the window of her bedchamber—most notably those emerald playing fields of Eton that George Orwell had written about, and the grandson who now played on them.

Every Sunday afternoon a car picked William up precisely at 3:50 P.M. and drove down Eton High Street, past Monty's Tavern and the aptly named Home on the Bridge restaurant, and over the short span connecting Eton to the village of Windsor. From there, the car sped up the hill to Granny's House. The entire journey took no more than a minute. On foot, William, always accompanied by two guards dressed in dark business suits and packing Heckler and Kock machine pistols in their shoulder holsters, usually made the trip in seven minutes.

The Queen and future king met for tea at 4 P.M. in the Oak Drawing Room, overlooking the quadrangle where foreign heads of state are greeted and the changing of the guard takes place. First, she would ask him about the events of his week at Eton—how his rugby was coming, which lessons were the most fun and which were giving him the most trouble, what the other boys were like. Then the Queen shared some of the details of her week—from affairs of state to the health problems of her favorite horses.

More and more, Prince William would turn to his grandmother for advice. Her Majesty could never remotely be described as warm or affectionate—she was never seen kissing or hugging anyone, in public or in private—but like grandmothers everywhere she wanted to indulge him, if only in her fashion.

Elizabeth also had other, weightier matters to consider: she was determined to prepare her grandson for the throne. William had grown accustomed to Granny trying to sneak in a history lesson here and there during their weekly teas together—a note from George III to William Pitt, perhaps, or a letter from Elizabeth I.

William also got a firsthand look at what it meant to be a modern monarch—chairman of what royal family members referred to sardonically as "the Firm." Wherever she was—at Windsor, Buckingham Palace, Sandringham, Balmoral, or even aboard the royal yacht *Britannia*—the Queen was forced to attend to the infamous "boxes" that followed her everywhere.

Red boxes contained paperwork pertaining to her schedule—from hospital walkabouts and wreath layings to state visits and the opening of Parliament. More mentally taxing were the blue boxes from the Foreign Office, each brimming with dispatches designed to keep the monarch apprised of government affairs.

Since more was expected of William, the

Queen was more apt to correct his behavior than she was Harry's or any of the boys' cousins'. Not long after the separation was announced, Diana decided to dispense with her Royal Protection Squad—a move that the Queen regarded as foolhardy. Around this time, William was riding at Balmoral when suddenly he took off alone, leaving his groom in the dust. When he got back to the castle, "the Queen tore a strip off Prince William," said a member of the royal household. "But it was out of concern for his safety."

Such outbursts on the part of the sovereign were rare—and indicative of the depth of feeling she had for William. For the most part, she ignored minor infractions of her many rules. At Windsor, for example, each volume in the royal library was clearly labeled inside as "The Queen's Book." Anyone who wished to borrow one of these books was required to fill out a card and put it in the space the book came from.

Not long after William started at Eton, the keen-eyed monarch noticed that several bound manuscripts were missing. Suspecting theft, she immediately called in Scotland Yard. Their investigation turned up the missing bound volumes—tucked away behind other books. Discreetly tucked away inside each of the hidden volumes were suggestive photographs of Cindy Crawford, a particular favorite of the young prince. "My goodness," the Queen said when investigators sheepishly showed her the photos. "Well, put the books back where you found them. There's no reason to embarrass the boy." Nothing was said to William, who would continue to hide photos of his favorite scantily clad models in this manner.

"I got the distinct impression," said one of the Scotland Yard investigators, "that Her Majesty was trying very hard to keep from laughing. She just thought it was rather innocent, even sweet."

Over the next five years, William would flourish at Eton. A natural athlete, he excelled at rugby and sculling, but truly shone at a sport that combined his mother's love of swimming with his father's love of the sport of kings—water polo. "On some subconscious level," Diana confided to her astrologer, "I think William chose to play it because it was a way of pleasing both Charles and myself." William, who had sailed through his entrance exams for Eton, would also prove to be a superb student with a flair for French and art.

If he did worry, it was about Harry and how he was faring back at Ludgrove without his older brother to look after him. "William was always very protective of Harry, and the boys missed each other in the beginning," Paul Burrell said. To soften the transition for Harry as well, Diana brought him to visit his big brother at Eton, and both the Princess and Charles made extra trips to Ludgrove to check up on Harry. To everyone's relief, Harry adjusted quickly to being the only royal at Ludgrove. "For someone who is always in his brother's shadow," said the mother of a Ludgrove classmate, "it's rather nice to have the spotlight all to yourself for a change. Prince Harry was always outgoing and full of fun, only more so once William left for Eton."

As for William, his first crisis at Eton would have nothing to do with homesickness or peer pressure or the stress of schoolwork. On November 19, 1995, William was summoned to Dr. Gailey's study to find his mother waiting for him. "William, I've done an interview for TV," she told him. "It's going to air tomorrow night, and I didn't want it to catch you by surprise."

Mummy went on to explain that she felt a lot of lies about both Charles and herself had been bandied about in the press, and it was time to "set the record straight." Meantime, she reassured him there was no cause for alarm. "Don't worry. Everything will be fine— I promise," she said. From Eton, Diana drove directly to Ludgrove to warn Harry.

Not surprisingly, over the years, every major broadcaster and talk-show host from Barbara Walters and Diane Sawyer to Oprah Winfrey had bombarded the Princess with interview requests. She automatically turned them all down. But in October Diana basically agreed to do for correspondent Martin Bashir what she had done for Andrew Morton.

Using compact cameras that had been smuggled into Kensington Palace through the service entrance, Bashir conducted a wide-ranging, three-hour-long interview that was cut down to fifty-five minutes for airing on the BBC's *Panorama* series. Even though she had preapproved the questions days earlier and thoroughly rehearsed her answers, she required numerous breaks to collect her thoughts.

On November 20, a Monday, William was called down to his headmaster's study shortly before 8 P.M. to watch the interview alone. Harry, given the option of watching the interview on his bodyguard's television at Ludgrove, opted not to watch.

As soon as his mother's face came on the screen, William would later confide to a classmate, the prince was "filled with dread." Looking up from beneath heavily mascaraed lashes and speaking in hushed tones, Diana either seemed very much in control or on the verge of a nervous breakdown.

William watched as his mother explained her rationale for doing the interview. "Friends on my husband's side were indicating that I was again unstable, sick, and should be put in a home of some sort," she said. "I was almost an embarrassment." Then, to her son's dismay, she went on to speak with startling candor about, among other things, her husband's affair with Camilla ("There were three of us in this marriage, so it was a bit crowded"), her suicidal depression, her eating disorders, her children, the Palace conspiracy against her ("There is no better way to dismantle a personality than to isolate it"), whether her husband was fit to be king, her own determination (" 'She won't go quietly—that's the problem.

I'll fight to the end' "), and her desire for "the man in the street" to know she would "always be there for him." She did not wish to reign as Queen of England, she said, but as "the queen of people's hearts... Someone's got to go out there and love people and show it."

William was happy to hear his mother say that she did not want a divorce. Although she had thrown down the gauntlet by airing her thoughts without Palace approval, the Princess insisted, "There is a future ahead. A future for my husband, a future for myself, and a future for the monarchy."

For all Diana's unprecedented, provocative candor, only one thing truly disturbed her eldest son. When asked about James Hewitt, Diana admitted that she and the former Life Guards officer had indeed had an affair ("Yes, I adored him, yes, I was in love with him"). She went on to say that she had felt betrayed by Hewitt, and was "absolutely devastated" when their affair was revealed in the book *Princess in Love*.

Watching this, William also felt betrayed—by his mother. She knew how upset both William and Harry had been when Charles confessed his infidelity on television the previous year. Even then, in his reluctant and cautiously phrased admission Charles never claimed he loved Camilla.

Equally significant was the fact that, while the boys had never even met Camilla, Hewitt had become a kind of big brother to William and Harry. For any boy to watch his mother talk on television about her extramarital sex life was humiliating enough. For William and Harry to learn that their mother's lover was someone they had known and trusted was doubly hurtful.

His face flushed with anger, William broke down. When his housemaster came to fetch him, he found William sitting on the sofa, eyes red from crying. The prince collected himself and rushed back to his room at Manor House. An hour after *Panorama* was aired, Diana phoned William. He refused to take the call.

For days, William refused to speak to his mother. Even after they resumed their habit of chatting over the phone several times a week, Mummy's unsettling confession concerning James Hewitt left an indelible mark on her relationship with William. From that moment, Diana felt William begin to pull away from her. "I wish I had never mentioned Hewitt," Diana told Ingrid Seward. "He was always so good to the boys—and to me."

Meanwhile, the interview caused a sensation on both sides of the Atlantic. After ABC paid $642,000 to broadcast the interview in the United States, Barbara Walters spoke with the Princess off-camera. "I thought," Walters said of Diana's *Panorama* appearance, "that it was a superb performance."

So did the British public. From the standpoint of her personal popularity, Diana had scored another media triumph. A Gallup poll conducted immediately after the program showed that 75 percent approved of the interview, 74 percent found her strong, 84 percent found her to be honest, and 85 percent felt she should be appointed as a sort of roving ambassador for Great Britain.

William was also angry about the manner in which his mother had cast doubt on his father's worthiness to be king. In that respect the interview had dealt a serious blow to Charles. Now fully 46 percent of the British people felt he was unfit to wear the crown.

Diana was elated by the public reaction. But she had miscalculated the impact the *Panorama* sneak attack would have on her own family. Diana had pointedly chosen Charles's birthday to inform him that the interview was forthcoming. Through emissaries, the Queen had asked her daughter-in-law for at least a preview. Diana refused.

Now, watching the broadcast in her private quarters at Buckingham Palace, the Queen was unprepared for Diana's broadside. Beyond the simple act of going before TV cameras without the sovereign's permission to air the Royal Family's soiled linen in public, Diana had gone a step further and cast doubt on the Prince of Wales's right of succession.

The Queen was right to suspect Diana's motives. Diana had always believed her astrologers' claims that Charles would not live to become king. But now she sought to hedge her bets by launching a full-frontal attack on the heir apparent's credibility. In a move that harked back to the days of Henry VIII, Anne Boleyn, and the first Elizabeth,

Diana was exploiting the public's growing desire as expressed through polls to see her son—not Charles—succeed Elizabeth. Once William V sat on the throne, Diana would be the power behind it, shaping a new, more compassionate monarchy for the new millennium. "No one in that place is streetwise in any way—nor do they want to be," Diana said of the Palace. It was a sentiment she frequently shared with William. "They don't believe they should relate to the world, the real world of today... They want me and my children to behave as if we were still in Victorian England."

Enraged, the Queen summoned Prime Minister John Major, the Archbishop of Canterbury, and several of her top advisers to Buckingham Palace. She informed them that there was no longer a place for Diana in "the Firm."

Princess Margaret, once Diana's friend and defender, now wrote the Princess of Wales yet another scathing letter in which she condemned her for not being able to make "even the smallest sacrifice." Such criticism was offset by the positive feedback from the public at large; Diana was left feeling vindicated. "You see—I'm right. The people understand that," she told her private secretary, employing her nickname for the Windsors, "even if the Germans don't."

Jubilant, Diana boarded the Concorde and flew to New York, where her old friend Henry Kissinger presented her with a Humanitarian of the Year Award from the United Cerebral Palsy Foundation. As she accepted the award before a crowd of one thousand at the New York Hilton, a heckler yelled, "Where are your kids, Di?"

"In bed!" she shot back. The crowd roared its approval.

In early December, the Princess was in rare form at the annual Christmas lunch party she and Charles put on for their staff. Diana joked and laughed as she mingled with the guests, but stopped abruptly when she spotted Tiggy Legge-Bourke across the room.

For two years, with every newspaper photo showing Tiggy enjoying another carefree outing with the princes or bussing Charles innocently on the cheek, Mummy's resentment festered. Diana now fantasized that Charles and the boys' attractive young nanny were having an affair.

Seizing the moment, Diana sidled up behind Tiggy and whispered in her ear, "So sorry to hear about the baby." Among those in the room, there was little doubt as to Diana's intended implication—that Tiggy had undergone an abortion and that the baby's father might even have been Charles. There was no basis whatsoever for Diana's malicious comment, but Tiggy was so upset that she nearly fainted. Several other guests helped her to an adjacent room, where she broke down and cried.

The next day, Tiggy instructed her solicitor to request an apology from William and Harry's mother and a withdrawal of her "false allegations." When she read the solicitor's letter on December 18, Diana was not surprised; she had expected Tiggy to seek swift legal redress. But another letter that arrived at Kensington Palace the same day would leave the Princess of Wales reeling—and change the lives of William and Harry forever.

I don't mind what you're called. You're
Mummy.

—*William, when
Diana asked him
if he minded that
she was losing
her royal status*

She felt her life fell into two parts: her public, humanitarian side and the side where she was a mother.

—*Family friend Lord Jeffrey Archer*

I will fight for my children at any level in order for them to be happy and have peace of mind and carry out their duties.

—*Diana*

6

W hat's wrong, Mummy? What is it?"
William always knew when something
was troubling her, even when the consummate
actress known to the world as Diana tried
her hardest to conceal her true feelings from
him. Finally, the Princess broke down and told
him what had happened: Just one week before
Christmas 1995, the Queen wrote letters to
both Charles and Diana expressing her anger
over the *Panorama* interview and her desire for
an "early divorce...in the best interests of
the country."

The letter's contents shocked Diana. She
had seen her *Panorama* interview as just another
public relations volley fired over the bow of
her enemies in the Palace. She hid her pain
from the public, but now deeply regretted
that she had lost the chance to be queen. "Yes,
yes. We would have been the best team in the
world," Diana later told magazine editor Tina
Brown. "I could shake hands till the cows
come home. And Charles could make serious
speeches. But it was not to be..."

Diana was, in fact, devastated. "When she
had to face the bitter truth from the Queen,
Diana fell apart," said Simone Simmons, the

"spiritual healer" who became her friend. "She couldn't sleep at night and started taking very strong sleeping pills. She was constantly in tears, reflecting over and over again on what might have been."

"D'you know, Patrick," the Princess said wistfully to P. D. Jephson after she read the Queen's letter to him over the phone, "that's the first letter she's written to me." Recalled Jephson, "She tried to laugh, but for once she couldn't."

Much to her mother-in-law's relief, Diana canceled plans to join the rest of the Royal Family at Sandringham. Instead, she spent Christmas Day 1995 alone at Kensington Palace while her sons opened presents and feasted on goose with their father's side of the family. Unlike Diana, Charles saw no need to bring up the painful subject of divorce. Instead, after depositing Wills at Eton, Papa celebrated the New Year by taking Harry on a ski holiday in Switzerland.

Soon, the contents of the Queen's letter were leaked to the press. The next day, Diana took William and Harry to the Harbour Club in Chelsea for tennis lessons and a dip in the pool. William and Harry were both still trying to come to terms with their mother's televised admission of infidelity. Yet they also wanted to stand by her at a time when she clearly was at her most vulnerable.

Just how vulnerable became clear in early January when Mummy, intercepted by the press as she came out of the offices of her therapist Susie Orbach, collapsed weeping against her car as photographers snapped away. Seeing the photos, William immediately called Kensington Palace from Eton to console her.

Yet Mummy was anything but meek when negotiating the terms of her divorce settlement. She wanted, among other things, to continue to live at Kensington Palace, to have access to perks such as use of the royal jets, seventy million dollars in cash, and, of course, shared custody of her sons.

Four months of intense and sometimes acrimonious negotiations would be required before a final settlement was actually reached. But on one issue the Queen made it clear that she was in agreement with her vexatious daughter-in-law. In a press release issued soon after the Queen's letter was made public, a Palace spokesman made it clear that the monarch was there for Charles and Diana and "most particularly their children in this difficult time."

In mid-February, the Queen met with Diana at Buckingham Palace to try to break the logjam in divorce negotiations. Granny had sole discretion in determining not only Diana's royal status or lack of it, but also the size of the settlement, whether Diana would be able to remain in Kensington Palace, and, most important, who would get custody of William and Harry. Her Majesty, saying that she wanted the best for all parties involved, urged Diana to meet with her husband and iron out the details of the divorce.

Around 4 P.M. on February 28, 1996—"the saddest day of my life," Diana would later say— Charles and Diana met for forty-five minutes at the Prince of Wales's offices in St. James's Palace. For the most part, both sides were businesslike, although at times Diana waxed emotional over the fact that she was turning William and Harry into children of divorce. "I loved you and I will always love you," Diana told Charles, "because you are the father of my children."

Unwilling to wait for the Palace to make the formal announcement, she promptly issued a statement of her own: "The Princess of Wales has agreed to Prince Charles's request for a divorce. The Princess will continue to be involved in all decisions relating to the children and will remain at Kensington Palace, with offices in St. James's Palace. The Princess of Wales will retain the title and be known as Diana, Princess of Wales."

Even as the press release was being typed up, Diana was calling her mother-in-law to inform her that she had agreed to the divorce. The Queen's feelings of relief quickly turned to rage when she learned Diana had unilaterally decided to go public with the terms. Granny promptly responded with a statement of her own, claiming that nothing had in fact been resolved, that all major issues "remain to be discussed and settled."

Diana countered that what the Palace objected to was a "strong woman" taking the initiative. The Queen seethed. While both sides dug in for the long battle ahead, William continued to make the seven-minute walk from Eton to Windsor for Sunday tea with Granny. Not a syllable was spoken about the divorce wars that waged outside the castle gates. "William and Harry loved Diana very much but they also loved their father and they loved the Queen," Elsa Bowker said. "They knew how to walk the tightrope in a way that, sadly, Diana did not." The royals, she went on, "have this ability to completely ignore the unpleasant things happening all around them. They are detached, removed, so cold—the opposite of Diana. I suspect the Queen is teaching them well…"

There were moments, however, when William seemed to share his mother's distaste for the Windsors' stiff formality. "Mummy," he asked her after paying a call on his grandparents at Buckingham Palace, "do I really have to be a part of this family?"

On August 28, 1996, the divorce was finalized. Diana would be allowed to remain in her apartments at Kensington Palace, and would receive a lump-sum cash settlement of $22.5 million as well as $600,000 a year to maintain her offices. Diana would also retain all her titles: Princess of Wales, Duchess of Cornwall, Duchess of Rothesay, Countess of Chester, Countess of Carrick, and Baroness Renfrew. She would also have access to the fleet of royal jets and be allowed to keep her royal jewelry—with the understanding that upon her death it would be passed along to the wives of her sons.

Charles and Diana would share custody of William and Harry, continuing the arrangement that had existed since their separation was announced in 1992. As the mother of the future king, Diana would be, a Palace spokesman stressed, "regarded as a member of the Royal Family." That meant she would, the statement continued, "from time to time receive invitations to state and national public occasions." At these events, she would "be accorded the precedence she enjoys at present."

But there had been a catch. Diana wanted to hold on to her designation as "Her Royal Highness"—a title reserved primarily for those who are in line for the throne and their wives and children. Without the HRH, Diana would technically be required to curtsy to nearly every member of the extended Royal Family, including her nieces Beatrice and Eugenie.

Not likely. But Diana still worried that this demotion would somehow diminish her in her own children's eyes. As she often did, the Princess asked William his opinion. As far as he was concerned, the HRH designation was superfluous. To both her sons, he said, she would always possess the most important title of all: "Mummy."

Diana, who had described William as a "deep thinker" in her *Panorama* interview, was moved by his Solomon-like answer. Minutes after their conversation, she phoned her lawyers and told them to accept the terms. From now on, Diana vowed, she would focus on the things that mattered most to her. "I've got my boys," she would tell friends who asked how she was bearing up. "I've got my work."

At twelve, Harry was relatively cloistered at Ludgrove; although he spoke to both parents often, his mother did not seek out his opinions the way she routinely sought out advice from fourteen-year-old Wills. Conversely, Diana did not worry about Harry as much, either. She viewed her younger son as living a vastly different, infinitely less pressured life.

"She was very conscious that both had a role to play," said Rosa Monckton. "She was grooming Prince Harry to be of support to his brother." But for the moment, the opposite was true: William was intensely protective of Harry, particularly now that he was left alone back at Ludgrove. William checked up on him by phone every few days, making sure that he was not at loose ends after his big brother's departure for Eton.

Feeling responsible for his brother's well-being as well as his mother's happiness, William began to show the strain. "He had," a friend said, "the weight of the world on his shoulders."

So oppressive was that burden that on more than one tearful occasion William told his parents he did not want the job he was born to do. "William is waiting patiently for the monarchy to be abolished," Diana joked. "It will make life so much easier for him!"

"Perhaps," Wills told his father, "I shall go

backpacking in Nepal and never come back." At times like these, when the heir to the throne of England voiced his desire to step aside, his feisty brother seized the moment. "I shall be King Harry!" he declared. "I shall do the work."

Easygoing by nature, Harry continued to play the role of royal rascal. He was reprimanded more often than William, and his modus operandi was to mimic whoever was disciplining him, then dash away laughing. At one point Prince Charles suggested in mock earnestness that perhaps Harry should indeed be made king if his brother didn't want the job. "I'd love it!" the spare replied.

Convinced that William's reluctance to be king was merely an adolescent phase, the Princess continued to rely on him for advice on matters both large and small. She had her eldest son's blessing that summer of 1996 when, in an effort to define a new life for herself as a divorced woman, she decided to focus on those issues dearest to her. Toward that end, she slashed the number of charities she was actively supporting from more than one hundred to just five: the Leprosy Mission, the National AIDS Trust, the Royal Marsden Cancer Hospital, the Great Ormond Street Children's Hospital, and a charity for the homeless called Centrepoint. She would also remain as patroness of the English National Ballet.

William knew that his mother would be accused of abandoning the other ninety-five causes that had counted on her support. But he also worried about what impact divorce might have on her already fragile emotional state. Papa could rely on Camilla and the Royal Family for support. With the exception of only a handful of friends, Mummy could really count only on her boys. If cutting back on her schedule could reduce the stress on his mother, William was all for it. So was his younger brother. "Mummy," Harry observed, "works too hard. I worry about her."

While Wills fretted about his mother's well-being, the rest of the world pondered the future of the monarchy. Three weeks after his fourteenth birthday, *Time* magazine ran Prince William on its cover with the headline CAN THIS BOY SAVE THE MONARCHY?

There were also those who wondered what toll all the scandal and speculation was having on the heir and the spare. "I hope for the best for Wills," said commentator Julie Burchill, echoing the sentiments of many of her countrymen. "But I would be very surprised if he turns out to be normal, because that's the maddest family since the Munsters. Every day there's something new. We wouldn't be shocked if he turned out to be a cross-dresser who wanted to marry a corgi. We all feel we know everything about them, and that's a very bad thing for a ruling family."

Indeed, beyond suffering the hammer blow of their parents' divorce, Wills and Harry had spent most of their lives dealing with one mortifying revelation after another. At Eton, the school administration took pains not to embarrass the prince. During Founders Day ceremonies in 1996, a series of speeches on the Seven Deadly Sins was amended to eliminate Lust; there was concern that, given what everyone knew about the Royal Family's antics, any references to adultery might be awkward.

Wills's fellow students were decidedly less politically correct. Every time a new scandal regarding the royals erupted, someone could be counted on to point it out to Wills. No sooner had an Italian magazine published nude photographs of Prince Charles—taken through his hotel window while he was on holiday—than someone (presumably an Eton upperclassman) faxed copies to William.

After sharing them with his brother, Wills could laugh off the photos of Papa in the altogether. But the fact remained that both William and Harry knew more intimate details about their parents' lives than any child should have to know—and so did the rest of the planet.

The torrent of scandalous headlines—from their father's desire to be his mistress's tampon to their mother's bulimia and her numerous obsessions (James Hewitt, Oliver Hoare, and Will Carling, to name a few)—left Wills not with a resentment of his unstable parents, but with an abiding antipathy toward the press.

When he read in one tabloid that Princess Diana had an "infatuation" with Tom Hanks, her son insisted she issue a denial through her press office. "It made my mother," William angrily told a fellow classmate, "look like a prostitute."

Ironically, as Mummy's popularity soared in the immediate wake of the divorce and more and more photographers thronged around her, William dreaded being with her in public. Both boys came to realize that it was far less stressful to be in the company of their father, who never inspired this sort of frenzied adulation.

"Wills is happier with Charles," said one Fleet Street photographer. "Physically you notice the difference—he is relaxed. It's clearly an easy relationship. But when William is with Diana, it's heads down."

Battle lines had actually been drawn in early 1996, when Diana brought her boys to the Austrian ski resort of Lech. At first it was Diana who got into a screaming match with a photographer. "Harry," said a witness to the incident, "just shrugged his shoulders very exaggeratedly and rolled his eyes as if to say, 'What can I do if she's nuts?' "

William, however, empathized with Mummy. Later, when paparazzi persisted in their pursuit of Diana after agreeing to leave her alone for the rest of the day, it was the prince who rushed to her defense. Skiing up to the offending photographers, he angrily demanded that they leave his mother alone. "You've already ruined most of the day, so if you don't let her have some peace," he said, motioning to his bodyguards, "I'll have your cameras taken away." Fully aware that they had no right to confiscate anyone's camera, the bodyguards persuaded William to calm down while they gently persuaded the photographers to return the following day.

Convinced that the British tabloid press was far more aggressive than its foreign counterparts, both princes urged Mummy to consider living abroad. Diana briefly toyed with the idea of moving to New York, where, she had convinced herself, the paparazzi would be less tenacious. P. D. Jephson observed that by 1996 her "natural affinity for much of American life was at a high pitch," and that her visits to the States were a "soothing antidote to the simmering acrimony of her daily life in London."

But there were two reasons why Diana felt she could not leave her homeland. "I think in my place, any sane person would have left Britain long ago," she said. "But I cannot. I have my sons."

No one understood her boys' lingering hostility toward the press better than Diana, who was variously a victim of the media and master manipulator of it. But she also appreciated the fact that William and Harry would never escape the media spotlight. "She was trying so hard to teach her sons how to cope with media attention, how to accept that it was something they were going to have to live with," said her friend Liz Tilberis. "William understood her fury with them, and he also understood that she courted them from time to time."

In the midst of all the chaos, William understandably welcomed the order and regimentation of life at Eton. Up every day at 7:30, breakfast at 8:00, then compulsory chapel at 8:30. At 9:00, morning lessons began, with a ten-minute "biscuit break" at 11:20. At precisely 1:25 P.M. Wills and the other first-year "F-tits" trooped to the dining hall for lunch—two vegetables, a meat (usually beef or mutton), and a traditional English pudding.

After lunch, Wills and his fellow Etonians headed for those legendary playing fields. Already towering over many of his fellow fourteen-year-olds at five feet ten inches tall (in two years he would top off at just over six feet one inch), the prince quickly proved himself to be a determined and at times fierce competitor. In the summer months, most students were classified as either a "drybob" (a cricketer) or a "wetbob" (a rower). William chose to be a wetbob, though he also played soccer in the fall.

But there were also rugby, squash, judo, karate, golf, tennis, and the inexplicable Eton Wall Game, in which one team defends a wall against the onslaught of another team. Players, caked with mud, are virtually plastered against the wall in a solid mass, making it virtually impossible for anyone to score. The last time anyone played the Wall Game and scored a goal was 1909.

At 4 P.M., afternoon classes began—everything from standard college prep fare like English literature, biology, Latin, computer science, and music to such eyebrow-raising electives as cooking, printmaking, Mandarin Chinese, car maintenance, and Swahili. Dinner followed at 7:00, followed by study and lights-out at 10 P.M.

Infractions of the rules—and there were many rules, both large and small—usually carried an automatic punishment. Any student who came late to class, for example, was required to get up at dawn the next morning, walk to the office of the headmaster, and sign the "tardy book." One infraction, staff and students alike were informed, would result in immediate dismissal: revealing anything about Prince William's life at Eton to the outside world.

Eton's hands-on approach included a personal tutor for each boy. William's was one Mr. Stuart-Clarke, a young English teacher charged with monitoring the prince's overall progress. Each week, William would go to his tutor's office and do nothing but talk about himself—his favorite subjects, his athletic endeavors, his relationships with other Etonians—for two hours. William was also invited to drop into Stuart-Clarke's home for an evening chat twice a week, where he often socialized with fellow students. Based on all he gleaned from the prince, his tutor would mark up an "order card" (report card) for William every three weeks.

Wills would also have to learn Eton's peculiar argot. Classes were "Divs." The headmaster: "head man." Teachers were "beaks," and their offices "elevenses." At the cafeteria, "Can you lend me some money for a Coke float?" became "Can you sock me a brown cow?"

Not even the school uniform of striped trousers and swallowtail coat was as simple—albeit a tad effete—as it seemed. The academic overachievers known as "tugs" sported their own version, as did Pop, a self-anointed group of school leaders denoted by their colorful, one-of-a-kind vests.

"William has that Etonian look already," said royal watcher Sue Townsend. "The boys are burnished, they are like angels, you know, and they float around the world."

Protocol may have demanded that his peers at the very least call him "Sir," but Wills would have none of it. He insisted that everyone simply call him Wills. By the end of his first year, a significant number of his classmates were addressing him as "Bill."

As at any other prep school that catered to the children of wealth and privilege, Eton was forced to cope with drug and alcohol abuse on campus. "William was not above having a beer or a shot of whiskey," a school-mate recalled. As for drugs, "He was just accepted as one of us, so no one hesitated to offer him pot or even cocaine. But he turned it down flat. It may have had something to do with those bodyguards of his always being about."

Even after entering Eton, William wanted above all else to be seen as just another kid.

Like everyone else his age, he was an avid fan of video games. He also mountain-biked, and for a time held the record at Chelsea's F1 go-cart track—until his brother unseated him. At Balmoral, William, who under British law could not obtain a driver's license until he was seventeen, often took the wheel of his father's Land Rover.

Away from school, his taste in clothes ran to baseball caps, designer sneakers, and sweats from Benetton and the Gap. Musically, the fourteen-year-old shunned alternative bands for chart-topping groups like Oasis and Pulp.

At Eton no posters were allowed in any of the boys' rooms. But the inside of Wills's locker was covered with pinups of super-model Claudia Schiffer, *Baywatch*'s Pamela Anderson, the Barbi twins, Emma "Baby Spice" Bunting of the Spice Girls, and his favorite at the time, Cindy Crawford. (Later, Christie Brinkley would be added to Wills's gallery.) In April of 1996, William walked into his mother's sitting room at Kensington Palace and, as he later said, "nearly fainted" when Cindy Crawford rose to greet him. For over a year he had been begging Mummy to invite the supermodel for tea, but the Princess had been waiting for "just the right moment." (When Harry complained that he felt left out, another American supermodel, Cindy Margolis, sent him calendars and posters of herself along with a note. "I'll be your pin-up girl," it read.)

Crawford was impressed by the bond between

mother and son ("They had an unspoken language") and touched by William's obvious concern for the embattled, mercurial, and palpably vulnerable Princess. When Diana left the room for a moment, William confided to Crawford, "I want Mummy to be happy at all costs."

As was the case for Diana, William's own search for happiness—and that of his brother—would largely depend on how he adapted to his fishbowl existence. In October of 1995, William pleaded with his parents to be allowed to join one thousand other well-heeled teenagers attending the "Toff's Ball" at London's Hammersmith Palais nightclub. Charles initially said no, and with reason. The event was generally regarded as an excuse for the spoiled sons and daughters of Britain's elite to go wild. Although alcohol was banned from the party, revelers often arrived drunk and were soon shedding their clothes and gyrating on the dance floor. In its coverage of the party the previous year, Britain's no-holds-barred tabloids had run photos of partygoers in various states of undress, some barely conscious and others actually engaging in one form or another of sexual conduct.

Mummy, eager to see both her sons enjoy something approximating the life of a normal teenager, thought it was time for William to attend his first teenage dance. Eventually, Charles grudgingly agreed to let his son attend the ball—so long as he went with a group of his friends from Eton.

The ball was already a bacchanal by the time William arrived with his buddies and two Scotland Yard detectives, adding to the frenzy. Over the next three hours, scores of miniskirted girls pursued the handsome, nearly six-foot-tall prince. William's friends tried to fend off some of the more aggressive admirers who literally threw themselves at him. Several had to be pried from the prince. One witness said William looked "shocked" when girls kept offering to "snog" (neck) with him.

Undeterred, William took to the floor, waving his hands in the air and generally having a good time. Then, like everybody else, he waded into the wall of suds spewing from a foam machine. But after the dance was over, he told Mummy, "Lots of girls tried to kiss me but I didn't do anything because the cameras are everywhere."

There would be plenty of other chances. Already towering over the heads of nearly all his classmates (not to mention his father), the handsome blond prince possessed a star quality that was evident to all. "Isn't he superb?" Diana told friends. "And he's so tall, too! The girls will be mad for him!"

Diana repeatedly referred to Wills as "DDG" (Drop Dead Gorgeous). "Oh, *Mum*," Wills would protest as he rolled his eyes skyward, "don't say that. *Please.*"

Mum was not alone in her assessment of William's appeal. When he was still four-teen, the British teen magazine *Smash Hits* included a centerfold pullout of the prince wearing a blue blazer. The issue sold out instantly. Later, the magazine distributed a quarter of a million "I Love Willy" stickers. To his horror, William's classmates began referring to him as "Dreamboat Willy." Nor did it help matters that his Eton warm-up jacket read "W.O.W."—for William of Wales.

That summer of 1996, Diana hoped to escape the paparazzi with her sons when she rented a hideaway in the south of France. Armed with telephoto lenses, photographers camped in the woods some six hundred feet away. Every time Diana or one of the boys stepped outside for a dip in the pool or to sunbathe on the patio, they were captured on film. William took to hiding behind a towel.

Once again, rather than threatening the spying photographers, Diana's bodyguards tried to reason with them. This was, after all, a family. And like all families, the detectives argued, Diana and her boys were entitled to at least a few moments of peace. None of which mattered to the paparazzi.

"Prince William was very frustrated," said one of the photographers. "Of course he knew he could not control the press. At the same time, he is a member of the Royal Family and used to getting his own way. Princess Diana must have tried to explain to him that we were on public property and there was nothing she could do, but he sulked anyway."

For his part, Harry simply ignored the intruders and enjoyed his holiday. But William holed up in the house all day, determined not to have his picture taken. Despite pleas from his mother and brother to make the best of the situation, William would not budge. Their holiday ruined, Diana cut it short and returned to London.

Away from the prying eyes of photographers at Balmoral, Wills and Harry could at last enjoy themselves. Nothing made the boys happier than picking up a rifle and slogging through the marshes with Prince Charles and Grand-papa. In October of 1996, fourteen-year-old William killed his first stag, with a single shot from a high-velocity rifle fired at a distance of 150 yards. Charles watched as Wills went through the ritual of being "blooded"—having hunting guides daub the boy's forehead with the deer's blood.

Once again animal rights activists were outraged, and refused to be mollified by the Palace's explanation that William had merely participated in efforts to thin out the herd. Mummy, meanwhile, was grateful that she had taken William's advice and not become head of the Royal Society for the Prevention of Cruelty to Animals. The controversy did nothing to dampen William's spirits. The stag's head was stuffed and mounted on a wall in Balmoral Castle alongside the scores of other hunting trophies displayed at Balmoral.

Diana understood the royal blood lust that was her sons' birthright. But she also worried about what effect all the killing might have on the boys' tender psyches. "All William wants to do," she told a friend, "is have a gun in his hand."

Even at Balmoral, Wills and Harry could not escape the detectives who monitored their every move and shadowed them twenty-four hours a day. At Eton, bodyguards tried to stay between sixty to one hundred feet away from the prince, but whenever he ventured into public that gap narrowed to twenty feet or less. "For God's sake!" he would say to anyone who would listen when it all got to be too much. "Why must I always be *followed*?"

Neither Charles nor Diana had any easy answers for their sons. Both William and Harry, along with their father and grandmother, were symbols of the state and obvious terrorist targets. "It's annoying, I know," Charles would tell his sons. "But try to cooperate. These men have a job to do."

The Princess of Wales was another matter entirely. Although the Palace implored her to retain her bodyguards following the divorce, Diana was eager to break free of them. As a member of the Royal Family, she had always felt those Royal Protection Squad detectives assigned to guard her were an unwarranted intrusion on her privacy. She also suspected, with good reason, that they were spying on her. She now notified Scotland Yard that she no longer desired the kind of round-the-clock protection provided Charles and their children.

Divorce also freed Mummy to fashion a

new life for herself as a single woman. To be sure, there were many lonely moments as she sorted things out. "Imagine, incredible adulation during the day," said her friend Lord Palumbo, "then dinner on a tray in front of the television in Kensington Palace—alone."

But there were also plenty of admirers, from legendary tenors Luciano Pavarotti and Placido Domingo to British businessman Christopher Whalley and Pakistani electronics mogul Gulu Lalvani. But it was another Pakistani—paunchy, chain-smoking, thirty-nine-year-old heart surgeon Hasnat Khan—who captured the heart of the young princes' mother.

For months, Diana managed to keep her relationship with "Natty" Khan a secret—even from William. They first met in September of 1995, when Khan performed a triple bypass on the husband of Diana's acupuncturist, Oonagh Toffolo. For Diana, it was love at first sight. "Oonagh," she said as Khan left the hospital room after their first meeting, "isn't he drop-dead gorgeous!"

Diana became obsessed with "Mr. Wonderful," as she called Khan, spending two or three days with him at Royal Brompton Heart and Lung Hospital, where he worked. She bought a copy of *Gray's Anatomy* and studied everything it had to say about the heart. At the Princess's request, Khan arranged for her to don scrubs and witness a heart operation close-up.

William and Harry watched with no small

degree of curiosity while Diana added Pakistani-style silk dresses to her wardrobe and began burning joss sticks in Kensington Palace. She scoured London for videos of Pakistani-made movies. "Aren't they a good-looking race?" she asked her hairdresser Natalie Symonds. "The men are so handsome."

In February 1996, while British newspapers speculated endlessly about the impending divorce, Diana made the first of two visits to Pakistan to learn more about Natty Khan's homeland. When Harry saw photographs of his mother cradling a child dying of cancer at Lahore's Shaukat Khanum Memorial Hospital, he was visibly moved. William, who was also following press accounts of the trip, was proud of his mother but knew that exposure to such overwhelming sadness took a heavy toll. After holding the hand of a sick child or hearing horrifying stories of domestic abuse, she would call William or a close friend like Rosa Monckton and, said Monckton, "simply cry, totally drained and exhausted."

On her return, Diana decided it was time to tell her sons about her deepening feelings for Khan. Although Harry was too young to be given anything more than the broad brush strokes of the relationship, the Princess would share certain details with William—boasting how she had managed to conceal their "special friendship" from the press. Often wearing a disguise—a favorite consisted of a dark wig, eyeglasses, a bomber jacket, and jeans—Diana would drive a borrowed Range Rover or her butler's car on a circuitous route to Royal Brompton Hospital. Then, with Khan concealed in the backseat under a blanket, she would drive him back to Kensington Palace.

More significant, Mummy's fascination with Khan triggered an interest in all things Muslim. Diana studied the Koran every night, and spent time in the company of cricket star turned politician Imram Khan and his wife, Jemima. The daughter of Diana's longtime friend Lady Annabel Goldsmith, Jemima had caused a sensation in 1995 when she converted to Islam and married Imram Khan, who was twenty-two years her senior.

For a young woman from a broken home whose own marriage had just ended in bitterness and acrimony, the Muslim concept of a close-knit extended family was enormously appealing. Jemima lived not only with her husband and their children, but with her in-laws and their brothers and sisters and *their* spouses and children. Diana also became fascinated with the dietary laws of Islam.

In July of 1996, Hasnat Khan introduced Diana to his grandmother "Nanny" Appa, and the two women hit it off instantly. Soon photographs of Khan and his grandmother were on Diana's nightstand along with those of William and Harry.

"She told me she was going to convert to Islam if that was necessary for her to marry Dr. Khan," Elsa Bowker said. But before she took any action, she took Khan to Kensington Palace to meet her boys. According to Simone

Simmons, Khan, unaccustomed to dealing with adolescents, was nervous about meeting William and Harry.

The meeting turned out to be cordial, the conversation awkward and strained. Diana suggested that in order to bond with her sons, Khan might move to Kensington Palace—into the suite Prince Charles once occupied. Media-shy Khan, knowing that the life he enjoyed as a private citizen would cease to exist once he became Diana's live-in lover, declined her offer.

The Princess was sensitive to Khan's need for privacy. After the *Sunday Mirror* broke the story that Diana was seeing the Pakistani surgeon, Diana fired back in the *Daily Mail* that the *Sunday Mirror* story was "bullshit." She was upset by such reports, she said, because of "the hurt they do William and Harry." Instead of being grateful that Diana had effectively discredited the *Sunday Mirror* scoop, Khan was insulted and would not speak to her for days.

Nevertheless, the Princess was now telling friends that she intended to wed Dr. Hasnat Khan. "Diana wanted more children," Lady Bowker recalled. "She said, 'Elsa, I want two girls.' "

It was no small irony that in November, William and Harry were cut off from their aunt Sarah and Fergie's children Beatrice and Eugenie—the closest thing Diana had to girls of her own. In her tell-all book *My Story*, Fergie had made the fatal error of claiming that she had contracted plantar warts after borrowing a pair of her sister-in-law's shoes. Largely because of that, Diana "cut Fergie out of her life," Natalie Symonds said. "But she missed all the good times they had together."

As much as Mummy missed her friend, she missed Fergie's daughters even more. On her bedroom wall next to some framed letters from William and Harry, Diana hung two drawings the princesses had done for her. They were inscribed with love to "Aunt Duch."

"I literally adore them," Diana said of the nieces she cut out of her life and out of the lives of her sons. "They are the daughters I never had."

Harry and Wills both asked their mother why they no longer spent time with the cousins they had always been so fond of. "Don't worry," she assured them, "it was just a silly misunderstanding their mother and I had, but it's all done now. We'll see them soon, you'll see."

During the remainder of Diana's life, William and Harry never spoke to the aunt who had been one of their mother's closest allies in the Windsor wars. Fergie flooded "Duch," as she called Diana, with letters and calls, but to no avail.

However powerful the desire to marry Khan and have children by him, Diana, Lady Bowker said, "knew that to marry a Muslim would create enormous problems for William and Harry..." Finally, Diana told William point-blank that she was in love with Khan, and wanted to marry him. But she would only do so with both her sons' blessing. She also knew that Harry would follow his older brother's lead. "Mummy," William told her, "you have to do what makes you happy."

William's answer to his mother's question said much about the trust each had invested in the other, and the significance of both boys in her life. Diana viewed her sons, her journalist friend Richard Kay observed, as "the only men in her life who had never let her down and never wanted her to be anything but herself."

While still secretly studying the Koran and pondering the possibility of converting to Islam, Diana drove her black BMW alone to Eton for the school's annual Christmas service. Prince Charles arrived five minutes later in the back of a chauffeur-driven Vauxhall Cavalier. They each went to Manor House, where they were welcomed inside by housemaster Andrew Gailey. The Prince and Princess of Wales then avoided photographers by entering the Eton College Chapel through a side door.

When William stood up to read "The Prophet Micah Foretells the Glory of Bethlehem," he looked out on the crowd and spotted his parents—it was the first time they had appeared together in public in over a year. "You could see a flicker of recognition across his face, and then he smiled faintly in their direction," the mother of another Eton boy observed. "It must have been a bittersweet moment, because his mother and father stayed just long enough to congratulate him, then went their separate ways."

Just as they had the previous Christmas, William and Harry celebrated at Sandringham with Papa, Granny, and the rest of the Windsors. Mummy, once again feeling the sting of ostracism in the Christmas season, swam and sunbathed in Barbuda, in the British West Indies.

It was just after Christmas 1996 when William phoned his mother in Barbuda. He was headed back to Eton, while Papa was getting ready to take Harry to Klosters for their annual father-son holiday on the slopes. Wills did not think it necessary to mention the fact that Tiggy would be tagging along.

With a little time to himself, William had been pondering ways to raise cash for his mother's favorite causes. "I've had a brilliant idea, Mum," said the media-savvy prince. "Why don't you have a sale of your dresses for charity? And I'll take ten percent!"

Mummy thought it over while lolling on the beach, then called Wills back. "It *is* brilliant," she told him. For the next hour they discussed where the auction should be held ("The Americans would go wild for this," Wills told his mother), which house should conduct the sale, and where the money might go.

Arriving back in London, the Princess summoned Simone Simmons to Kensington Palace. For three hours, they scoured the Princess's closets, pulling one designer gown after another off the rack and laying it out on the floor. Two weeks later, after running the final details past William, Diana announced that she would be auctioning off her dresses at Christie's in New York the following June, and that the proceeds would be divided between the AIDS Crisis Trust and the Cancer Research Fund for the Royal Marsden Hospital.

Diana was also relying on William's counsel as she contemplated a bold, even outlandish, career move. A month before Diana and her former sister-in-law had their falling-out, Fergie had met Kevin Costner on a trip to China and told the actor how obsessed Diana was with his 1992 hit film *The Bodyguard*. The Princess had strongly identified with the hunted pop diva played in the film by Whitney Houston.

When Costner told the Duchess that he was planning a sequel, Fergie suggested he offer Diana the lead. With the backing of his studio, Costner called Diana and discussed the possibility. "Look, my life is maybe going to become my own at some point," she told Costner. "Go ahead and do this script and when it's ready I'll be in a really good spot."

Costner then set out to create a role tailor-made for his new star. In *The Bodyguard II*, she was to portray a princess who falls in love with her bodyguard after he rescues her from a kidnapper. The fee: ten million dollars, which Diana intended to spread among her charities.

"Her life was complicated," Costner said. "She wanted the right to reinvent herself. But she wanted to be delicate about it."

251

Costner's partner, Jim Wilson, headed up the top secret project, making sure that the script "didn't take her beyond her qualifications as an actress... It played beautifully into her hand."

William was a main reason she tentatively agreed to take the role. Like their mother, both princes were starstruck, and the idea of starring in a Hollywood film was irresistible. When Diana asked William for his opinion, he did not hesitate to give it. "Mummy, *Kevin Costner*. Ten *million* dollars," William gushed. "You have to do it!"

While the script for *The Bodyguard II* was being worked on Diana embarked on a new and daunting task—focusing public attention on the human suffering wrought by land mines. In January of 1997, under the auspices of the Red Cross, she flew to Angola, where there was an unexploded land mine for every one of the country's twelve million inhabitants. William had encouraged her to go; she had comforted so many sick and injured people around the world, he knew she could do the same for people who had lost limbs to land mines.

Diana did just that. But the emotional toll was high. She phoned Wills at Eton several times during the trip, confessing that she was so moved by what she was witnessing that she cried herself to sleep every night. She told William that, as she hugged one eleven-year-old girl who was crying because her leg had been torn off by a mine, Diana had to bite the inside of her lip to keep from crying herself.

What neither William nor Harry nor anyone else had counted on was Diana's willingness to risk her life to make an important point. When photographs ran in newspapers around the world showing the Princess strolling through a minefield marked with skull-and-crossbones pennants, the princes were upset. Wearing a flak jacket and face protector, Diana looked confident as she strode through the minefield. In reality, she told William, she was "absolutely terrified."

William and Harry asked their mother not to take chances like that again. But they also told her how proud they were of her for making a difference in the world. Despite criticism from elements in her own government, which officially opposed a land-mine ban at the time, Diana persevered. Later in 1997, she would visit war-ravaged Bosnia, where she would again hug children whose limbs had been blown off, and bite her lip to keep from weeping. Her efforts unquestionably laid the groundwork for the anti-land-mine treaty eventually signed by more than 120 nations in Ottawa.

Even Charles was impressed, and told his sons so. Since the divorce was finalized, the acrimony that had been the hallmark of their marriage had been replaced by admiration and, oddly enough, affection. Diana would trace the turning point to the day they both stood looking over William's shoulder as he enrolled at Eton. Gradually, as they shared responsibility for raising their sons, Charles and Diana became, in her words, "very best friends." "Her love for him never really died," said her hairstylist Natalie Symonds.

Relations between the boys' parents had thawed to such a degree that the Palace readily approved Charles's plan to make his first public appearance with Diana since William's confirmation six months earlier. As part of a move to trim the monarchy's budget, the royal yacht *Britannia* was being decommissioned, and Charles was scheduled to board the ship at Cardiff on one leg of its farewell tour around the United Kingdom.

Charles called Diana and asked if she and the boys would be interested in sailing with him. The Princess was, said one of her own staffers, "thrilled and touched that he asked. It was a sign that they really had put all that ugliness behind them and reached a new plateau in their relationship. She wanted peace more than anything for the boys."

"They were both very excited about being seen in public as a family again," said one Palace official. Not nearly as excited as their sons. "Every child of divorce knows what it is like to feel like you're part of a family again," Diana said, "even if it's only for a few hours."

At this stage, Mummy even came to harbor a grudging admiration for the woman she used to call "the Rottweiler"—in part because Diana was so besotted with her Pakistani heart surgeon. "She became so devoted to Hasnat," Symonds recalled, "that she said she at last began to understand the undying love

Prince Charles shared with Camilla Parker Bowles. She was wildly in love, totally obsessed by Dr. Khan."

One person she still could not bring herself to warm to was Tiggy Legge-Bourke. Diana still resented Tiggy's "surrogate mother" status, and in the words of her hairdresser Tess Rock, "went potty" every time she saw a photo of Legge-Bourke with her boys. Under pressure from his ex-wife, Charles had asked Tiggy to be less conspicuous around the boys in public. But on March 9, 1997, when William was confirmed in St. George's Chapel at Windsor, Diana complained that Tiggy had drawn up a guest list that slighted her side of the family. In a matter of weeks, Tiggy was off the Prince of Wales's payroll. This did not prevent Tiggy, who remained a friend of the Royal Family, from spending time with William and Harry.

At around the same time William, aware of his father's low standing in the polls, surprised his mother by insisting that they watch a televised debate on the state of the monarchy. Harry joined them in front of the television set in Diana's Kensington Palace sitting room. The debate had raged for less than five minutes before the name Camilla came up. Harry turned to his mother and asked, "Who's Camilla?"

William and Mummy looked at each other for a moment before collapsing with laughter. "Harry," William told his brother, "that's something you'll have to ask Papa about."

Diana now concentrated on the new man in her life. Without telling Khan, she flew to Pakistan in May of 1997 to visit his family. "I met his parents and they love me," she told her hairdressers. "There is absolutely no problem about me not being Muslim. So we can definitely get married now! Spread it around," she told Rock and Symonds, "we're going to get married."

Khan was in no hurry to rush to the altar. "He was devoted to his career," Symonds recalled, "and not willing to live in Diana's shadow." He also rightly suspected that Diana was leaking stories about their affair to the press. After one angry confrontation, he stormed out of Kensington Palace vowing not to speak to her again.

Diana had already asked William how he would feel if she married Khan. Now she asked if, as a young man, he could understand Khan's behavior. Wills had always been his mother's closest confidant, but she drew the line at discussing her lovers. Now that he was a teenager, William found his mother far less reticent to discuss the state of her love life with him.

"William was always far older than his years—Diana had said that since he was a very little boy," Elsa Bowker said. "He was not embarrassed when his mother asked why Hasnat Khan was behaving so oddly. He told her, 'If Dr. Khan doesn't appreciate you, Mummy, there are lots of gentlemen who will.'"

Diana, as was now more often the case than not, took her son's advice. She was seen around town with old friends Gulu Lalvani, fifty-eight, and the handsome young property developer Christopher Whalley. The dates had the desired effect. Khan, consumed with jealousy, showered the Princess with roses and apologies.

Few sons would have felt comfortable giving advice on romance to Mom. But growing up in the midst of chaos, Wills often assumed an adult role—if only to bring some semblance of order to his life. The seven-year-old boy who bossed the other children around on the playground was now exhibiting signs of leadership on those fabled playing fields of Eton. Even when he was not technically in charge, the prince took the initiative, coming up with ideas and cheering on his fellow players. "He wasn't always trying to show people who's boss or anything like that," a schoolmate said. "He was just very enthusiastic, very committed to everything he did. If someone was having a rotten time of it, he would encourage them. Or he'd kid with them—but never mean, always in fun. Will got on with everybody. I don't think I can say that about anyone else at Eton."

As sensitive as he was to the feelings of his peers, William stunned both Mummy and Papa when he asked them both not to come to Parents Day at Eton. "There will be press about," he told Diana, "but if you come it will truly be unbearable. Of course I'm used to it, but I don't want to ruin things for all the other boys and their parents. You understand..."

They might have understood—had William not then invited Tiggy Legge-Bourke. Tiggy, who had formed a particularly strong bond with Harry and still went riding and shooting with both boys at Sandringham and Balmoral, was flattered but embarrassed. Knowing that Wills's mum would be furious, she called Charles for advice.

Papa, as it turned out, was also nursing a bruised ego over being excluded from the Parents Day festivities by his own son. He shared his feelings with Wills, and warned him further that it could fuel speculation that there was a rift between him and his parents. Or—even worse—Wills's actions could be seen as a sign that Diana and Charles could no longer stand to be in each other's company, even for the sake their children.

Still, when Tiggy called and expressed doubt about the wisdom of accepting Wills's invitation, Charles was loath to discourage her. "Don't be silly," he reassured her. "William wants you there. So pack a picnic lunch and some wine and have a good time."

She did, bringing along one of William's friends, Edward van Cutsem's younger brother William. Wearing his striped pants and tails like the rest of the Etonians, the prince sat with Tiggy and van Cutsem on a plaid blanket spread out on the grass, drinking wine and eating sandwiches, pâté, and potato chips. When three giggling girls in miniskirts stopped over to introduce themselves, the prince eagerly invited them to join him and his friends. Later, in true royal fashion, William and van Cutsem embarked on a "walkabout," visiting each family group, chatting up his friends and their parents—and meeting scores of beautiful young women in the process.

The next day, William would report to his mother that he had had a wonderful time—without ever mentioning Tiggy. Diana was happy to hear that her son had had the presence of mind to write down the names of several of the girls he had met. "At this point," the Princess said of her elder boy, "it's all raging hormones—theirs and his."

Like Charles, Mummy was angry and hurt that he had excluded her from Parents Day—a slight compounded by the fact that Tiggy went instead. Nevertheless, it was now that William decided to try and settle things between the two most important women in his life. He asked Mummy if she would be willing to meet with Tiggy, and to his delight, the Princess agreed. She had her secretary call Tiggy and invite her to join her and William for lunch at the aptly named La Famiglia ("the Family"), an Italian restaurant off the King's Road in Chelsea. But Tiggy, still wary of the princes' mum, respectfully declined.

Diana fretted about more than just her sons' affection for their "surrogate mother." Worried that her own celebrity was driving a wedge between herself and the children,

Diana had been feeling particularly vulnerable when she attended a benefit performance of *Swan Lake* the same week.

At the dinner that followed, she happened to be seated next to the controversial Egyptian tycoon Mohamed Al Fayed. Over a thirty-three-year period, the self-made billionaire had acquired an impressive number of British icons—Harrods department store, the satirical magazine *Punch*, royal shirtmaker Turnbull & Asser, and Scotland's Balnagown Castle among them—in his quest for respectability. Spurned by England's aristocracy and denied British citizenship, Al Fayed nonetheless counted Diana's beloved father as a friend.

For years, Al Fayed had been inviting Diana to spend the holidays with him at his family's villa in St.-Tropez. Now, for the first time, she told him she would mull over his offer. She had no doubt about what her sons would say: understandably, they harbored a special fondness for Mohamed Al Fayed, who on past occasions had given them the run of Harrods' extensive toy department.

For the next several weeks, William and Harry wound down their school years while Mummy made one of her periodic public relations assaults on the United States. For his part, William was increasingly given to open displays of his contempt for the press. When the Royal Family posed for an official photo marking the Queen Mother's ninety-seventh birthday, William tried to hide in the back of the pack. Instructed to take his place of prominence next to Charles and Harry, Wills did so—but turned his face away from the camera. Similarly, following the Queen Mother's annual tea party for Eton boys, Wills walked backward toward his father's car so that photographers could not snap a shot of his face. Whenever photographers spotted Prince William sculling on the Thames, as he frequently did that summer of 1997, he quickly turned his face in the direction of the opposite bank.

Conversely, Mummy basked in the spotlight of an adoring American press. Papers on both sides of the Atlantic were filled with photos of Diana—with Hillary Clinton at the White House, attending the eightieth birthday party of *Washington Post* publisher Katharine Graham, visiting her friend Mother Teresa at an AIDS hospice in the Bronx, attending a Red Cross fund-raiser and the preview party for the auction of her dresses at Christie's.

William's idea would pay off handsomely: Bidders wound up spending $3.26 million for seventy-nine of Diana's gowns. As soon as she heard the staggering figures—the midnight-blue velvet dress she wore the night she danced with John Travolta went for $222,500—the Princess called her son to congratulate him.

"Isn't it wonderful? Three million dollars for some old frocks!!!" she squealed.

"So," Wills replied, "where's my ten percent?"

As they did every summer, the boys shuttled between Kensington Palace and their father's various quarters at St. James's, High-grove, Sandringham, and Balmoral. Charles and Diana were discussing the boys several times a week in person or over the phone, and it occurred to William and Harry that they had never seen their parents behave so warmly toward each other.

The boys also noticed that, unlike the Diana of the past, their mother was now determined not to offend their father or the Queen. Not that Papa or Granny was aware of everything that transpired between Diana and the boys. When William turned fifteen on June 21, 1997, Diana asked the chef to prepare something special for her centerfold-obsessed son. At a small party at Kensington Palace sans the rest of the Windsors, William blew out the candles on a cake decorated with six topless models.

The next day, she took William and Harry to see *The Devil's Own,* starring Harrison Ford and Brad Pitt. No sooner did they leave the theater than there was an uproar over Diana's choice of film fare for her sons. Many felt the movie was sympathetic in tone toward the Irish Republican Army.

Unnerved by the latest spate of headlines, Diana called Charles at his offices in St. James's Palace. "I didn't know what it was about," she explained. "We just wanted to see a movie, and we picked it out of the paper because William likes Harrison Ford." To her relief, Charles told her not to worry. Granny, he pointed out, was also a big fan of Harrison Ford.

Diana's concern for Charles's feelings was not entirely reciprocated—a fact that did not go unnoticed by their children. Despite opposition from the Queen, the Prince of Wales was planning to throw an elaborate fiftieth birthday party for Camilla at Highgrove—his first public declaration of love for his mistress.

Diana, determined not to be outshone in the birthday department, celebrated her thirty-sixth on July 1 as guest of honor at a gala benefit marking the centennial of London's Tate Gallery. Afterward at Kensington Palace, William and Harry sang "Happy Birthday" and watched as she blew out the candles—for what would be the very last time—on a cake prepared by the palace chef.

A week later, Diana took William and Harry to Chequers, the Prime Minister's official country residence. There they played outside with Tony Blair's young sons Euan and Nicholas while Blair discussed a possible role for Diana as a roving goodwill ambassador for Britain. On the ride home to London, Diana asked her boys what they thought of the Prime Minister. They both agreed that Blair seemed "incredibly nice." Yes, Mummy nodded in agreement, "and quite sexy." William and Harry, mortified, rolled their eyes and changed the subject to the Blair boys.

On July 11, William and Harry joined their mother aboard Harrods' Gulfstream IV jet, with its pink upholstery and pharoahs-head carpets, and took off for Nice. Their flying companions: Mohamed Al Fayed, his Finnish-born wife,

Heini, and their four children, aged ten to sixteen. Once they touched down in France, the party was whisked off to the harbor at St.-Laurent-du-Var, where they boarded the *Jonikal,* Al Fayed's spectacular 195-foot yacht.

Five hours later, the *Jonikal* dropped anchor in St.-Tropez. Following their mother up the gangplank, William and Harry looked up to see most of the yacht's sixteen crew members gawking. "We weren't told in advance," said Debbie Gribble, the *Jonikal*'s chief stewardess. "Diana and her sons were the last people we expected to see."

Shortly after sunset they arrived at Al Fayed's seventeen-million-dollar Côte d'Azur compound. Diana and her sons were promptly escorted to the "Fisherman's Cottage," the estate's lavishly appointed thirteen-room guest house.

Boasting a private beach, two swimming pools, a terraced garden, and waterfalls, the Al Fayed villa seemed the perfect antidote to the pressures Diana and her boys had been under. Every morning, William and Harry walked down to the beach with their mother to sail, Jet Ski, snorkel, surf, and just splash around in the waves.

Lunches aboard the *Jonikal* always consisted of a glass of champagne (William was allowed one glass; Harry drank Coke) followed by caviar and fresh lobster—all served under a white awning on the upper deck. The boys, more accustomed to the comparatively meager culinary offerings at Ludgrove and Eton, devoured dish after epicurean dish but still wound up turning food away. "William couldn't believe it when a whole fish was sent back to the kitchen untouched," his mother told Gribble. "I don't think he's ever seen so much food."

Although Diana had dismissed her bodyguards, two detectives assigned to the princes hovered in the background. Their presence hardly seemed necessary; at least a half dozen of Al Fayed's own armed bodyguards were watching the billionaire and his kids at any given time.

They were powerless, however, to do anything about the paparazzi who swarmed in small motorboats one hundred yards from Al Fayed's private beach. Harry was, as usual, able to ignore the interlopers, but William reacted by retreating to his room. "Who told them we were going to be here?" he demanded. "Don't you have the right to enjoy your vacation? Why can't they just leave us alone?"

He had asked her these questions a thousand times, and Diana still had no easy answers. Now William was adding concerns for his mother's safety to his usual litany of complaints about the press. Wills and Harry both wondered aloud if the frenzy over Diana, fueled by the nonstop tabloid coverage, might lead someone to try and harm her.

Diana's boys were also troubled by the way their mother was literally chased through the streets by photographers. Despite the fact that she always wore a seat belt and would not start her car unless they were wearing theirs, William and Harry had also been along on some hair-raising rides through the streets of London as Mummy tried to elude the press pack. "They could cause an accident," William pointed out to her. "Someone could get hurt."

More ominously from Diana's viewpoint, William pointed out to her that when he was with his father and Tiggy Legge-Bourke, they were never pursued by "those maniacs. I don't see how you can bear it, Mummy," William said. "I can't."

"She told me William was an incredibly sensitive soul," said her friend Richard Greene, "and she was very concerned about him. She said he needed to be protected."

The Princess certainly understood William's inherent shyness. Indeed, whenever press photographers appeared—even during an official Palace-sanctioned photo opportunity—Wills kept the downcast gaze that had been the hallmark of "Shy Di" at the beginning of her public career. Harry had no problem grinning on command, but his brother's scowl became the bane of press photographers throughout Britain. William would be even less apt to break into a smile when he returned to Eton in September of 1997; Mummy, concerned with correcting her son's overbite, was insisting that Wills get his first set of braces.

As much as they clearly preferred the country to London, Kensington Palace continued to be, according to royal biographer Anthony

Holden, "the happiest, least stuffy royal residence I have ever visited." When Holden drove up to Kensington Palace with a video Diana had asked to borrow, he "nearly ran down the future King of England... As I pulled up the gravel driveway, two laughing boys came charging out, nearly colliding with my car." Holden observed that "nothing could have been more natural—and, therefore, less royal—than the sight of the Princes William and Harry, home from boarding school, galloping into the garden."

William's reticence aside, Diana was convinced that her son would not only be able to bear the media scrutiny, but that like her he would ultimately turn it to his advantage. Toward that end, she was confident he would make a first-rate king—and that with his brand of youthful humanism, William would be able to save the monarchy from itself.

"All my hopes are on William now," Diana said. "But I don't want to push him... I try to din into him all the time about the media—the dangers, and how he must understand and handle it. I think he understands. I'm hoping he'll grow up to be as smart about it as John Kennedy Jr. I want William to be able to handle things as well as John does."

Diana was confident that her son was up to the task. A firm believer in divine providence, she told her friend Richard Greene that it was her destiny to transform the monarchy. "Yes, I believe in destiny," she said, "and I'm not coming back."

Greene thought for a moment. "Are you talking about reincarnation?" he asked her.

"Yes, this is my last lifetime," she replied. "I'm going to do it all now. This is it. I'm not coming back to this place."

For the moment, however, the Princess was intent on salvaging her boys' St.-Tropez vacation. While Wills and Harry headed off on Jet Skis, Diana climbed aboard one of Al Fayed's powerboats and headed straight for a boat full of British photographers.

Wide-eyed, the paparazzi were taken aback by Diana's direct approach. "How long do you plan to keep this up?" she demanded to know. "We've been watched every minute that we've been here. There's an obsessive interest in me and the children... William is freaked out—he's worried about the family's safety. My sons are always urging me to live abroad to be less in the public eye, and maybe that's what I should do—go and live abroad."

The Princess's appeal on her sons' behalf accomplished little. The boats remained. Grateful that his mother had made a valiant effort, William had a sudden change of heart. "We mustn't let them spoil our holiday," he told Mummy. "So let's just give them what they want."

At 11 A.M. each day, William and Harry ran out onto the beach with Mummy and spent several hours diving, swimming, boating, Jet Skiing, and splashing in the surf—all in full view of the photographers.

Diana did not tell her sons that she had an

ulterior motive for finally relenting and cooperating with the media. Shots of her swinging off the deck of the *Jonikal* and cavorting with her princes in the water appeared on front pages everywhere. Consequently, Charles's long-planned birthday party for Camilla came and went virtually unnoticed. The Prince's longtime mistress, suspecting that this was intentional, now took to calling William and Harry's mother "Barbie."

On July 14, the *Jonikal* dropped anchor in Cannes Harbor so that Mohamed Al Fayed's guests would be afforded a perfect view of the resort's spectacular Bastille Day fireworks. That evening Al Fayed had arranged for his son Dodi to fly in from Paris and join the Princess for a candlelight supper aboard the yacht. The sometime film producer (*Chariots of Fire*) with a reputation for pursuing beautiful women had met Diana and the boys several times but only in passing.

Within moments, the elegant supper for two deteriorated into a full-blown food fight, with Dodi and Diana hurling bits of fruit at each other and laughing hysterically. "They were chasing each other and laughing and giggling like a couple of kids," said Debbie Gribble.

William and Harry, meanwhile, had come up from belowdecks to watch the fireworks. They stood transfixed at the sight of their mother, her white sleeveless dress stained with food, pushing a ripe mango full into the face of their host's son.

The boys recognized the impromptu food

fight for what it was: a defining moment in their mother's relationship with Dodi. Over the next few days, the Princess and the playboy were engrossed in conversation. Fayed (Dodi dropped the Arabic "Al" from his surname) listened intently as she told him about her travels to Pakistan and Africa, her crusade to ban land mines, and the role she hoped to fashion for herself as Britain's roving goodwill ambassador. "Something had passed between them," said Gribble. "Suddenly they seemed to fit as a couple."

With their mother duly occupied, William and Harry engaged in horseplay with members of Al Fayed's security force, some of whom were former Royal Seals, or played in the surf with Mohamed Al Fayed's children. While Harry took his mother for rides on the back of his Jet Ski, William practiced swan dives into the Mediterranean off the yacht's thirty-foot-high diving board.

Savoring these days away from regimented boarding school life, the boys also liked to spend time with the crew. "They loved being on their own," one *Jonikal* employee observed, noting that everyone on board the yacht was impressed with the princes' manners. "They'd help themselves to ice cream from the galley, then insist on doing the wash-up. They were very down-to-earth, with no airs at all, and always volunteering to help out. Harry was eager to work in the machine room, or in the galley. He'd have climbed up a mast and manned the crow's nest, if we had one."

Fayed bodyguard Trevor Rees-Jones, who would later be the sole survivor of the fatal crash in Paris, was also impressed with Diana's boys. "William was a lovely lad, very genuine, similar to his mother. He was level-headed and had a lot of her compassion," Rees-Jones said. "There was none of the future king bit. He remembered your name and had time for everyone. He was a great lad, not what you'd expect the Royal Family to be like." As for Harry: "He was a bit of a scamp, but a thoroughly decent, well-mannered boy. Their mother taught them both extremely well."

William and Harry had seldom seen their mother happier. But her reverie would be short-lived. Shortly after meeting Dodi, news came that Diana's friend the Italian designer Gianni Versace had been shot to death in broad daylight outside his Miami Beach mansion.

As devastated as Diana was, the Versace murder gave her children new cause for concern. If this crime was the work of a mentally unbalanced fan, as television reports were already speculating, then surely no celebrity was safe—certainly not the world's most famous woman. William and Harry, whose own bodyguards were always close at hand, begged their mother to consider reinstating her royal protection detail. Dodi agreed with the boys. From now on, he told Diana, his father's small army of bodyguards would protect her.

But for the moment, Diana was too distraught

to deal with questions of her own safety. Determined to cheer them up, Dodi hired a St.-Tropez disco for two nights so that Diana, Wills, and Harry could dance in private. The following day, he took them to an amusement park. There, Diana and the boys let off steam crashing bumper cars into one another.

When it finally came time to end their idyll on the French Riviera, William and Harry shook the hands of the crew members and thanked their hosts. Except for the shocking news of Versace's murder, the vacation with her boys had, in Diana's words, been "very nearly perfect." It would, sadly, be their last together.

On their return to Kensington Palace, William and Harry had managed only a few steps toward their rooms when Mummy let out a squeal of delight. Waiting for her were four dozen roses, a twelve-thousand-dollar Jaeger-leCoultre gold watch—and a love note from Dodi.

On June 22, Diana flew to Milan for Versace's celebrity-packed memorial service. The next day she joined Dodi for a weekend in Paris, where his father numbered among his holdings the legendary Ritz Hotel and Villa Windsor, former residence of the Duke and Duchess of Windsor.

For Mohamed Al Fayed, there could be no sweeter revenge on the aristocrats who had rejected him than to have Dodi become step-father to William and Harry. Should marriage be in the offing, Al Fayed told his son, there would be no more fitting place for them to live than at the Villa Windsor.

Returning to London, Diana was confronted by her two very bored sons, biding their time until they joined their father and the rest of the Royal Family for six weeks of hunting and fishing at Balmoral. William, in particular, was eager to use the two hunting rifles Papa had given him as a confirmation present.

"There's nothing for you here," Diana told them. "Why don't you go up to Scotland to join your papa a day early?" They happily complied, leaving their mother free to rejoin Dodi aboard the *Jonikal*—this time on a cruise from Nice to Sardinia.

As they left Kensington Palace for the train that would take them to Scotland, William and Harry hugged their mother and kissed her goodbye as they always did. At Balmoral, away from the yachts, the sun-washed Mediterranean villas, and the hordes of paparazzi, the boys quickly settled into the royal life they had learned to love. There were the hunting parties that lasted from dawn until dusk, the days spent fishing by the River Dee, horseback riding along the moors, and afternoons spent taking turns behind the wheel of a Land Rover.

But, while Granny, Great-granny, and the rest of the royals were already in residence, Papa was nowhere to be seen. He had taken a few days to be by himself on the Spanish island of Majorca when his Mercedes careened out of control on a winding mountain road. The driver managed to regain control of the car, but the Prince, believing he had narrowly escaped death, returned to his hotel visibly trembling. Over the phone to Balmoral, Charles downplayed the episode, but his sons were concerned nonetheless. "Be careful, Papa," William told his father. "Tell your driver to drive more slowly on those roads."

The same day their father's mishap went unreported, coverage of Mummy's trip to Bosnia—part of her ongoing anti-land-mine crusade—filled the papers and the airwaves. Diana had visited clinics and hospitals, sat cross-legged on the gymnasium floor to chat with a volleyball team made of paraplegic land-mine victims, and hugged small children whose limbs had been blown away. Each day, she called Dodi at his lavish Park Lane apartment in London. She also phoned William and Harry, sharing every heart-tugging detail.

The next day, August 10, Mummy was on the world's front pages yet again—only this time pictured in the *Sunday Mirror* necking with Dodi aboard the *Jonikal*. "Locked in her lover's arms," read the subhead, "the Princess finds happiness at last." The tabloid ran ten more pages of photos inside—of Diana and Dodi rubbing suntan lotion on each other, romping in the surf, embracing.

In one of her daily phone calls to Balmoral, Diana had warned her sons that "The Kiss," as the shoot soon came to be known, would be hitting newsstands everywhere. She also told William that she, with Dodi's tacit consent, had orchestrated the entire thing. To make sure that the photos were as aesthetically pleasing as possible, Diana had leaked information regarding the couple's whereabouts to Gianni Versace's personal photographer, Mario Brenna. When Brenna materialized, the couple simply pretended not to notice.

Unlike the wary and secretive Hasnat Khan, Dodi was one Muslim man who did not feel the need to conceal his affection for Diana from the public. The fact that Fayed was eager to trumpet news of their affair to the world was immensely appealing to the chronically insecure Princess. In her conversations with William, she pointed out these important differences between the two men, and repeatedly sounded her son out on the subject of her new love. "She ran everything by William that even remotely affected him," Rosa Monckton said. "She valued his judgment."

To William it seemed painfully clear that, while both men had made his mother happy, with Dodi Fayed there were none of the fights and recriminations that characterized her relationship with Hasnat Khan—at least not yet. The fact that Dodi was Muslim was no longer an area of concern in their conversations; when she had approached them about marrying Khan, both William and Harry registered surprise that she raised the issue of religion at all. "They were still children," Elsa Bowker pointed out. "They were unaware of the enormous problems marrying a Muslim would have created for their mother. All they knew was this man made her very happy and seemed to honestly care for Diana."

In numerous phone calls to her friends that August of 1997, Diana left no doubt that she "simply adored Dodi," Bowker added. "But she knew that to marry a Muslim would create enormous problems for William and Harry, and she would never subject them to that."

Yet other friends conceded that the idea might have appealed to the mischievous streak in Diana. "It probably gave her a lot of chuckles," Richard Greene said, "to think she could embarrass the Royal Family by having a half-Muslim child. She did have a very sharp sense of humor about those kinds of things."

Whether or not he was husband material, Dodi did provide Mummy with the kind of undiluted attention she craved. "Diana was obsessive," Bowker observed. "She wanted the person to abandon *everything* for her. Very few people are willing to do that... Harry was too young to realize it, but Prince William knew that his mother needed this special kind of man in her life—someone who would completely devote his life to making her happy."

Charles soon caught up with his children at Balmoral and, unbeknownst to the Princess, they would be joined a week later by Tiggy—not in an official capacity, but simply as a guest of the Royal Family. Papa did not have to convince the boys that, given Mummy's feelings about their former nanny, there was really no need to mention Tiggy's presence to her.

By this time, however, Diana had even managed to come to terms with the presence of Tiggy in her boys' lives. "She is devoted to the children," she told Lady Bowker, "and they are devoted to her. Because she gives them happiness, I now accept her."

For the remainder of August, the papers were filled with stories about the Princess of Wales and her Egyptian playboy lover. William and Harry did not have to read them; Mummy was calling at least once a day with updates on the state of the romance. She never missed an opportunity to sound her boys out on the subject of Dodi. William's response never varied. "As long as you're happy, Mummy," he would say, "that's the important thing."

Charles echoed his son's sentiments. When a friend asked what he thought of Diana's new love, the Prince of Wales replied, "Whatever makes her happy, makes me happy."

Diana did indeed sound happy—deliriously so—to William. But her affair with Dodi Fayed now meant that Mummy was being more hotly pursued than ever by the voracious tabloid press. On August 15, Diana managed to sneak away with her friend Rosa Monckton for a five-day Aegean cruise aboard a small motor cruiser, the *Della Grazzia.*

One morning, Diana and Monckton stopped in at a Greek Orthodox church in a small village and lit candles for their children. Suddenly, the Princess became emotional. "Oh, Rosa," she said, "I do so love my boys."

Throughout their voyage through the Greek Isles, Diana "talked constantly about her sons," said Monckton, "about her concern to protect them from their position... not to be isolated and to live a balanced life."

From the Greek Isles, Diana continued to stay in touch with her sons daily by phone. Often the Balmoral Castle switchboard operator, speaking in a thick Scottish brogue, would tell the Princess that her boys were "oot."

"Out killing something," Diana would mutter as she hung up the phone.

She was right. During their sojourn in the Scottish wilds, Charles and their boys bagged dozens of grouse, ducks, and pheasants. Harry, coached by Tiggy and Grandpapa, was proving to be a superb marksman— although not as good as his brother. William chided his brother whenever he missed a shot, and did not hesitate to mention that when he was Harry's age, he had shot fifteen pheasants in a single morning.

But duty called for the princes—even at Balmoral. While Mummy zoomed around the world pursuing her romance with Dodi, Wills and Harry negotiated the rocky banks of the River Dee with their kilt-clad father as part of a scheduled photo opportunity. Easygoing Harry grinned obligingly. Charles and William also managed to smile for the cameras, but both princes privately continued to refer to members of the press as "reptiles."

Winding down what had been another perfect season at his beloved Balmoral, Charles sat in his study on the night of August 30, 1997, pulled a piece of the Queen's stationery from a drawer, and penned a brief letter to Diana. The note was addressed to "My Dearest Diana," and discussed whether Harry, who seemed to be struggling with his grades, should stay an extra year at Ludgrove before joining William at Eton. Ending the note, "Lots of love, Charles," the Prince sealed the envelope and handed it to a secretary. "Make sure this goes straight out," Charles said. "I want Princess Diana to have it on her desk when she returns from her holiday. First thing Monday morning."

In Paris, where she had stopped off with Dodi on their way home to London, Mummy also had Harry on her mind. Once settled in the lavish Imperial Suite of the Fayed-owned Ritz, she sent a hotel employee off to find the Sony Playstation he had asked for. With the press camped just outside the hotel in the Place Vendôme, there was no way she could pick the Playstation out herself, as she had originally intended.

As she waited for the Ritz staffer to return with Prince Harry's gift, Diana placed one call after another to friends and family. When she called her friend Rita Rogers with the news that she was in Paris, Rogers was thunderstruck. The psychic had warned Dodi not to go driving in Paris—she saw him exposed to grave danger in a tunnel there—and she shared that premonition with Diana. "I'll be careful, Rita," the Princess said, "I promise... I'm looking forward to seeing my boys. I'm going home tomorrow."

Then there was what she always considered her most important call of the day—the call from William expressing concern about Harry. This time, Wills was being ordered by the Palace to pose alone for photographers at Eton, and he did not want Harry to feel he was being ignored.

Harry was not the only topic of conversation. For the next twenty minutes, Diana shared more details of her holiday with Dodi while Wills bragged about the number of game birds he'd shot. After a month apart, William and Harry were looking forward to spending at least a couple of days with Mummy in London before returning to school. Diana would be arriving late Sunday morning, and when they asked if they could meet her at the airport, she replied, "Of course."

Diana hung up the phone and turned to the new man in her life. "Dodi, I do so miss my boys," she said. There was an urgency to her voice. "That's all anyone really has to know: William and Harry are everything to me. Everything."

They adored their mother, and she loved them passionately. I can hardly bear to think about them.

—*Rosa Monckton,*
Diana's friend

William and Harry will be properly prepared. I am making sure of this. I don't want them suffering the way I did.

—*Diana*

The rest of us have lost a superstar and a very important ambassador. But the children have lost their mother. Our hearts should go out to them first.

—*Lord Jeffrey Archer*

Your mum cares for you and looks after you. It's really sad for William and Harry that they won't have that. No one can replace her.

—*Twelve-year-old Peter Burrell, friend of the princes*

7

It was late afternoon, and gathering clouds threw shadows across the emerald lawns of Althorp. William and Harry stood, hands folded before them, staring at the flower-draped coffin as the final prayers were said. Then, as Diana was slowly lowered into the freshly dug grave, the rays of the late-afternoon sun suddenly sliced through the clouds and fell on the casket. Tears flowed freely down the faces of Diana's sons as they, and the rest of her family, were overcome with emotion.

At first, Earl Spencer had planned to bury his sister in the thirteenth-century Church of St. Mary in the nearby village of Great Brington. Their father was buried in the family crypt there, along with nineteen other generations of Spencers. But there were fears that pilgrims would turn the village into another Graceland. "I couldn't bear the thought," Diana's mother said, "of people walking all over her grave and gaping."

So the Spencers decided to provide the deceased Diana with the privacy she never had in life. Ringing down the curtain on a mind-numbing week of sorrow and pageantry,

Mummy was laid to rest away from the media glare on a secluded island in the middle of what was known as the Round Oval, a small ornamental lake on the grounds of Althorp.

The tiny, 75-by-180-foot island, which would soon be carpeted with the flowers that had been left at the gates of Althorp and brought over by rowboat, had been a favorite spot for the young Diana and her brother. It was here they fed the ducks, chased butterflies, and tried to frighten each other with stories of ghosts that inhabited Althorp manor. Now this would be the site of Diana's grave, marked by a simple east-facing monument and shaded by beech, oak, and willow trees. Their mother had been known as Lady Di, the Princess of Wales, the People's Princess, and the Queen of Hearts. Locals would add to those Diana, Lady of the Lake.

When it was time to leave, William and Harry and the rest of the mourners walked across a pontoon bridge that had been hastily erected by the Corps of Royal Engineers. Then they made their way along dirt paths, through an arboretum filled with rare trees, and on toward the stately Tudor mansion where Mummy had spent much of her own childhood. There they stayed for tea and sandwiches with Frances Shand Kydd (their other granny had returned to Buckingham Palace), their uncle Earl Spencer, and their Spencer aunts, Sarah and Jane—all red-eyed and drained.

September 6, 1997—a sun-drenched Saturday—would go down in history as the day the world witnessed one of the largest outpourings of grief in modern times. It was also the day William and Harry bid a final farewell to their mother.

That evening the boys returned with their father to Highgrove, arriving in time for dinner with Tiggy. Over this last terrible week since Diana's fatal crash in Paris, hers had been the shoulder they cried on most. Fifteen-year-old William was also old enough to insist on following news accounts of what had happened to his mother—reports that left him confused and angry.

Why was a drunk driver put behind the wheel of the doomed Mercedes? Mummy wore her seat belt even when dressed in elaborate formal gowns and was obsessive about the boys belting up. How could she not have worn a seat belt that fatal night in Paris? Why did French medical personnel take so long to get Mummy to the hospital—the ambulance arrived at the hospital, located just 3.8 miles from the crash site, a full *ninety minutes* after the accident. "Do you think she could have been saved, Tiggy?" he asked. "Could she have been saved?"

Yet these questions would be secondary to William. From the beginning, he blamed the press for chasing his mother to her death and—despite mounting evidence to the contrary—would continue to do so.

For a young man who already harbored a grudge against the media, early reports of what happened in the Alma Tunnel seemed only to confirm his feelings. Wills pointed to the accounts of witnesses, such as American tourists Jack and Robin Firestone, who claimed that the paparazzi not only did nothing to help the victims after the crash, but actually interfered with rescue efforts. "Photographers were swarming all over the car, snapping as many photos as they could," Robin Firestone said. "I still feel dirty now when I remember I saw humans behaving in that way."

Ten photographers who had pursued Princess Diana into the Alma Tunnel that fateful night were arrested and charged with "involuntary homicide and nonassistance to persons in danger." Eventually, French authorities would conclude Diana died as the result of a drunk driving accident and drop all charges against the men.

For the moment, Diana's sons, like their uncle Earl Spencer and millions of others around the world, preferred to think the press was at fault. If William in particular hated the media, few people were willing to blame him. But the potential consequences for the monarchy were unsettling. "How on earth is William going to deal with the media all his life," asked writer Anthony Holden, "if he thinks they killed his mother?"

There were other questions that vexed Wills. Why, he wanted to know, had Granny taken so long to express the Royal Family's grief? And why had it taken a public outcry of almost unparalleled proportions to convince the Queen to honor his mother by lowering the flag at Buckingham Palace to half-mast?

Charles's explanations—that Granny was only listening to her Palace advisers and that she had always been reluctant to show emotion—seemed sufficient. "Wills loves and respects the Queen a great deal," one Palace insider said. "As long as he could focus his anger on the media, it was easier to forgive his grandmother."

Shortly after 10:30 that night—less than seven hours after they watched their mother's casket being lowered into the ground—William and Harry went to bed. It had been the longest day of their lives.

No sooner were the boys up the next morning than their father urged them to take advantage of the uncharacteristically sunny weather. Charles was determined to distract the boys with physical exertion. Over the next five days, Papa rode horses with them, splashed with them in the pool, and joined them on long walks through the countryside. For her part, the tomboyish Tiggy, who promised their father she would stay by the boys' side as long as she was needed, spent hours with the boys kicking a soccer ball around the Highgrove grounds.

Whatever Diana may once have felt about Tiggy, the Princess's friends agreed she would have been grateful to her onetime nemesis for shepherding the boys through this difficult time. "Above all else," Elsa Bowker said, Diana "would not have wanted her children to be lonely. She would have wanted them to have had real affection."

By the end of the week, the boys were ready to return to the safe haven of their respective schools. But William, who had always been his brother's protector, did not want to leave Harry's side.

Their mother had always been afraid of the dark. Diana kept a light on in the hallway or slept with a night-light—but not her sons. Until now. Although William harbored no such fears, Harry now asked that a light be left on in his room when he slept. He was also suffering from nightmares about his mother and the gruesome manner in which she died.

Tiggy would be the one to pull Harry through this terrible period. At times, she even cradled the young prince to sleep. "It was entirely natural," a friend noted, "and just the kind of thing Diana would have done."

"Diana smothered Harry in love," said another, "and at least Tiggy has been there to give him the hugs and kisses the Princess could not." As for William: "Harry misses his mother dreadfully and far more openly than William. With William, you never really know what he is feeling, what he is thinking. Harry wears his heart on his sleeve."

"I'm very worried about Harry," Wills told his father and Tiggy. "I don't want to go away from him now." But they assured him that Harry would be allowed to call his brother at Eton anytime he wished. In the meantime,

Onlookers were stunned when, less than a year after Diana's death, Harry (*center*) and William rappelled down a dam without helmets or safety harnesses.

Harry in—and out—of uniform. Joining Wills at Eton, Harry led his schoolmates as they marched to class. *Below:* Harry goes for the grunge look in T-shirt and jeans.

40

William was at first rattled by the pandemonium that broke out when he visited Vancouver with Prince Charles and Harry in March 1998. Within hours, he was working the crowd with ease.

41

Offering a future glimpse of royal father-hood, William holds his godchild, Greek prince Konstantine, at the infant's 1999 christening.

42

43   "How humiliating," new driver William
muttered when the press gathered to record
his first official driving lesson in July 1999.
His brother looked on in amusement.

44 William, captain of his house soccer team at Eton, explains a play to his teammates. A natural athlete, he also excelled at rugby and water sports.

45   Animal rights groups were livid when William (*center*) and Harry (*right*) took up foxhunting. Scotland Yard beefed up security when one extremist organization marked William for death.

The sport of kings. Left-handed William had to learn to play polo—his father's favorite pastime—right-handed. While Harry distracts a teammate, his brother gives him a friendly goosing with a polo mallet (*below*)—and later kids around with Papa (*opposite top*). Usually guarded in public, Wills cuts loose behind the scenes at a July 2000 match with an explosive laugh reminiscent of his mother's (*opposite bottom*).

46

48

49

50

51

52

In celebration of his eighteenth birthday in June 2000, the Palace allowed glimpses of William strolling the halls at Eton, taking a cooking class, and studying. Struck with a golf club and badly injured when he was eight, William still bears a noticeable scar over his left eye.

Diana called Charles's longtime mistress "the Rotweiller," but Wills and Harry have grown fond of Camilla Parker Bowles. Still, they are not ready to call Mrs. P.B., here in a rare public appearance with Charles in June 2000, stepmum.

53

54

William leaned over to listen to Granny after a service at St. Paul's Cathedral marking the Queen Mother's one hundredth birthday in the summer of 2000.

Among William's closest friends: Camilla's children Laura and Tom (*left*), Lord Frederick Windsor (*below, with his sister Gabriella*), and Edward van Cutsem (*bottom*), who joined Wills and Victoria Aitkin at a party in 1999. Tom and Frederick were two of at least five William intimates whose drug use caused the Palace concern.

55

56

57

58

59

60

During his precollege gap-year adventure doing volunteer work in a remote Chilean village, William chopped and sawed wood, taught children like six-year-old Alejandro Heredia English, cleaned toilets, and was a rap deejay on the local radio station.

61

William had a crush on Camilla's niece Emma Parker Bowles (*right*). Family friend Tara Palmer-Tomkinson (*below*) made Charles furious when she whipped off her bikini top in front of Wills. Papa worried even more when both women sought treatment for substance abuse.

63

62

The ladies. Pop star Britney Spears did not strike up a cyber romance with William. But model Lauren Bush (*right*), niece of President George W. Bush, did. Fellow polo player Tamara Vestey (*opposite top*) got the royal treatment at a party in 1999. Model Davina Duckworth-Chad (*opposite middle*) and Devonshire's Emilia d'Erlanger (*opposite bottom*) have both been along on an Aegean cruise.

64

65

66

67

"Of course they're close,"
said a family friend of the
princes', who conferred
after a church service in
July 2000. "Look what
they've been through
together." Later, Harry and
William teamed up to greet
well-wishers in London.

70

he would be in good hands with Ludgrove head-master Gerald Barber and his wife, Janet—the same couple that had helped Wills weather the storm surrounding the breakup of his parents' marriage.

As for friends, Harry, like his brother and in stark contrast to his father's lonely experience at Gordonstoun, proved to be one of the most well liked boys at Ludgrove. Yet there were moments when Harry could seem sadly, almost painfully withdrawn. One courtier remembered seeing Harry at Highgrove one afternoon, lost in his thoughts as he bounced a ball against a wall for more than two hours straight.

There had, in fact, been much discussion among the boys' classmates at Ludgrove and Eton about how best to behave toward the motherless princes. One father advised his son, "It will be your duty never to mention her. You must pretend that nothing has happened and just carry on." One member of Eton's faculty conceded that Diana's death had been "a terrible tragedy. But Prince William is not a little boy. He cannot grieve forever. He must learn to take it."

Both Spencers and Windsors showed up at Highgrove to wish Harry a happy thirteenth birthday on September 15, and over the next few weeks the princes showed signs of adjusting astonishingly well to their mother's sudden death. Given Wills's close relationship with his mother, it was surprising to her friends how quickly he seemed to recover.

Harry, though noticeably quieter and more introspective, also seemed to be easing back into the life they had known.

"William in particular has quite unexpectedly displayed a remarkable stoicism, almost leadership, in the quiet manner of his grief," Earl Spencer observed. "His mother would be proud."

Papa certainly was—of both his sons. On September 19, Prince Charles gave a speech to business and community leaders in Manchester in support of the Salvation Army. But his thoughts—and those of his audience—were clearly with the boys. Prince William and Prince Harry were, their father said, "quite remarkable" and had handled an "extraordinarily difficult time" with "quite enormous courage and the greatest possible dignity." But, he added, "Obviously Diana's death has been an enormous loss as far as they are concerned, and I will always feel that loss."

Charles went on to thank the public for its "expressions of warmth and support," while at the same time pointing out that the global outpouring of grief only intensified his sons' pain. "As many of you will know from the experience of family loss in your own lives," Charles said, "it is inevitably very difficult to cope with grief at any time. But perhaps you might realize it is even harder when the whole world is watching at the same time."

The healing process was accelerated by the British press, which agreed to keep a respectful distance while the boys coped with their grief.

Following guidelines set down by the Press Complaints Commission, a government watchdog agency, Fleet Street agreed not to photograph the boys in private situations until they each turned eighteen. When paparazzi offered candid photos of the princes, the tabloids—aware of how protective the British public had become toward the motherless princes—generally refused to print them.

For William and Harry, there would be added comfort in a return to routine. For thirty-eight weeks a year, William and Harry would be protected behind the wrought-iron gates and brick walls of Ludgrove and Eton. William would remain at Eton seven days a week. But Harry would be allowed to join Papa and thirty-two-year-old Tiggy at Highgrove for eight weekends a term. Where once they split vacation time between Kensington Palace and Highgrove, now all their holidays would be spent with Papa.

That October Wills had to remain at Eton, but Harry's half-term break happened to coincide with his father's planned official visit to South Africa. For Charles, the trip afforded a chance to both bond with Harry and lift the boy's spirits just eight weeks after the crushing blow of his mother's death. It also gave Papa an opportunity to show a disbelieving world that Diana was not the only nurturing force in the family. To play it safe, Prince Charles brought Tiggy along to keep Harry company when he was otherwise engaged.

For any thirteen-year-old boy, this was a

dream vacation. First, Harry went on a safari in Botswana with Tiggy and his Ludgrove pal Charlie Henderson. Then Harry met up with Papa in Johannesburg, where they attended a Spice Girls concert. After the show Charles and Harry, dressed in a purple polka-dot tie and navy blue suit, went backstage to have their pictures taken with the girls. While Papa looked on, members of the group sidled up to his blushing son and bussed him on the cheek. "My brother," said a beaming Harry, "will be very jealous when he sees this."

Harry was still grinning after he and his father left Tiggy behind to visit the remote Zulu village of Duku Duku—although this time the young prince was not quite sure where to look. Bare-breasted women greeted them at the gates of the village, and later did a spirited dance of welcome a few feet from the seated princes, their nipples at Harry's eye level. "My," Prince Charles said as the dancers jumped up and down in front of his wide-eyed young son, "what amazing energy." Harry, taking a cue from Papa, smiled benignly and tapped his feet to the music "as if," said one reporter, "he'd been in that position a hundred times before." Added another eyewitness: "Maintaining his dignity in a delicate cross-cultural situation, under the eyes of seventy television cameras and photographers, was a remarkable achievement."

Harry mastered the Zulu handshake—grasp the thumb and wrist and shake vigorously—and laughed when his father picked up a Zulu shield and club and waved them in the air like a warrior. Examining local crafts, Harry noticed a bracelet of brightly colored beads and told Prince Charles he wanted to buy it to give to Tiggy. Since no member of the Royal Family actually carries cash of any kind, Harry had to borrow a twenty-rand note—about five dollars—from his bodyguard, Ian Hugget.

Father and son also participated in a local ritual that smacked of Mann's Chinese Theater. Instead of signing the guest book, Charles and Harry were asked to get on their knees and plant their handprints in wet cement. As he did throughout the tour, Harry threw himself into the proceedings, chatting with his hosts and smiling broadly for the cameras.

Charles could not disguise his sheer joy at having Harry with him. As he shook hands with locals outside Durban's city hall, the Prince of Wales spotted his son taking photos of him from the balcony of his suite at the Royal Hotel. Harry, standing just below the hotel sign, snapped away as the crowd below began chanting, "Harry! Harry!" Papa pointed up and told the crowd, "He's right there—under the letter H."

The Palace was thrilled with the press coverage, which gave the world its first real glimpse of the easy rapport that existed between Charles and his children. Although Wills regretted not being able to go along and feigned outrage with his Eton pals over Harry's backstage antics with the Spice Girls, he was delighted to see his brother's face light up in a way it hadn't for weeks.

In addition to the feature pieces chronicling Harry's travels with Papa, William was carefully following the investigation into their mother's death. There was no doubt that the Mercedes's driver, Henri Paul, had a blood alcohol content that was three times the legal limit. But questions remained about the mysterious white Fiat Uno that the car carrying Diana and Dodi had grazed in the moments before impact. French investigators would ultimately interview the owners of more than three thousand white Fiat Unos and still not locate the owner of the mystery car.

William could not ignore the most sensational, disturbing theory, which held that it was no accident at all, but rather an assassination carried out by British intelligence. Mohamed Al Fayed believed from the beginning that Dodi and Diana had been murdered by elements of the British establishment who could not accept a Muslim as the stepfather of their future king. The controversial Al Fayed even offered a one-million-pound reward to anyone who could prove it.

There was no hard evidence to support Al Fayed's assassination theory. The investigation would, however, establish the fact that MI6, Britain's foreign intelligence agency, and other agencies did keep a close eye on the Princess before and after her divorce. (So, incredibly, did the United States. Over a year after the crash, a Freedom of Information Act request would reveal that the CIA, FBI, and National Security Agency have more than a thousand pages of classified files on Diana.)

When his father returned from Africa, Wills asked him if there could be any truth to the rumors that Mummy's death was not an accident. Charles assured him that there was "not a shred" of truth to the stories; out of grief and his ingrained hatred of the British establishment, the Prince of Wales told Wills, Al Fayed was fanning the flames of conspiracy theorists.

As disturbing as the conspiracy theories were the new "details" of the crash making their way into the tabloids. In late November, the *Sunday Times* of London quoted Dr. Frédéric Mailliez, the Good Samaritan who arrived on the scene moments after the crash, as saying Diana cried, "I'm in such pain. Oh, God! I can't stand this!" Other reports had her saying, "It hurts so bad."

Mailliez, who did not recognize the Princess at the time he was treating her, would later concede that Diana did moan and cry. But he also insisted there were no last words to pass on. As he worked to save her life, the young French doctor did not try to decipher what she was uttering between her anguished cries of pain.

William and Harry had hoped that their mother was knocked unconscious at the moment of impact. This confirmation that she had suffered upset William—so much so that he asked his father to make sure school officials at Ludgrove stepped up their efforts to hide the tabloid stories from his younger brother.

William and Harry were soon dealt another blow—this time by Inland Revenue, England's equivalent of the Internal Revenue Service. Diana had left the bulk of her $35 million estate to her sons. Of the $35 million estate, Inland Revenue was demanding that 40 percent—$14 million—be paid in taxes. That left $21 million—$10.5 million to be left in trust for each of the boys.

At first, Charles objected on his sons' behalf, but then backed off. "Charles was trying to take legal action to protect their inheritance," his spokesman said, "but abandoned his plans so there would be no question of the Royal Family receiving preferential treatment."

Notwithstanding Fleet Street's new hands-off policy toward them, William's status as a heartthrob was becoming increasingly evident. When he showed up at the Royal Naval College in Greenwich for a lunch to celebrate his grandparents' fiftieth wedding anniversary, six hundred screaming girls were there to greet him.

That Christmas season of 1997—their first without Mummy—was an emotional roller-coaster ride for William and Harry. On December 15, they showed up unannounced with their father at a fox hunt outside London. There, for the first time, they got their first look in person at Camilla Parker Bowles, one of the red-jacketed competitors.

It would be some time, however, before they actually met Camilla. That evening, William and Harry appeared nothing short of euphoric when they attended the premiere of the Spice Girls' first feature film, *Spice World,* with Papa.

But two days later, there was yet another sober duty to perform. Since their mother's death, the princes had been dividing their time between their respective schools and Highgrove while a new residence was readied for them at St. James's Palace. Charles, who wanted his sons near him, had hired interior decorator Robert Kime to redesign the five-bedroom York House to include a pool table, their own computers, a video room, and a room for Tiggy.

Now they went back to the apartments at Kensington Palace where they had once lived with Diana, ostensibly to pick out things to bring to York House. The Princess's butler Paul Burrell, the man she used to call "my rock," opened the black front door and welcomed the boys. William shook Burrell's hand; Harry embraced him. Then, with a tearful Harry holding on tight to Burrell's hand, they walked from room to room picking out mementos.

They selected several of Mummy's favorite stuffed animals, arranged on a sofa near her bed, as well as silver-framed photographs of their mother, several of her favorite paintings, and her prized collection of Herend porcelain animal figurines. Both boys asked that the carpets in their rooms be moved to their new quarters at York House. In William's new suite there, the television and kilim wall hanging she had given him shortly before her death would also be part of the decor.

Wills also took a small silver figurine he had made for his mother in the metal workshop at Eton. But his most prized possession was the Cartier "Tank" watch that had been given to Diana by her father.

As they went through the rooms at Kensington Palace, William moved at a determined clip. Harry, savoring every memory, would not be rushed. When it was finally time to leave for the last time, both boys thanked Burrell and then looked back as the door shut behind them. Harry's eyes were filled with tears.

The pain of losing Mummy intensified as they approached Christmas. Even their Christmas card—Charles and the boys had posed, relaxed and smiling, on the deck of the soon-to-be-decommissioned royal yacht *Britannia* just days before Diana's death—was a poignant reminder of happier times.

As they had in previous years, the princes spent Christmas with the Windsors at Sandringham. On Christmas Eve, William and Harry gathered by the tree and exchanged presents—they had purchased a silver paperweight and cuff links for Papa—with the rest of the Royal Family. The next morning, the princes attended services at the Church of St. Mary Magdalene on the grounds of the royal estate. Unlike the services at Balmoral during which Princess Diana's death was not mentioned at all, on this day Canon George Hall offered thanks "for those whom we love but see no more, Diana, Princess of Wales, and all loved ones who have departed this life." The boys then stood outside the church and shook hands with thirteen hundred of their fellow worshipers, many of whom thrust bouquets into their hands or mentioned how much they missed Di.

Even the Queen, still trying to repair the damage done to the monarchy by her reticence to give Diana her due, mentioned her former daughter-in-law during her annual Christmas Day address. She noted Britain's "shock and sorrow" over the Princess's tragic death, and went on to describe the loss as "almost unbearably sad."

The boys' other grandmother, Frances Shand Kydd, also spoke out. "I'm fed up," she announced. "I just want the media to shut up. I'm hurting." Shand Kydd went on to point out that "Christmas is as difficult for her beloved sons, William and Harry, and for all her family and close friends, as it is for all families who have suffered a bereavement. I ask, on behalf of Diana's family, that we may all be left in peace and silence by the media." Shand Kydd also voiced her concern that the growing "cult of Diana" would make it impossible for her grandsons to forge personalities of their own. "I don't want them growing up," she said, "to be a shadow of their mother."

To help the boys cope with the holidays,

Queen Elizabeth enlisted the help of her eldest grandchild, Princess Anne's son, Peter Phillips. Four years William's senior and a student of sports science at Exeter University, Peter had been a comforting presence in the boys' lives in the week leading up to their mother's funeral.

So, too, was Peter's younger sister, Zara. Starting with their Jell-O-gargling, mayhem-raising Willie the Wombat days, funloving Zara was always one of the princes' favorite cousins. For the first time, she would accompany them on their New Year's ski trip to Klosters, Switzerland, with Papa. "Obviously Her Majesty is delighted," a Palace spokesman allowed, "that the younger members of the family are pulling together through these difficulties."

William's friends at Eton were also intent on helping him through this time. The Prince would occasionally stay for the weekend at the home of a schoolmate, or invite his pals to spend a few days with him at St. James's Palace. During the Christmas break, he invited several Eton boys over to York House. For four nights in a row, they changed into black tie before heading out to a series of holiday dances. "He was totally determined to have a good time," said one of William's fellow Etonians. "It was, we all supposed, one way to avoid thinking about the death of his mum."

At fifteen, he was also showing a healthy interest in girls. At the holiday parties he attended, Wills was not the least bit reluctant to introduce himself to the most attractive girls in the room. "He seems awfully normal, sort of salt-of-the-earth," said a guest at one of these functions who witnessed Wills in action. "And surprisingly good at breaking the ice. He seems to know how to put a girl at ease, which is a rather tall order, considering."

One of these girls, the daughter of a prominent London businessman, would for a short time boast the distinction of being referred to by Prince William's pals as his "girlfriend." She would be replaced within a few months by the daughter of an aristocrat, whose tenure would be even shorter. Even with the press's new hands-off-the-princes policy, the ever-present Royal Protection Squad made any serious romance virtually impossible.

Wills appeared to have found a way to cope with Mummy's absence during the holidays. The same could not be said for Harry. "He has been causing his father some concern," acknowledged a friend of the Royal Family. "One minute he is up, rushing about without a care in the world, and the next he is crying."

Aware that William was handling the situation far better than his brother, Tiggy concentrated on buoying Harry's spirits. Legge-Bourke, Charles conceded, continued to be a "central figure" in his sons' lives.

The Queen, meantime, struggled to repair her image. In the wake of Diana's death, the public was outraged at Her Majesty's seeming disregard for Diana and the fragile emotional state of her two young sons. Her insistence that

William and Harry attend church only hours after learning of their mother's death (and that Diana's name not be mentioned during the service), her reluctance to interrupt her Balmoral vacation to join mourners in London, and her initial refusal to fly the flag over Buckingham Palace at half-mast still angered and mystified her subjects.

In the early months of 1998, the Queen was forced to concede that she had grossly underestimated the British people's fondness for the Princess of Wales. As part of a calculated plan to repair relations between the Firm and the people, Buckingham Palace turned to an outside public relations company.

Over the next two years, Her Majesty would take several unprecedented steps to win back her subjects. She released certain previously top secret financial records of the Royal Family and did not oppose Prime Minister Tony Blair's proposal to end primogeniture, making the monarch's eldest child—not just the eldest son—heir to the throne. The Queen also decreed that all bowing and curtsying to royals should be strictly voluntary. Borrowing a page from Diana's people-to-people approach, Queen Elizabeth also visited a pub (although she declined to drink) and rode in one of London's famous cabs—both firsts for Britain's monarch.

The most potent weapons in the Royal Family's goodwill arsenal were, of course, Diana's boys. In March, Charles brought them along on an official visit to Canada—

William's first major public appearance since the funeral. In keeping with the Palace's long-standing reluctance to have more than one royal heir flying on the same plane, Charles and Harry took one flight while William and Tiggy, invited to provide moral support, took another.

When they arrived at Vancouver's Waterfront Centre hotel, where their suite was stocked with CDs by the Spice Girls, Savage Garden, and Oasis, several dozen photographers and more than three hundred teenage girls were waiting for them. "William, William, William," they chanted in unison—a refrain the heir would eventually become accustomed to.

But for now, William, rattled by such hormone-fueled adulation, managed only a nervous smile before slinking into the hotel. Wills was so upset by the attention that he asked that the press be barred from the premises when he and Harry visited Vancouver's Pacific Space Centre museum.

It hardly mattered to the hordes of hysterical schoolgirls who waited for Wills and his brother outside the space center and at every other stop during the trip. Inside the center, however, the two brothers were left alone to enjoy themselves. Both fiercely competitive, they spent two hours playing computer games, shooting off rockets, and taking turns at the controls of a spaceship on a simulated voyage to Mars.

By the time they joined their father on a tour of Burnaby South High School, William was relaxed enough to take a cue from his brother and smile. Harry actually found his brother's heartthrob status to be nothing short of hilarious. "Go on, wave at that lot," he would urge the reticent William as they went by another group of sobbing girls. When they reacted with deafening squeals, Harry could, in the words of one Canadian official, "scarcely control himself."

By the end of the day, when they made their last scheduled appearance onstage at the Vancouver Heritage Center, William almost seemed to enjoy being treated like a rock star. Although his father was supposed to give a speech on the environment, five hundred shrieking, weeping teenage girls made that impossible. They tossed flowers, cards, teddy bears, and hankies at Wills, who reciprocated by working the crowd. "Thank you," he would say as he accepted the gifts, shook hands, and made eye contact—something Diana had tried to get both her sons to always do. "It was nice to meet you. Thank you..."

A defining moment came when the boys and their father were presented with the red-and-white jackets and caps of Canada's Olympic team. Without hesitating, William whipped off his suit coat, slipped into the jacket, and put the cap on backward. Then he did a seamless break-dancer's roll of the shoulder and wrist and struck a rap star pose. The reaction from the crowd was deafening. "It was a totally spontaneous moment that surprised everybody," said a reporter in the crowd. "He reminded everybody of the early Diana—shy and reticent at first, but then without warning able to make the crowd-pleasing gesture." What's more, said the journalist, "at some point he obviously started to like being the center of every young girl's fantasy." Concurred a friend of William's: "He can protest all he wants about girls chasing him. He loves it."

From Vancouver, Charles and the boys were off to spend four days skiing at the exclusive Whistler resort in the Canadian Rockies. On the slopes, fearless Harry was generally conceded to have the edge. But when a local reporter called out, "Hey, dudes, who's the best skier? I hear it's Harry," William was quick to protest.

"I don't know about that!" responded Wills, who then raced off with his brother in hot pursuit. Within seconds, they had both pitched headlong into the snow. Over the next four days, they snowboarded, played hockey with some locals, and tried some of the most challenging ski trails.

The whole time, William's female fans were never far away. One group, which had followed the royal trio from Vancouver by bus, was not adequately dressed for the snow or the bone-chilling temperatures. Not that they minded. "He looks so much better in person than he does in pictures," said Leah Pereira, fourteen. "He is cute and looks vulnerable when he blushes." While watching Wills, Harry, and Papa Charles line up for a photo shoot, Jessica Towes, also fourteen, sighed, "He is rich and he is gorgeous and he is a prince. What more could you ask for?"

Miss Towes was not alone. Wherever he went on his Canadian sojourn, Wills was met with cries of "I love you, Wills!" and "Will you marry me?" Americans were no less smitten. When the teen magazine *YM* put Wills on its cover, more than twelve thousand readers wrote in—some signing their fan letters "The Next Mrs. Windsor."

Harry, though obviously destined to live his life in his brother's looming shadow, managed to garner some female attention of his own. Many of the girls who reached out for the heir reached out to touch the spare as well. Harry also had planned something special upon his return to England. Careful to wait until Wills resumed his studies at Eton, Harry invited his old friends the Spice Girls for tea at Highgrove.

The boys sent flowers to Princess Diana's grave on their first Mother's Day without her. "It was a painful time for them," said a family acquaintance. "But they tried not to dwell on their loss." Instead, they poured themselves into their schoolwork. William added ten subjects to his course load at Eton, focusing primarily on English, French, art history, and economics. He was also proving to be an exceptional athlete. William excelled at rowing, tennis, soccer, rugby, polo, team clay-pigeon shooting, and in particular swimming—his mother's favorite sport. By the summer of

1998, Will had broken several Eton records and ranked among the United Kingdom's top one hundred swimmers his age in the fifty-meter freestyle.

In June, Charles was relieved when Harry, always less academically inclined than William, easily passed his Eton entrance exams—no doubt helped by the fact that he had spent an extra year at Ludgrove. Harry would now be able to join his older brother at a time in his life when they desperately needed each other's support.

Although William had basically outgrown his dependence on Tiggy Legge-Bourke, she remained another pillar of emotional support for Harry—sometimes to his father's chagrin. During a visit to Wales, the high-spirited Tiggy watched calmly as both boys went rappelling down the face of a dam without helmets. Photographs of the incident appeared in the next day's papers, causing nationwide concern for the boys' safety and calling into question their nanny's judgment. Both the Queen and Prince Charles were, in the words of one courtier, "appalled" that the boys would be placed in such perilous circumstances.

Gradually, Charles began easing Tiggy out of the boys' lives. This time she did not attend Parents Day festivities at Eton, and was dropped off the guest list for a number of functions at which the boys were scheduled to be in attendance. By the summer of 1998, she was no longer at Highgrove every time

William spent a free weekend there. "It is so nice," Charles told friends, "to have William on his own."

Still, the Prince of Wales and his sons would always have warm feelings for Tiggy and continued to consider her a member of their family. It was a feeling apparently not shared by Camilla Parker Bowles, who referred to her as "the hired help" and reportedly came up with her own less-than-charitable nickname for Legge-Bourke. The woman Diana used to call the Rottweiler allegedly referred to Tiggy as "Big Ass" behind her back.

If Tiggy was allowed to remain a presence—albeit a somewhat diminished one—in the lives of the princes, Diana's family was another matter. Following Earl Spencer's elegiac pledge to take up where Mummy left off in the raising of her sons, the Royal Family raised the drawbridge on the Spencer clan. Cape Town–based Earl Spencer rarely saw the boys and spoke with them only infrequently over the phone. At Charles's behest, the princes declined an invitation from their aunt Sarah McCorquodale to spend two weeks during the summer with her family in Cornwall. And while Charles invited her to spend a July weekend with Prince Harry at Highgrove, Frances Shand Kydd lived as a virtual recluse in Oban, Scotland, and seldom saw her grandsons. "The meeting was simply a gesture," said a friend of Diana's. "The Spencers are treated with the same disregard as they always have been."

While the Spencers were being phased out, Camilla Parker Bowles—still referred to around St. James's as "Mrs. P. B." despite the fact that she had been divorced from Andrew Parker Bowles since 1995—was gradually insinuating herself into the lives of the princes. Banished from public view in the months following Diana's death, in March "the Rottweiler" had begun spending nights at Sandringham and St. James's Palace.

On June 12, just nine days before his sixteenth birthday, William left Eton for London, where he planned on going to the movies with friends. When he called his father from the car to say that he would be stopping by at St. James's Palace to change, Prince Charles warned him Mrs. Parker Bowles was there—an awkward situation resulting, Papa explained, from a "clash of diaries."

Then, on the spur of the moment, Charles asked his son if he wouldn't like to meet Camilla. Wills said yes, but Mrs. Parker Bowles, unnerved by the prospect, offered to make a hasty exit. Nonsense, Charles told his mistress of twenty-six years. William was looking forward to at long last meeting her. "Won't you stay, darling? Please," Charles pleaded.

When William appeared, Camilla curtsied as he took her hand and Charles introduced them. At first Camilla, not knowing whether Diana's sons blamed her for breaking up their parents' marriage, was literally shaking. But William, kind and self-assured beyond his years, tried to calm her with talk of foxhunting and polo.

After a half hour chatting over tea and soft drinks, William excused himself and left for the movies. Camilla then turned to Charles. "I really need a vodka and tonic," she said. The meeting, Camilla allowed, had left her "trembling like a leaf."

In truth, the chance encounter between Diana's eldest son and her ex-husband's mistress was nothing of the sort. Wills had planned the entire thing. "William had heard about Camilla for years from his mother," one of Diana's friends said. "He was eager to see for himself what all the fuss was about. In the end, William discovered he rather liked Camilla."

Over the next few weeks, William would arrange to have lunch with his father and Camilla and meet her once alone for tea. Pleased with the outcome, Charles arranged for Harry to meet Parker Bowles at Highgrove. Like his brother, Harry warmed to the informal, sometimes self-deprecating woman Papa had chosen over their mother.

Camilla was in many ways the diametric opposite of Diana. Sixteen months older than Charles and looking every minute of it, Camilla was an unrepentant chain-smoker with manners described in some quarters as slovenly. Her own home, a former mill house located seventeen miles from Highgrove, was classic English shabby, with threadbare furniture, fraying carpets, and muddy boots in the foyer.

As outdoorsy as Diana was urbane, Camilla

was no fashion trendsetter. And again in stark contrast to the Princess's hands-on parenting style, Camilla's approach to child rearing was decidedly laissez-faire. All of this—the studied messiness, the lack of introspection and self-consciousness—may have accounted for Camilla's appeal. "If she had resembled their mother in the slightest way," said a friend of Charles's, "I think they would have seen her as someone trying to replace their mum. They would never allow that to happen. It's precisely because she is nothing like the mother they loved that Camilla is so non-threatening in their eyes."

William and Harry had also seen enough domestic strife to last a lifetime, and what they wanted now was, said one Etonian, "peace and harmony in their household. The only way to get that was to go along with Papa."

Charles, encouraged by his sons' positive response to his mistress, asked William how he felt about the prospect of Camilla playing a more public role. Wills answered his father in much the same way he had answered Mummy when she asked a similar question: "Whatever makes you happy, Papa."

Elsa Bowker, Annabel Goldsmith, and other close friends of Diana's felt the meetings were a betrayal of her memory. "Diana had more or less come to accept Charles's love for Camilla," Bowker said. "But that doesn't mean she would have approved of her becoming a stepmother figure to her boys. Not at all. Diana would have been very upset that the woman who destroyed her marriage and made her life hell was now being embraced by her sons. And so soon after her death."

The timing, in particular, rankled many of those in the Princess's camp. Calling the decision to let William meet Camilla "astonishingly insensitive," one friend told British journalist Richard Kay, "In view of the wretched history of the triangle which caused Diana so much misery, it seems incredible that such a meeting should happen before the first anniversary of the Princess's death."

Neither did the Queen approve. Still blaming Camilla for the breakup of her son's marriage, Her Majesty avoided any public function Camilla might attend, and ordered her courtiers to do likewise. One, the Queen's newly appointed private secretary Sir Robin Janvrin, refused to join Prince William and Camilla for tea at St. James's Palace because he had not received royal permission. "How could he," asked an enraged Charles, "be so rude to me in my own house?"

More significant, the Queen let it be known that any marriage plans would be met with strong opposition from the Crown. Still, in the words of Charles's former private secretary, Sir Richard Aylard, Camilla remained "the non-negotiable part of his private life."

On June 21, 1998, William marked another milestone without Mummy. The Palace, in an unprecedented effort to satisfy the public's thirst for information about the future monarch on the occasion of his sixteenth birthday, released a profile of William. Among other things, it revealed that he now had a pet Labrador named Widgeon, had a particular fondness for fast food, felt uneasy about his newfound sex symbol status, and listened to techno music. The official profile was seen as a reward to the British press for essentially leaving the princes alone.

Underscoring a new streak of independence, William celebrated his birthday—and the completion of his Eton exams—with friends. The only family members he spoke with were Papa and Harry—and then only by telephone.

For teenage girls throughout the realm, it was a special day. Answering thousands of call-in requests, radio stations across Britain played songs like the Beatles' "Birthday" and "You're Sixteen," by Ringo Starr. "My God," Wills asked another Etonian, "I'm going to have to listen to this sort of thing my entire life?"

On July 1, which would have been Mummy's thirty-seventh birthday, the Princess Diana Museum was opened in a converted stable hall at Althorp. For sixteen dollars, visitors could see, among other things, Diana's wedding dress, her childhood letters, and her school reports. Diana's children, further distancing themselves from their mother's "blood family," declined Earl Spencer's invitation to attend the opening ceremonies.

Understandably, William and Harry viewed the approaching first anniversary of Mummy's death with dread. Knowing the inevitable memorials and the global replay of grieving they would trigger would only dredge up painful memories, they searched for ways to distract themselves.

Toward that end, William came up with plans to throw Papa a surprise fiftieth birthday party—with a difference. They asked Academy Award–winning actress and screenwriter Emma Thompson and actor Stephen Fry to write a comedic playlet commemorating the occasion. Along with Thompson, Fry, and Rowan Atkinson (television's *Mr. Bean*), William and Harry would star in the production.

To pull off the surprise, the play would be given at Highgrove on July 31, 1998—three and a half months before the Prince of Wales's actual November 14 birthday. There was another reason for the July date: Camilla was planning a huge birthday bash of her own for her longtime lover.

Just ten days before the boys' carefully planned surprise party was to take place, details were leaked to the *Sunday Mirror*. "William and Harry are upset that information about a secret party they were planning for their father has reached the *Sunday Mirror*," said a spokesman for Charles. "They worked very hard to try to pull it off... The Prince of Wales is sad that the newspaper involved did not handle the information it received with greater common sense and courtesy." Still, the boys went ahead with the play—a takeoff on the British television series *Blackadder*. To cover the cost of dinner, dancing, and their costumes, William and Harry charged the one hundred guests at their father's birthday party forty dollars apiece.

As the countdown to the first anniversary of Diana's death continued, William and Harry ignored as best they could the flood of newspaper articles, magazine pieces, and television programs commemorating the sad event. There was no better place to accomplish this than Balmoral, where they enjoyed their usual late-summer holiday fishing, hunting, hiking, and riding with the rest of the Windsors.

William and Harry did ask for the one thing that was denied them on the very day of their mother's death—a church service at which Diana's name was actually mentioned. They also asked that all flags in Britain fly at half-mast in honor of Mummy. The Queen, recalling the uproar that resulted when she balked at making this same gesture a year earlier, granted her grandsons their wish.

Once again, the princes rode in a limousine to nearby Crathie Church—this time sandwiched between Princess Anne and Prince Edward.

Pointedly excluded from the service were Diana's relatives. The Spencers, in response, organized their own memorial on the shore of the tiny lake at Althorp that encircles Diana's grave.

The Queen did invite Prime Minister Tony Blair and his wife, Cherie, to the twenty-minute service, which included a reading of the Twenty-third Psalm and prayers for Diana and her family. Charles, the Queen, and the boys all read along from a special prayer sheet. "Today I have to come to this quiet place to offer my prayer of remembrance and thanksgiving for Diana, Princess of Wales," the congregation intoned. "She was a person whose life touched the hearts of so many people. She knew sorrow as well as happiness in her own life, and through this she grew in compassion for the suffering of others. I pray for those who were closest to her. I pray especially for her two young sons, Prince William and Prince Harry. Surround them with your loving care. May the love and assurance of their family protect them."

"Our main concern was for the boys," said the Reverend Robert Sloan, "that they be allowed to remember their mother in the way they want." Those in the crowd who waited patiently outside Balmoral hoped that William, Harry, Charles, and the Queen might stop to chat with them. Instead, the cars swept past and through the gates to the castle. "Today is not about the Queen's subjects," conceded Marjorie Black of Aberdeen, one of those who waited for hours in the late summer sunshine. "It is about the princes, and how they are feeling. There is no reason why they should want to stop and talk to people on today of all days."

By now, William and Harry were held fast in the embrace of the Royal Family. Diana's influence was dwindling rapidly, in part because—unbeknownst to the princes—her friends were being denied access to the boys. "When I try to speak to them at the palace," said Diana's friend Roberto Devorik, "I am told they're unavailable." Lady Elsa Bowker was similarly snubbed.

Despite the princes' long-standing affection for their cousins Beatrice and Eugenie, they were barred along with their mother, the Duchess of York, from even attempting to see William and Harry. "I miss them desperately," said Fergie, who because of the strict terms of her own divorce settlement was in no position to defy her former mother-in-law.

The Princess's friends were the first to note the absence of Diana's humanizing influence on her sons. Instead of spending weekends with their mother visiting homeless shelters or amusement parks, the boys now enjoyed the rural pleasures of Balmoral or spent weekends at Highgrove with their father and, increasingly, his mistress.

"The departure of their mother," said Richard Greene, "pushed the princes into the traditional 'maleness' of the Royal Family— the foxhunts and polo—and away from the emotional, raw, open, honest side of their psyches that Diana was reinforcing." Observed another friend: "William and Harry belong to the Windsors now."

Perhaps. But, in death even more than in life, Diana had an undeniable impact on the way the Royal Family now conducted itself. While the Queen visited a pub, rode in taxis, and even chatted amiably with twenty-one-year-old rock singer Julie Thompson, Papa now engaged in previously unheard-of displays of public affection. Where once there seemed to be only chilly formality between Charles and his boys, he now regularly hugged them in public. Before boarding separate planes for a brief vacation in Greece that summer of 1998, Charles allowed himself to be photographed standing on the tarmac at Heathrow, kissing William goodbye. Harry, who would unselfconsciously hold his father's hand or hug him, even engaged in a game where he covered his father's face with kisses while Papa jokingly tried to fend off his advances.

Just days later, William was fending off advances of a different sort as he and his father were once again cruising the Aegean aboard billionaire John Latsis's opulent yacht *Alexander*. Among other accoutrements, the *Alexander* boasted a ballroom, a disco, a billiard room, five swimming pools, a piano lounge, several oak-paneled reception rooms, a movie theater, a video library stocked with one thousand films, gold plumbing fixtures, and a helipad. As they often did, the Prince of Wales's old friends Charles and Patty Palmer-Tomkinson tagged along, and brought with them their daughter Tara.

On board the *Alexander,* Tara, then twenty-seven, rushed up to William and greeted him in the same playful manner she had since they were both children: she thrust her hand down the front of his pants. At other times, in the middle of a conversation she would reach over and begin playing with his zipper. "It started when he was younger," a friend said, "but she keeps doing it. He wishes she would stop."

During the same voyage, Tara was sun-bathing on deck when she noticed that William was staring at her. She sat up, whipped off her bikini top, and told him, "Come on then, have a proper look!" Mortified, William walked off as Tara burst out laughing. "She thought it was hilarious," said a crew member who witnessed the event. "He obviously didn't."

It was not the only time William was taken aback by the young model's behavior. At one of their regular ski vacations in Klosters, Papa winced when, in the words of one observer, she "launched herself into William's lap." Said one of Charles's aides, "They are teenage boys, and like all boys of that age are sensitive about such blatant behavior. They squirm when she gets up to her antics."

Prince Charles may have been able to over-look Tara's disconcerting lack of decorum. But when she confessed to being a cocaine addict who routinely snorted the drug at parties and in the bathrooms of friends, he barred her from any further contact with his boys. Or, as his spokesman delicately put it, "It is unlikely that she will be seen on holiday in the foreseeable future with the Prince or his sons."

Tara's familiarity with William in particular

gave rise to gossip that she had given herself to William as a birthday gift. After spending a month at the Meadows, a one-thousand-dollar-a-day drug clinic in Arizona, Palmer-Tomkinson returned to London and added fuel to the rumors—by publicly denying them.

"This is so far from the truth," she insisted. "I'm a cocaine addict, not a pedophile. I've messed around with lots of friends, young and old, by the pool, with everyone playing striptease and de-pantsing one another. But then the rumors kick in and instead of ten people clowning around, you have only two. Before you know it, you're branded a sexual deviant. William is a mate but that's something I'm not going to go into."

Increasingly, Charles and the Queen were relying on the stalwart, clean-living likes of Princess Anne's son, Peter Phillips, to serve as a model for the boys. His attractive sister, Zara, was another matter. Now sporting a metal stud in her tongue, the self-styled family rebel would invariably sidle up to William at royal gatherings and start chiding him about his sex symbol status. Zara "loves to tease William and make him blush, which he does easily," said British writer Brian Hoey. "She has a wonderful ability to deflate egos."

The Queen, who originally encouraged Zara's involvement in the boys' lives, was less than amused when Zara and William giggled uncontrollably at a reception in honor of Her Majesty's fiftieth wedding anniversary. She was also taken aback when Zara became one of Wills's chief allies in his efforts to loosen the reins on his private life.

When *The Mail on Sunday* published what it described as a "warm tribute" to William on his sixteenth birthday, Palace officials branded the contents of the story "grossly intrusive and completely untrue." What upset them was a passage that claimed young women were "vetted" by his aides before they could be invited for tea with the prince.

Denials aside, Palace aides did investigate the backgrounds of each girl William showed a particular interest in. "Several government agencies, including MI6 and Scotland Yard, have watched Prince William and Prince Harry just like they watched Diana," said one former member of Parliament with close ties to the Palace. "They are not about to let anyone who might be a threat get close to the princes."

As for determining whether a girl is socially "suitable" for either prince: "After all the scandalous headlines, the Queen pays *very* close attention to the girls in William's life. The last thing she wants is another Diana or Fergie on her hands. Her Majesty has access to all the dossiers on these young women, and if one of her advisers points out that a girl might be a problem for one reason or another, she makes her feelings known to Prince Charles. He's the one who has the job of putting his foot down when the need arises."

For the time being, at least, there was little cause for concern. William remained focused on his studies and school sports at Eton, with Harry poised to join him. The difference between the two boys became obvious on September 3, 1998, when Harry registered for classes just as his brother had done three years earlier. This time, rather than being flustered the way William had been, Harry obliged with a warm smile every time a photographer called, "Over here, lad!"

Charles, hovering over the boy, remembered how William had to be told to put down "Church of England" in the blank space next to "Religion."

"Make sure you sign in the right place," he cautioned, half in jest.

"Oh, shut up!" Harry cracked.

Later "the spare," resplendent in Eton's striped trousers and swallowtail coat, strode out ahead of the other F-tits on the way to morning prayers at Eton's Lower Chapel. Then, with his ubiquitous armed guard just a few paces behind him, Harry headed off to French class.

Sharing his father's artistic flair (Charles had long been an accomplished amateur painter), Harry would decorate his frequent letters home with drawings and caricatures that depicted life at Eton. His impish sense of humor also shone through in his writing. Once Prince Charles had been made an honorary Rear Admiral in the Royal Navy, Harry addressed his letters home "Rear Admiral Papa."

Charles and the Queen were delighted that

Wills would now be close at hand to help his brother through the tough transition period—not to mention the lingering effects of his mother's death. In fact, both boys would be staying under the watchful eye of Andrew Gailey at Manor House—largely for security reasons.

Within a month, however, an incident would occur at Eton that would raise serious questions about just how safe the princes really were. In a startling breach of security, a convicted armed robber and kidnapper was found prowling the halls of Eton within feet of the princes. Floyd Stevenson had served time in prison for holding four men, a woman, and a baby at gunpoint during a robbery, and then forcing one of the victims to drive his getaway car.

Stevenson apparently had no plans to harm William and Harry, and was released without being charged. But his mere presence at the school served as a chilling reminder that, despite the $1.5 million spent each year to guard them at Eton, the princes remained vulnerable.

The biggest threat to their safety, however, may well have been themselves. Over the next two months, both princes would wind up in the hospital with injuries suffered on the playing fields of Eton. "Having two rapidly growing offspring who continuously injure themselves in one sport or another," Charles said of the doctors who treated Harry's broken arm and William's various fractures and sprains, "I'm glad that someone takes care of these sort of things."

Such offhand remarks aside, Charles had met the challenge of replacing Diana as the most important person in the princes' lives. So strong was the bond between father and sons that they now seemed eager to do whatever it took to please him—even so far as accepting Camilla into their lives.

Charles's official fiftieth birthday party at Highgrove, planned with military precision by Camilla and the boys, also marked a coming-out of sorts for Camilla and Charles as a couple. In honor of Charles's passion for organic growing, Camilla used leaves, vines, branches, wildflowers, and tree stumps to re-create the Prince's beloved walled garden indoors.

A few of the 340 guests had already arrived when William rushed in from Eton wearing combat gear. He explained that he was a member of the school's cadet force and had to come straight from field exercises. William was "rather proud," recalled one guest, "that he had spent the last night in a ditch." Within minutes, he changed into a tuxedo and bounded downstairs to greet the new arrivals.

No longer willing to linger in the shadows, Camilla made the most of her entrance by instructing her chauffeur to slow down for photographers as she pulled up to the estate. She emerged from the car wearing a low-cut emerald-green velvet dress and a dazzling turquoise, diamond, and sapphire necklace.

At the dinner, William stood up and raised a glass of pink champagne. "I want you all," he said, "to wish my father a happy fiftieth birthday." Toward the end of the meal Harry, seated at a separate table, burst into an impromptu solo rendition of "Happy Birthday." The rest of the crowd quickly joined in.

During the dancing that followed, William and Harry served as willing deejays. At one point, they huddled with Camilla and culled through a formidable stack of CDs before she picked out a disco tune that had been a hit back in the early days of her affair with their father: "YMCA," by the Village People.

The boys started stamping their feet to the music, and Camilla moved onto the dance floor with Papa. Camilla's children, Tom and Laura Parker Bowles, were soon standing beside William and Harry. All four looked on in mock horror while Charles and Camilla gyrated to music by Abba, the Bee Gees, and Chic.

"They all behaved like a family," one of the guests said. "It had only been fourteen months since their mother's death, but William and Harry showed real affection for Camilla and for her children." Said another: "The thing they want most of all is for their father to be happy. And they like Camilla—that's obvious."

As the party dragged on past 3 A.M., William and Harry, fans of the British film *The Full Monty,* decided to entertain the remaining guests by reenacting the movie's final strip scene. To "You Sexy Thing," by Hot Chocolate, the princes whipped off their shirts and unbuttoned their pants before collapsing with laughter. "They know every step of the dance routine," said an Eton pal, "and it has become their party piece whenever they get together with friends."

Notably absent from the proceedings was the Queen, as intransigent as ever on the subject of her son's relationship with "Mrs. P. B." Even though Her Majesty remained steadfast in her opposition to marriage, the Church of England seemed willing to bend. The same institution that once forced a king to abdicate because of his intention to marry Wallis Simpson, a divorced woman, now seemed willing to step aside if Charles insisted on wedding Camilla.

For their part, William and Harry told Papa they had no objection to Charles marrying again. If he chose to officially make Camilla step-mother to his sons, she would become consort— not queen—once he ascended the throne. Contrary to prevailing rumors at the time, Camilla made it clear to friends that she very much intended to eventually marry Charles. In the meantime, they divided their time between London and Highgrove. "They have settled into life," an aide said, "like any other married couple of twenty-eight years."

Meantime, Camilla seemed to relish her role as royal mistress. She continued to flaunt Alice Keppel's jewels and hung a portrait of the Edwardian mistress in a prominent spot in her home. When the American philan-thropist and grande dame Brooke Astor dined at St. James's Palace, Camilla was eager to speak with her because as a child in New York Astor had met Keppel.

While the press debated the wisdom of Charles marrying his longtime mistress, an insidious threat to the health of William and Harry—not to mention the rest of the Royal Family—was literally festering inside the walls of Buckingham Palace. Wills and Harry were visiting Granny and Grandpapa Philip there shortly before Christmas when the deadly bacteria that causes Legionnaires' disease was discovered in the Palace's antiquated plumbing system. The disease—so named after it killed twenty-nine people attending an American Legion convention in Philadelphia in 1976—was deemed an immediate threat. The most contaminated pipes, investigators determined, led directly to the Queen's own showers and bathrooms.

While the Palace's pipes were disinfected and flushed with scalding water, the Queen, Prince Philip, and their staff fled to Windsor. Everyone, including William and Harry, was given a blood test to determine if they had become infected with the disease, which if not fatal can still produce severe long-term lung damage. Understandably, everyone breathed a collective sigh of relief when all the tests came back negative.

A few days later, on December 20, William, Harry, and fourteen of their chums dined with the Queen and Prince Philip at Windsor. Her Majesty had gone to Eton to watch William in a school production of *The Tem-*

pest, and according to a Palace spokesman, "thought it would be a pleasant gesture" to invite some of his schoolmates to the castle.

Shortly after their arrival, the boys went to their rooms to change into suits before having drinks with Her Majesty in the Green Drawing Room. All the boys—including several as young as fourteen—were offered one alcoholic drink before sitting down to dinner with the Queen. Of all fourteen boys, Harry alone abstained.

Elizabeth and Philip chatted with their callow guests as they dined on sole, pheasant, and a variety of cheeses. White wine from the royal cellars was served with the fish course, and red throughout the remainder of the meal. Two hours later, at 10:00, the Queen retired to bed. She had, she told William and Harry, "loved every minute."

Her Majesty was "delighted the dinner party went so well," said a Palace spokesman, "and that William and Harry can entertain their friends in her home. She is incredibly fond of her grandsons... she wants them to feel as relaxed and at home at Windsor as she is."

What Granny did not know, however, was that after she left for bed, the young men put their favorite CDs on the stereo system and proceeded to empty out the liquor cabinet. At around 11:30, Harry, apparently the only one at the party who had not been drinking, announced that he wanted to go sledding.

He took his guests to the pantry, where they grabbed several large silver serving trays and went out to the steep, grass-covered embankment beneath Windsor Castle's nine-hundred-year-old Round Tower. For the next half hour, they whooped and hollered as they slid down the hill—all under the tolerant gaze of the princes' longtime bodyguards.

Early the next morning, Wills and Harry gave their hungover young guests twelve-gauge shotguns and then headed out with their gamekeepers to hunt rabbits in Windsor Great Park. At a picnic lunch served on the grounds, the princes' teenage guests, several of whom had only a passing familiarity with firearms, were again offered wine.

The potentially deadly combination of guns and alcohol was part and parcel of royal life. At Sandringham and Balmoral, hunting parties stopped several times during a day's shoot to imbibe liquor, putting themselves and those around them at risk.

The situation was scarcely better at school. Incredibly, Eton provided its students with their own pub, called The Tap. Boys sixteen or older were permitted to consume two pints of beer or hard cider a day, although former students claimed they could easily skirt the rules. "Drinking to excess is not uncommon at Eton," said one alumnus, "and that's not the only thing."

Indeed, for all its undeniable exclusivity, Eton dealt with the same problems of alcohol and drug abuse, violence, and sexual experimentation that characterized boarding schools on both sides of the Atlantic. Boys had been caught smoking marijuana, taking painkillers and speed, even sneaking knives and stun guns into the school.

For many of the younger boys entering Eton, the menacingly brawny upperclassmen posed a problem. Bullying was commonplace, at times causing the more sensitive underclassmen severe emotional distress. Some boys suffered nervous breakdowns, a few attempted suicide. Further complicating matters was the school's sexually charged atmosphere. In his book *Eton Voices*, Danny Danziger notes that the school was fraught with "adolescent eroticism, expressed (and sometimes fulfilled) in homosexual liaisons, sometimes amorous, sometimes lustful, sometimes innocent."

"It's hard for Americans to understand," explained British author Victor Bockris, "but this sort of early homosexual activity is very, very common in England. Most males go through it, but it doesn't mean they're gay at all—it's just sort of a rite of passage. The vast majority go on to become lifelong heterosexuals with wives and children."

By virtue of who they were and the bodyguards who accounted for their every move, William and Harry were both shielded from some of the seamier goings-on at Eton. But not all. The Royal Protection Squad did not try to intervene when William got drunk with his pals and threw up, or when those around him smoked marijuana. "He drank the way everyone does," a schoolmate said, "but that's as far as it went. Some of the other boys moved on to cocaine. He was not one of them."

Nor was he a participant in one of the deadlier nocturnal pastimes on campus. Called the "Fainting Game," it involved two students tying a bathrobe belt around the neck of a third, then pulling it until the classmate passes out. The person being "fainted" taps on his thigh while the other boys tighten the noose. Once the tapping stops, that is the sign that the classmate has lost consciousness and the pulling should stop.

A bizarre sexual practice called autoerotic asphyxiation, this form of voluntary strangulation is intended to produce an orgasmic state in the victim. Often, however, it leads to severe injury or death. It was a gamble that a surprisingly large number of William's classmates were prepared to take. The game was played nearly every night, and one boy claimed to have personally witnessed it on more than seventy separate occasions.

When he was approached by schoolmates in late 1998 to participate in the deadly game, William would later say his first reaction was "total shock." He not only refused but went immediately to Harry and made him promise not to join in. In early 1999 one of William's schoolmates, sixteen-year-old Nicholas Taylor, was found hanged to death in his room, a bathroom belt around his neck. Apparently he had tried to play the game alone.

Prince Charles seemed less concerned with

the deadly games being played at Eton than the future of his life with Camilla Parker Bowles. In January, they made their first public appearance together on the steps of London's Ritz Hotel. Significantly, the occasion they chose was a party celebrating the fiftieth birthday of Annabelle Elliot, Camilla's sister. It was at Annabelle Elliot's fortieth birthday party that Diana had confronted Camilla, then went home to Kensington Palace and "cried like I have never cried before. I cried and cried and cried..."

As they left the Ritz together, Charles and Camilla ignored the shouts of 150 cameramen and a cheering throng of well-wishers. Reluctant to walk beside him at first, Camilla followed a step behind, and when Charles turned to check on her they briefly collided. When they reached their car, Charles put his arm around Camilla, publicly cementing the relationship that had been conducted surreptitiously for over a quarter-century. Standing behind them at the top of the stairs, Tom and Laura Parker Bowles smiled broadly as their mother finally stepped out of the shadows to take her place as the Prince of Wales's true love. Noticeably absent: William and Harry, who despite their fondness for Camilla refused to be party to what many called a betrayal of their mother's memory. "Harry, in particular, hated the whole thing," said a friend of Charles's. "He had been slower than William to warm to Camilla, and he just did not like the idea of her stepping into his mother's shoes." When it came to his sons' feelings for Mummy, Charles was careful to "never force them to do anything they didn't want to do."

Besides, the princes were less interested in black-tie affairs at the Ritz than they were in testing themselves on and off the playing field. Both ferocious competitors, William and Harry were frequently treated for injuries sustained playing rugby and soccer. And with Tiggy Legge-Bourke looking on, neither had hesitated to rappel down the steep face of a dam with only a slim cord around his waist and no helmet. For that stunt, Tiggy had received a royal reprimand from Papa.

But in March of 1999 the boys' former nanny was given an opportunity to redeem herself. Ever since Papa and Harry returned from their South African sojourn with tales of exotic wildlife and spectacular scenery, William had been pleading to experience an African adventure of his own. Charles, whose own hectic schedule precluded him from going, once again turned to Tiggy.

For ten days William and Harry (along with Tiggy and a supporting cast of five) trekked through two of southern Africa's great game preserves, Moremi National Park and the sprawling Okavango Delta. They slept under the stars, navigated the shallow waterways of the Okavango in dugout canoes, and from the safety of their Range Rovers spied on herds of elephant, giraffe, antelope, and zebra.

William, still craving privacy, had asked

to be "completely cut off from the outside world," so only one satellite phone was taken along by the princes' bodyguards in case of an emergency. It was never used—not even to check in with Papa.

What made the princes' African adventure even more unusual was the fact that the public was unaware of it until after the boys were safely back home, spending Easter with the rest of the royals at Balmoral. "We want the public to know that we were working with the press to protect the boys' privacy," said a spokesman at St. James's Palace, "and that the Prince of Wales is extremely grateful."

The press's decision not to print the story had less to do with altruism than it did with the harsh realities of dealing with the Palace. Even though photographers had been absolved of all blame in the death of Diana, public sympathies remained with the boys, if not with the rest of the Royal Family. Any publication that dared to print an unsanctioned article about Wills and Harry, however benign, risked more than just a backlash from the public. It risked an official rebuke from the Press Complaints Commission and the threat of being cut off from access to the Palace.

But as speculation concerning the young woman in Wills's life continued to churn, it was a risk more and more publications were willing to take. With good reason. Although he cherished his privacy and shared the Windsors' inborn passion for country life, William had also inherited his mother's love of London's nightlife. With the peripatetic likes of Tom and Laura Parker Bowles as his after-hours guides, Wills made the rounds of such nightspots as K-Bar, Mimo, China White, and Crazy Larry's.

Moreover, the soon-to-be-seventeen prince was bringing girls home to his top-floor suite at York House—ostensibly for tea. With security ringing St. James's Palace, this was, ironically, the only place he could escape from the watchful gaze of his security detail. To ensure that not even Papa would barge in on him, Wills insisted that he have the only key to his suite.

Before he left on safari, Wills had been spotted at Foxtrot Oscar with a stunningly beautiful blonde. "He was gazing adoringly into her eyes," said the waiter, "and hanging on to her every word." The mystery woman was in fact Camilla's niece Emma, who at twenty-four was eight years William's senior and had just given up a lucrative modeling career to pursue a career in journalism.

Charles's circle acted quickly to squelch rumors of a romance that, given the distinct possibility that Camilla would become Wills's stepmother, seemed vaguely incestuous. "There is nothing improper about their relationship," a friend of Emma's was quoted as saying. "Emma is someone William can trust." Concurred an aide to Prince Charles: "The boys rather look up to Tom as a young man about town, and they took to Laura and Emma because they're pretty, and they like pretty girls."

But William was in fact smitten with Emma,

and for a short time the two were insepa-
rable. "He was infatuated with her," said one
Eton buddy, "and she was obviously very
fond of him. But it was obvious that she was
treating him like a younger brother."

"William is so sweet," Emma told one of her
circle, "but he mustn't get the wrong idea..."
Whatever misconception Wills may have been
laboring under, it was cleared up when newspapers carried a photo of Emma strolling
arm-in-arm with another, considerably older
man.

The prince took his frustrations out on the
Eton rugby field, where in late April he
fractured the index finger on his left hand. With
his left arm in a sling and several bracelets he
picked up in Africa dangling from his right wrist,
William attended the christening of Konstantine
Alexios, grandson of King Constantine of
Greece. King Constantine was William's
godfather, and now he returned the favor by
naming William the baby's godfather.

With the aid of Crown Princess Victoria of
Sweden, Wills maneuvered his injured hand
to bathe baby Konstantine in holy water as the
bearded, berobed, somewhat wild-eyed Greek
Orthodox Prelate repeatedly plunged the
hapless infant into the gold baptismal font.
William struggled to keep from laughing at the
bizarre scene.

After the ceremony William, who at six
foot two stood to be the tallest English king
since Henry VIII, knelt down to chat with several of the small children in attendance. Then

he told the proud parents, Prince Pavlos and the former Marie-Chantal Miller, that he was grateful for the chance to be part of their son's life. "William and Harry have a natural ability to be relaxed with children," observed a family friend. "They got it from their mother."

All my hopes are on William now. It's too late for the rest of the family. But William, I think he has it.

—*Diana*

William lives in his father's world now.

—*A friend of Diana's*

It's a pity Diana isn't around to keep an eye on her boys, because she'd be appalled at what's been going on.

—*British journalist Judy Wade*

I think he'll find it easier being king of Hollywood than I shall being king of England.

> —*William on being compared to Leonardo DiCaprio*

William knows how much Diana would want him to do the job he was born to do. He will be conscious of that and, in her memory, do it even better.

> —*BritishLord Jeffrey Archer*

8

He is really quite splendid, isn't he?" the Queen asked her private secretary as she studied the front-page photos of Will cradling the infant Prince Konstantine in his arms. "Quite splendid."

Her Majesty had watched proudly as William carried out his first few high-profile ceremonial duties with the good-humored grace of his mother. By contrast, she had scarcely noticed when he dropped in on a low-income housing project two months earlier, or when on the spur of the moment he joined a soccer game in Shepherd's Bush, a gritty West London neighborhood—and then celebrated at a local pub. "He was rather quiet," said a fellow player, "but quite effective."

She never spoke of the problematic Diana—and saw no value in exposing the boys to homeless shelters and AIDS clinics the way their mother had—but Elizabeth was grateful for both the beauty and charisma Wills inherited from his mother. For a time, it may have even seemed to the monarch that scandals and torrid tabloid headlines were a thing of the past. "The future of the monarchy really rests on William's shoulders, and the Queen knows that," said a former member of Prince Charles's staff. "She invested a great deal of time grooming him to be king—more time than she ever spent with her own son." It was important to Her Majesty "that William not be tainted by scandal the way his parents were. She was very impressed with the kind of person he was becoming—a serious, responsible young man. And she was very grateful that he had not fallen in with a bad crowd."

That illusion would soon be shattered, and the Windsors would all have misgivings about the company William kept. Camilla's son Tom had been an unrepentant hell-raiser since his days as a student at Oxford. Two of the clubs he joined as an undergraduate—the Assassins and the Piers Gaveston Society (named after the gay lover of Edward II)—were notorious for their bacchanalian bashes. One, the Assassins' "Fetish Party," featured whips, chains, studded dog collars, rubber underwear, and *Silence of the Lambs* masks. Tom, in his self-assigned role as a dominatrix, showed up in full makeup, a plastic dress, and stiletto heels.

With a 1995 arrest for possession of marijuana and the drug Ecstasy already on his record, Camilla's son was now snorting cocaine at some of the same clubs he frequented with Wills. At one club Tom, who was then working for a public relations firm, openly bragged to a young woman that he "did a line with someone I found last night." Then he asked the woman if she was in the market for "gear" (heroin) or weed. Confronted with the evidence,

Tom publicly admitted that he was in fact a cocaine user.

News of Tom's drug taking sent shock waves through the Palace. The Queen, enraged that yet another Parker Bowles was tainting a member of her family with scandal, retaliated by barring Camilla from the June 19, 1999, wedding of her youngest son, Prince Edward, and Princess Diana look-alike Sophie Rhys-Jones.

The Tom Parker Bowles drug scandal dealt a severe setback to the rehabilitation of Camilla's image—not to mention her plans to become stepmother to William and Harry. By now, Charles had been seen at the same public event as Camilla on at least three separate occasions. As for Charles's continued entreaties that the Queen finally meet his mistress, Granny remained intransigent. "Charles," Elizabeth replied firmly, "understand that I have absolutely no desire to meet her."

Papa, meanwhile, called his mistress's son. "You've done a very stupid thing, Tom," Prince Charles told the boy. "Your mother is very upset. For God's sake, at least think of what all this is doing to her." He urged Tom to seek professional help, and then made it plain that he was not to go near either William or Harry so long as he was continuing to use cocaine.

Then Charles summoned William to his office at St. James's Palace and asked him point-blank if Tom had ever offered him drugs. Others had, Will conceded, but not Tom.

Besides, Wills assured his father, he had no intention of trying cocaine or any other drug; he had visited enough clinics and rehab centers with Mummy to know the havoc they wrought. Still very much the protective older brother, he was also conscious of not setting the wrong example for Harry.

As for the possibility that Tom's behavior might rub off on his young friend, Wills refused to take the notion seriously. "He just laughs it off," said a friend of Charles's. "He is much more sensible than these people realize."

Charles believed his son, but soon there was more cause for alarm. That spring it was revealed that one of the boys' cousins, Lord Frederick Windsor, was also a cocaine user. Lord Frederick, son of Prince and Princess Michael of Kent and a friend of William's, was four years ahead of William at Eton. A gifted scholar and a favorite of the Queen's ("His manners are impeccable," she once commented), Frederick had gone on to pursue classical studies at Oxford.

There was, according to leading British psychiatrist Dennis Friedman, legitimate cause for concern. Lord Frederick Windsor's grandfather—the Duke of Kent, Queen Elizabeth's uncle and William and Harry's great-great-uncle—was also a cocaine addict. "There is a history of addiction on both sides of the Royal Family," Dr. Friedman pointed out. "Therefore, the genetic loading is quite high. Charles must tell William it isn't something he could try like other boys might. 'Just try a bit of marijuana or have a few more drinks' is not an option for them." Both William and Harry "run a far higher risk of addiction than most people."

In apologizing for his drug abuse, Lord Frederick Windsor underscored the dangers confronting William and Harry. "It is very difficult to avoid getting into this sort of thing," Windsor said, "when you move in these circles."

Dealing with Tom Parker Bowles presented special problems for Prince Charles. William had come to regard him as the big brother he never had. Moreover, Charles had watched him grow up, the only son of the woman he ever loved. It would be virtually impossible to cut Camilla's son out of the princes' lives the way he had Tara Palmer-Tomkinson.

For now, Charles and Camilla asked William and Tom to stay away from each other. The two complied, although they still spoke to each other on the phone almost daily. Papa was aware that the problem was bigger than just Tom, and ordered the princes' bodyguards to ferret out the drug users among William's expanding circle of club-crawling friends.

No easy task. A few months later, another pal of William's, a young woman named Izzy Winkler, would confess to using cocaine. So, sadly, would the young woman who was the object of Wills's first serious infatuation—Emma Parker Bowles—bringing to five the number of admitted substance abusers belonging to William's inner circle.

"It's all very upsetting," Emma conceded

after she returned from thirty-five days at the same Arizona clinic where Tara Palmer-Tomkinson had been treated. In Emma's case, the problem was not just cocaine but alcohol abuse. "Her problem is the booze," Emma's father, recovering alcoholic Richard Parker Bowles, explained. "I blame myself. It's been passed on through the genes."

He also chalked up Emma's problems to the added pressure of being Camilla's niece. So reviled was Charles's mistress in the aftermath of Diana's death, Emma's father said, that it "affects everybody with the Parker Bowles name. I've even considered changing mine."

Still, Richard Parker Bowles admitted that the primary force behind his daughter's substance abuse was peer pressure—the same peer pressure now brought to bear on Diana's boys. What made the specter of alcohol and drug use even more pressing was the fact that, when he turned seventeen on June 21, William would be old enough to drive under British law.

William, who had been tooling around Balmoral in Grandpapa's Range Rover since he was twelve, had no trouble passing his test the first time out. When Papa turned down his request for a 125cc Kawasaki motorcycle, William asked instead for a sporty but decidedly understated white Volkswagen Golf—an identical match to the car driven by one of Wills's closest friends, Edward van Cutsem. The prince's license plate left no doubt as to which VW was his. It read, simply: WILLS 1.

Persuaded to cooperate with a photo op outside Highgrove, Wills showed off his driving skills behind the wheel of a borrowed Ford. Scores of cameras whirred and clicked as he pulled into the gravel drive and climbed out. "How humiliating," he muttered under his breath to his father, never letting his smile drop. Dwarfed by his six-foot-two-inch son, five-foot-ten-inch Charles cracked, "This is just to show how quickly I'm shrinking."

That summer, William proudly took friends for spins around London and environs—with a bodyguard at his side and another following at a discreet distance. Amid the scandalous headlines and scalding revelations, the fact remained that William was on one level that most typical and uncomplicated of creatures: a teenager besotted with his shiny new car.

In his first two weeks as a licensed motorist, William took more than a passing interest in his fellow drivers. Software salesman Simon Thompson and his passenger, off-duty policeman Steven James, were pushing Thompson's broken-down BMW down a Chelsea street when a woman in a green Range Rover drove up. "Do you want a hand?" Tiggy Legge-Bourke asked.

"Before I knew it," Thompson recalled, "the back door of the car had opened and Harry came up." Followed by William. The princes rolled up their sleeves and started to push while Thompson maneuvered the wheel. "It was hard to concentrate on the steering," he said. "They acted as though it was no big deal, but it is amazing when there are two princes pushing your car down the road."

Then Wills and Harry jumped back in the Range Rover and sped off. It was only then that Thompson noticed the princes' bodyguards, who, under strict orders to remain as "invisible" as possible, sat in their car while the princes played Good Samaritan.

Aside from the questionable company Wills sometimes kept, he and Harry were shaping up to be, in Charles's own oft-repeated words, "ideal sons." Perhaps nothing delighted Papa more than watching both offspring follow him onto the polo field. Harry, who like his brother was a gifted horseman, showed an early interest in the game at which Papa and Grandpapa excelled.

But for Wills, polo presented special problems. He was left-handed, and the game required for safety reasons that all players "meet" right hand to right hand. According to Diana's friend Richard Kay, William "had to literally become right-handed." To accomplish this he trained for months, and eventually became so proficient that Charles rewarded him with his own polo pony.

Increasingly, Wills viewed Highgrove as a refuge. He no longer felt compelled to fill the house with friends during school breaks, instead preferring to spend quiet weekends there with Papa and Harry. With his father's permission, William had one of the first-floor rooms converted into his private study. Anyone trying to reach him directly on the telephone would have to consult Highgrove's in-house directory. Making bittersweet reference to the room's previous occupant, the number for Will's study was listed under the heading HER ROYAL HIGHNESS'S DRAWING ROOM.

Princess Diana was still very much a presence at Highgrove. Since her royal apartments at Kensington Palace had been shut down a year earlier, Highgrove was the one place that still held memories for William and Harry of what life with their mother was like. Out of deference to his sons, Charles still displayed photographs of the Princess around the house. For their part, William and Harry kept framed pictures of their mother on their nightstands.

William felt his mother's comforting presence at Highgrove. "I still look up and for a split second I think I see Mummy standing in the doorway," he told a friend. "I feel her with me always." Prince Harry understood perfectly. He, too, had seen the same apparition and at times told his father that he thought he had heard Mummy's voice.

Understandably, both boys said they occasionally dreamt of their mother. While Harry's dreams were replays of happy times with Mummy, Wills's were often dark and foreboding. In the weeks and months following Diana's death, Wills, in his search to determine what caused the accident, had demanded to know all the details. Ever since, he had been haunted by a recurring nightmare in which he witnessed the horrific crash. "He said the dreams were a lot worse at the beginning," recalled a schoolmate. "Back then he would take long walks alone just trying to get the thoughts out of his mind. The dreams don't happen that often anymore, but he also said that he doesn't think they'll ever go away forever."

One person who was careful to stay away from Highgrove when the boys were there was the Princess's old nemesis. While William, who now called her Camilla—and insisted she call him William—greeted her with kisses on both cheeks, Mrs. P. B. did not wish to intrude on their father-son weekends.

Camilla went a step further, and at one point promised William and Harry that she could never replace their mother and "would never try." She also told Charles that, even if the Queen agreed to their marriage, she would not go through with it without the blessings of both boys.

However fond they were of the easygoing Camilla and her family, in the scandal-ridden summer of 1999 neither of Diana's boys were eager to see a marriage to Camilla and the uproar that would inevitably ensue. "Robbed of his mother," observed Richard Kay, "William is not ready for a mother figure—nor, incidentally, is Harry."

They were also reluctant to see Camilla become queen consort, as she automatically would if she married Charles and he ascended the throne. "Diana was not allowed to be queen," Lady Bowker said. "They would not *let* her be queen. For Camilla to become

Charles's queen consort when she caused Diana so much heartache—unthinkable."

Whatever she may have felt about Diana, the Queen was not about to forgive Camilla. "She's made it clear," a Palace official confirmed, "that any rapprochement is out of the question."

There was one member of the Royal Family who was even more adamant in her opposition to Charles marrying Camilla. England's beloved Queen Mother was, in the words of one courtier, "livid" at the prospect: "The Queen Mother was not fond of Princess Diana. But she detests Camilla and believes her to be a wicked, selfish woman. She has made the Queen promise that, as long as she is alive, no marriage between Charles and Camilla will ever take place."

With the memory of headlines tying William to two drug-dabbling Parker Bowles children still fresh in her mind, the Queen was nonplussed when Charles invited Camilla to accompany him and the boys on holiday for the first time. To make matters worse, Charles had also invited Tom and Laura Parker Bowles, along with the family of the notorious Tara Palmer-Tomkinson—although not the zipper-tugging Tara.

Aware that a significant number of Britons still despised Camilla, Charles's operatives at St. James's acted preemptively to soften the blow. They leaked false information to the effect that inviting Camilla and her children along had been "William's idea."

This time, as the royal party embarked on

its annual ten-day cruise of the Aegean aboard the *Alexander,* it was clear that Camilla was on board to serve "in the role of stepmother... sort of a mother hen," as one observer put it. "She was chiefly in charge of saying, 'Hurry up, boys, get ready for dinner,' and the other things most stepmums do."

"It's ironic," added Judy Wade, "knowing how much Diana hated Camilla, that Camilla would now be the main one in her son's life." Particularly ironic in view of the fact that it was aboard the *Alexander* that Charles and Diana's disastrous "second honeymoon" took place in 1992.

For all this, William—now dubbed "His Royal Sighness" by the tabloids—had other things on his mind during the cruise. So did Harry, who over the past six months had shot up six inches in height. To ensure there were enough young people aboard, William invited along three stunning beauties: Davina Duckworth-Chad, twenty-one; Emilia d'Erlanger, seventeen; and sixteen-year-old Mary Forestier-Walker. All three girls were from influential families, and had ties to the boys through both the Windsors and the Spencers.

Davina, a distant cousin of William through his mother, quickly emerged as the most intriguing of the three. The daughter of a wealthy landowner whose two-thousand-acre estate is close to Sandringham, the leggy blonde was dubbed "the Deb on the Web" after she struck a seductive pose to launch an Internet site.

"I think it is nice for Prince William to have such charming female companions," said Elizabeth d'Erlanger, Emilia's mother. "He's a lucky young man." Fleet Street wasted no time christening *Alexander* "the Royal Love Boat."

Not merely content to flirt with the current passengers aboard the *Alexander,* Wills started up a steamy e-mail correspondence with a young woman he had yet to meet. When he arrived on the yacht, there was a signed eight-by-ten glossy photo of an American model waiting for him in his stateroom. The *Vogue* model had been on board the *Alexander* the week before, and when she learned Prince William would be on board she decided to leave him her picture with a somewhat suggestive note. The model: Lauren Bush, granddaughter of former President George Bush and niece of soon-to-be President George W. Bush.

William promptly sent a photo of himself to Lauren, and began an e-mail romance that would heat up steadily over the next two years. Meanwhile, in an eerie replay of Diana's 1997 Mediterranean cruise with her boys and Dodi Fayed aboard the *Jonikal,* hundreds of boats and a dozen helicopters carrying paparazzi prowled the Aegean in search of the *Alexander.* This time, however, Tony Blair's office, Earl Spencer, and Britain's Press Complaints Commission warned them to back off or face government sanctions. The British press did disperse, but that still left an estimated two hundred foreign press photographers searching for the "Royal Love Boat." But without being tipped off as to their whereabouts, the press failed to locate the *Alexander* on the open sea.

William and Harry both returned looking tanned and rested and ready for three weeks of hunting at Balmoral before returning to school. This year, Harry would hold his own at Eton while his brother further distinguished himself as both scholar and athlete in his last year at Eton. Wills continued to be a standout at rugby, rowing, and water polo. As keeper (captain) of the swim team, the future king, in a black wet suit and yellow cap, would lead Eton to victory in the triathlon, coming in a full ten minutes ahead of the second-place finisher.

Wills also became an outstanding member of Eton's cadet force (akin to the Reserve Officers' Training Corps in the United States). He would go on to earn the coveted Sword of Honor, the highest honor bestowed on a cadet. An acknowledged student leader, he belonged to the Etonian society called Pop, whose members were, to a certain extent, given authority over the rest of the student body. As a "Popper," Wills was entitled to trade in his run-of-the-mill black vest for something of his own design: a Union Jack design emblazoned with the Austin Powers phrase "Groovy Baby." (Wills also had a polka-dot vest, a vest in the Manor House colors, and one with the slogan BAN THE BOMB.)

Harry was also coming into his own—and

drawing ever closer to his brother. "Harry was always rather young for his age," a family friend told Richard Kay, "but since he got to Eton he has grown up, physically and mentally." As for sibling rivalry: "William is very protective toward his brother. For his part, Harry worships William. There used to be a lot of fighting between the two—rivalry I suppose—but they're over that now."

Not entirely over it. William tried to avoid skiing with Harry, who was by far the superior of the two on the slopes. A superb marksman, the heir was none too happy that eagle-eyed Harry bested him in that department, too. The spare could also be an incorrigible cutup—a personality trait reminiscent of their mother that William found less and less amusing. In the middle of a cross-country race at Eton, Harry leapt out from behind some bushes, startling William. When the race was over, William blasted his brother for costing him the lead. Still, Harry's godmother, Carolyn Bartholomew, insisted, "They are getting on incredibly well."

Even though Prince William now ranked as the world's most eligible bachelor, Harry was not without his share of female admirers. At one Eton charity event that September, he volunteered to be dunked into icy water at the "Drown a Clown" stall. Other boys had been dunked two or three times each, but when Harry stepped up in the platform, a horde of teenage girls lined up to whack him in the rear with a hockey stick and send him into the tub.

When the first girl hesitated, Harry told her, "If you don't push me in, I'll throw you in instead!"

Hundreds of people gathered to watch the spectacle, and thirty dunkings later, Harry called it quits. "Harry looked like a drowned rat," said Colleen Birch, who witnessed the event. "But he had a huge grin on his face."

Not surprisingly, attention now focused on where Wills would go to college. It was assumed he might enroll in Prince Charles's alma mater—Trinity College at Cambridge University—or follow Diana's expressed wishes and attend Oxford. A generation earlier, Charles had had little say in the matter; the decision was made for him by a committee headed by the Archbishop of Canterbury. His headstrong son was hardly about to let that happen. "God help anyone who tells William what to do," said one of Charles's aides. "He listens, but he won't be pushed around."

Nor would William be pushed around when it came to one of his favorite extracurricular pursuits. He had been foxhunting on family estates for years, and in November 1999 made his public debut jumping fences and hedges with two hundred members of the Beaufort Hunt Club near Highgrove. Harry, still too young to ride at fifteen, trailed the pack on a motorbike.

Once again, front-page photos of tweed-jacketed Wills riding to the hounds sparked outrage. "SHAME-FACED," screamed the headline in the *Mirror,* which branded Wills "haughty and provocative." The *Express* blasted Prince William for his "upper-class arrogance" and accused him of showing a "blatant disregard" for public opinion. He was even denounced on the floor of Parliament. "It is insensitive and arrogant of the prince," MP Mike Foster thundered, "to so publicly endorse hunting."

But Papa, who had urged Wills to participate, was far from contrite. "Charles believes William should be involved in manly sports," *Burke's Peerage* publisher Harold Brooks-Baker said. "By encouraging his son and heir to take the risks involved in chasing foxes over dangerous terrain, Charles is telling the anti-hunting lobby to get lost."

Had she been alive, several commentators pointed out, Diana would have been disappointed in her son's actions. While she tolerated the shooting parties that went on at Balmoral and Sandringham, foxhunting seemed particularly cruel to her. "She would have eventually tried to talk them out of it," Lady Elsa Bowker speculated. "But in this I doubt that Diana would have succeeded."

Neither would Mummy have been pleased that her sons chose to attend Tiggy's October wedding to divorced father of two and former army officer Charles Pettifer. Harry stole the show at the reception when, on a dare, he plunged his hand into a bowl, pulled out a goldfish—and swallowed it.

Papa was not there to see it. Bowing to Camilla's distaste for Tiggy, he had declined the invitation. Later, when Charles and the boys sat down to watch a video of the wedding at Highgrove, Camilla left for her own home a few miles away. "I really do not need to watch *that*," she said.

Within a few months, Mrs. Tiggy Pettifer would move into her new home in Battersea, South London. No longer the surrogate mother Charles had hired her to be, Tiggy still kept in close contact with the boys. "We speak all the time," she said, "constantly. The way people who care deeply for each other do."

Camilla, meanwhile, filled the void left by Tiggy. When she fell ill with a serious case of the flu in mid-December 1999, it was Wills who took an active hand in nursing her back to health, each afternoon going to the kitchen at St. James's and bringing up a tray of hot soup. Harry also popped into her room daily to keep her spirits from flagging. This new intimacy, said Richard Kay, was "regarded with a suspicion bordering on repugnance" by those who had been in Diana's camp.

They need not have worried. Despite their undeniable affection for Camilla, William and Harry stressed to their father that they were still not in the market for a stepmother. The Queen had made her feelings clear: she would not even deign to meet Camilla, much less sanction her marriage to the Prince of Wales. But now Charles had a new impediment to contend with. Camilla had promised that she would not wed Charles without both boys' blessing. To their father's dismay, William and

Harry refused. "It was one thing to embrace Camilla as an unofficial member of their family," said the mother of one of Harry's close friends. "It was quite another to have her replace their mother as Prince Charles's lawful wife."

As the century drew to a close, it became increasingly clear that William was no longer willing to take orders from anyone—including his father. Without consulting Prince Charles or warning the St. James's staff, he would order the royal chefs to prepare elaborate dinners for his Eton friends. Once they had been served the meal by the palace footmen, William's guests would go to his room and spend the night on his floor in sleeping bags.

When Charles returned from a trip to discover six boys on his son's floor in sleeping bags, he demanded to know why they had not been given their own rooms. "There are," he pointed out to his son, "seventy-five rooms in the palace. I'm sure we can find enough space for everyone." Charles was also perturbed that no one had warned the staff of the boys' arrival.

William insisted, in turn, that he had every right to bring friends home without clearing it first. A quarrel ensued that only ended when Camilla, who understood William's need to operate independently from his father, intervened.

"Half the time Prince Charles has no idea what his son is up to," said one of Charles's oldest friends. "He doesn't know who he is with, who his latest friends are, or even which houses he is sleeping in." Agreed Richard Kay: "William likes to do his own thing without people knowing, which is frightfully difficult when you are second in line to the throne."

The young prince rejected Papa's offer to throw his year-end "Willennium" bash at Highgrove. But Wills was now so obsessively secretive that he refused to tell his father where he was planning on throwing the party.

It all added up to a security nightmare for the royal bodyguards, who often found themselves scrambling to keep up with the peripatetic young prince. Like his mother before him, William now continually questioned the need for detectives to be with him at all times.

There were exceptions. More and more young women were dropping by for "tea" at the top-floor York House suite to which only Wills had the key. When the prince was out on the town and showing particular interest in a young lady, Wills's security detail knew enough to "hang back, out of sight," said a former security expert assigned to guard the Royal Family. "He is a teenage boy, after all, and you've got to let him live his life."

There was mounting concern that Prince William was too independent for his own good—particularly in his insistence on continuing to frequent clubs where drug taking was rampant. "He knows he can pretty much do whatever he likes," a friend told the *Daily Mail,* "and Charles doesn't know how to say no to him." With reason: "He knows," said

Richard Kay, "that he cannot be too firm with a boy who has lost his mother."

Wills showed his independent streak again when he argued that Fergie be welcomed back into the royal fold. When the Duchess of York was once again pointedly excluded from the Royal Family's Christmas festivities, William refused to participate. Later, he and Harry took matters into their own hands and staged a reunion of their own. Without warning, they dropped in on Fergie and her daughters at Wood Farm, the cottage in a remote corner of Sandringham where the Duchess and her daughters spent the holidays.

As a rule, neither William nor Harry spoke of their mother in public; whenever there was a mention of her on television, they quietly left the room. But in defying his father and the Royal Family, William was not above invoking Diana's memory. When Prince Charles demanded that he do something he didn't feel like doing, Wills often replied, "Mummy wouldn't want me to do that," or "My mother would not have approved." A favorite all-purpose line of Wills's: "My mother said, 'Do only what your heart tells you.'"

"Prince William knows that he can stop his father dead just by mentioning Diana's name," said an ex-staffer at St. James's Palace. "No other member of the Royal Family ever spoke of the Princess, including Prince Charles. So whenever one of the boys mentioned

'Mummy,' conversation came to a halt. It was a powerful weapon, and William was not afraid to use it to get his way."

The 1999 holiday season was also memorable for the cyber-friendship Wills struck up with Britney Spears. For several months, Wills had a poster of the buxom pop diva hanging on the wall of his bedroom. "Someone called me and was like, 'Oh, the prince is such a big fan of yours,' " said Spears, who sent him several of her CDs and an autographed photo. As for their e-mail exchange: "We started back and forth. He's very, very cute."

Wills invited Spears to be his date at the millennium party he was planning, but she was in the middle of her world tour at the time and had to decline. Plans for a Valentine's Day meeting were in the works when, much to Wills's chagrin, word of the budding cyber-romance was leaked to the press.

The Palace immediately issued a denial, and eventually Prince William followed suit. "There's been a lot of nonsense put about by P.R. companies," Wills later said. "I don't like being exploited this way, but, as I get older, it's increasingly hard to prevent."

So, too, Prince Charles discovered, was the sometimes unsettling behavior of William and his substance-abusing friends. Instead of joining in any of the huge millennium eve celebrations in London, William opted instead to drink (mostly beer and champagne) the night away with friends in a tiny, tin-roofed village hall near Sandringham.

William was also intent on indulging another habit—one that Charles opposed and that Diana, in particular, had frequently railed against. William had become a smoker. Although she put up with Hasnat Khan's smoking, "Diana knew how unhealthy smoking was and would never have let William get hooked," said her hairdresser Tess Rock. "She would have nagged him until he stopped."

The future king of England would spend the first twenty-four hours of the twenty-first century recovering. Two days later, during a visit to Wales with Papa and Harry, William was asked by a British Airways flight attendant if he had enjoyed his New Year's. "I had a really good night at a party," he replied. "I'm still hung-over from the millennium. I suppose everybody is!"

The statement did nothing to dispel Wills's emerging image as a party boy. Nor did the actions of eighteen-year-old Nicholas Knatchbull, great-grandson of Lord Mountbatten, a distant cousin of Wills's as well as perhaps his closest confidant at Eton. On New Year's Day the lanky Knatchbull, who had dyed his hair rainbow colors, was pulled over for speeding at 10 A.M. after leaving an all-night party with several friends.

Officers searched Knatchbull's Fiat Punto and, beneath the seat where his sixteen-year-old girlfriend was sitting, found a wooden box containing marijuana and Ecstasy. Knatch-bull's two male passengers, one seventeen and the other eighteen, were found to have drugs stuffed inside their socks. All knew William, and partied with him frequently.

Charles was "apoplectic," said a staffer. Knatchbull himself had been cleared, but the cache of drugs found in the car only under-scored the Prince of Wales's fear that his son was "running with the wrong crowd."

William, meantime, was not about to let another drug scandal spoil his vacation at the trendy Swiss ski resort Crans Montana. He and Papa had already clashed over his insis-tence on flying commercial instead of char-tering a plane. When Charles called him with news that more close friends of his were enmeshed in a drug scandal, William shrugged it off.

At the resort's Club Absolut, William—closely followed by two bodyguards—headed straight for leggy blond twenty-two-year-old barmaid Annaliese Asbjornsen and ordered a lemonade. He was only drinking lemonade, he told her, because "I had enough last night."

Wills then took Annaliese, clad in a sequined miniskirt and skintight black top, out onto the dance floor. "He has no inhibitions," she said. "He was thrusting his hips, gyrating, and clapping his hands above his head. He knew all the moves. He was great."

Then Gloria Gaynor's "I Will Survive" came on, and Wills sang along at the top of his voice. "When he held me for the slow dances," Annaliese said, "I could smell his expensive aftershave, and it was really sexy."

By now Wills's bodyguards had made themselves invisible, sitting a discreet distance away from Wills and his friends and the action on the dance floor. For the next three hours, they danced to hits like Lou Bega's "Mambo No. 5" and "Smooth" by Carlos Santana.

Then the song "Closer Than Close" began to play, and Prince William pulled Annaliese to him. "We were *very* close together. He wound his arms around my waist and whispered in my ear, 'You're gorgeous!' " They began kissing. "I knew his friends were watching us so I was well behaved." Perhaps, but the Swiss beauty thought Wills "might invite me back to the apartment where he was staying with friends." Instead, at 3 A.M. he departed the club with only his snowboarding friends—and exhausted bodyguards—in tow.

The next night, he honed in on another comely barmaid, nineteen-year-old Lydia Truglio. Again, they danced until the early morning hours. "He's a beautiful young man," Truglio said, "and in a few years he's going to be extraordinary." In the meantime, she added wistfully, "I'll have gorgeous memories."

If the prince seemed a tad fickle, the father of an Eton chum had a simple explanation: "William is aware of his sex appeal. He's very cool and out to pull girls."

If the heir to the throne always seemed to have his hands full, so did his security detail. Several bodyguards asked their superiors at

Scotland Yard for "clarification" of their role in light of drug taking in William's presence. "It's come about because of his liking for the high life," a Scotland Yard official told London's *Sunday Times*. "The junior officers... want some direction from above on what they are meant to do. If they are in this scenario and see drug users, do they stay, do they go, do they nick [arrest] them? Their primary role is to protect the individual. That means getting him away from physical harm. Drugs would include harm. So your immediate aim is to remove him from the threat and the potential embarrassment."

For the time being, Charles let it be known that he did not want William's bodyguards embarrassing his son by causing a scene. Their job was not to make drug busts, but to gently steer him away from any "unpleasantness."

Now that he was boldly pursuing the opposite sex, the bodyguards sometimes found themselves protecting William from himself. During one evening at London's K-Bar, William and yet another attractive blonde were having a steamy encounter in a dark corner—unaware that they were being taped on a security camera. A restaurant employee caught a glimpse of what was going on on the monitor, and rushed to tell one of the prince's bodyguards.

The detective dashed over to the other side of the room, tried to get William's attention from a distance, and when that didn't work, blurted out, "Please, sir, stop—you're being filmed!" With that, William and the mystery woman stopped what they were doing and hastily straightened their clothes. Neither seemed upset. "They were just laughing," said a patron at the club. "You know, it was 'Oops, looks like we got a little carried away. Oh, well... ' But the gentleman with the Prince looked quite concerned." The tape was confiscated by the shaken bodyguard.

These were not the only challenges facing the royal bodyguards. Fully aware that his mother's decision to forfeit royal protection had cost her her life, William usually tried to make the best of it. When someone at a club asked him about his bodyguards, Wills cracked, "I don't know what their game is, but they are constantly following me around."

In the past, Wills had only rarely tried to elude his minders. But now, in a spurt of teenage defiance, he made the occasional break for freedom. Typically, he would go into the front door of a building, then duck out the back and meet up with friends. More than once, his frantic bodyguards found him wandering with a group of friends on the High Street just outside the school, or across the river in Windsor.

It was more than just a game for the prince. "Now I understand why my mother gave up her detectives," he told a friend. "No one can stand being watched *all* the time. It's... suffocating."

Yet the sobering fact was that, as he approached his eighteenth birthday—the age of majority under British law—William was fast becoming the number one target of terrorists. According to government documents, Diana's eldest son was the subject of no fewer than twenty serious threats in the year 2000 alone—all of which resulted in stepped-up security surrounding Prince William.

Scotland Yard was particularly concerned about animal rights extremists incensed by William's foxhunting. When authorities discovered that the prince was marked for death by a terrorist group called the Hunt Retribution Squad (HRS), they immediately doubled security at Eton and informed the Prince of Wales. Charles knew to take the threat seriously. In the early 1990s, the HRS had launched a series of firebomb attacks across Great Britain on stores selling fur. Not only had Prince Charles already been targeted by the group, but on several occasions the HRS had allegedly tried to blow up one of the Royal Family's most avid foxhunters, Princess Anne.

Another fringe group, the Animal Liberation Front, also gave William's bodyguards cause for alarm. The previous November, freelance photographer Graham Hall had been kidnapped by the group, stripped, and tied to a chair with a burlap sack over his head. Then the initials of the group, ALF, were burned into his back in letters six inches high with a branding iron.

"It doesn't surprise me that Prince William has received death threats," said Ben Ponton, a spokesman for the nonviolent animal rights group Hunt Saboteurs. "They should be taken seriously because they have committed some pretty desperate acts."

The alarm bells went off again when members of the radical Movement Against the Monarchy, or MA'M (a takeoff on one of the acceptable forms of address for the Queen), demonstrated in London. One of the hood-wearing protesters turned out to be a schoolmate of William's. Scotland Yard raided the boy's rooms at Eton as well as his home, and discovered information concerning the prince's movements that could have been used by terrorists. They uncovered no evidence of an active kidnap plot, but again William's security detail was put on alert.

By contrast, Harry never gave his minders cause for concern. The only thing he may have found suffocating was the insatiable—and at times overwhelming—public appetite for his older brother. In March of 2000, when Harry was confirmed in the Anglican faith along with thirty of his Eton classmates, one paper billed it as his "rare day in the limelight." But even then it was William, posing for the cameras alongside Harry and their father, who stole the show. "You can't help but feel sorry for the lad," said one of the photographers assigned to cover the ceremony. "It's supposed to be his party, and he's smiling away, but all you hear is, 'William, over here!'"

Privately, William struggled to blend in. Around the same time as Harry's confirmation, Wills and several Eton students went on a field trip to northern England. In the town of Thornley, the prince and his friends dropped into the bar of the Crossways Hotel. It was karaoke night, as Wills leapt onto the stage and led three chums in an off-key but loud rendition of the Village People's "YMCA."

"He wasn't the best singer of the night, but there was rapturous applause," said Crossways owner John Hudson. "Everyone thought it was wonderful that this lad who's second in line to the throne could act like one of the crowd."

Such moments, so reminiscent of Diana's populist bent, belied William's stature as the world's most famous young man. "Willmania," as the British now called it, reached a frenzied peak on June 21, 2000, when the eldest son of the Prince and Princess of Wales turned eighteen. Fiji, the Falklands, the British Virgin Islands, the Cayman Islands, and several other British protectorates and Commonwealth countries issued stamps commemorating William's birthday. But even this seemingly innocuous gesture caused a stir when Earl Spencer complained that the stamps, personally approved by the Queen, included Charles but not Diana.

The Crown Agents Stamp Bureau, which issued the various commemorative sets, scrambled to explain that while William's mother was not included in the original set of thirty-five stamps, she would be shown playing with Baby Wills on a stamp being issued in Gibraltar.

"There is no hidden agenda," insisted Nigel Fordham, head of the Stamp Bureau. "Prince William is a young guy and he lost his mother in tragic circumstances. We did not want to put her and William on all the stamps because we could be accused of exploitation. Everyone is very sensitive about it and we want Prince William to feel really good about his eighteenth birthday."

William also helped design his personal coat of arms—paying tribute to his mother by restoring her insignia, three red scallop shells representing the Spencer clan. The red scallop shells had been part of Charles's coat of arms, but were dropped after the divorce.

Magazines issued special birthday editions, newspapers ran multipart series on the prince's coming-of-age, and the airwaves were filled with documentaries and tributes. Anticipating the onslaught, William, who had yet to be interviewed by anyone, agreed to answer questions submitted in writing by Peter Archer, longtime royal correspondent for the British Press Association.

Among other things, William "revealed" that he was still a fan of dance and pop music, that he enjoyed playing water polo, soccer, and rugby, that his dog Widgeon had given birth to eight puppies, and that he felt "uncomfortable" with all the media attention. He also confirmed that, before starting college, he would enjoy the traditional "gap year" of self-exploration so popular among upper-class Britons.

In his answers to Archer, however, Wills would not disclose how he coped with all the female attention ("In my own way. Trying to explain how might be counterproductive!"). Neither would Wills say anything about the girls he was dating ("I like to keep my private life private").

But he was, in fact, in the middle of a romance with seventeen-year-old Alexandra Knatchbull, the beguiling younger sister of his friend Nicholas and a favored godchild of Princess Diana. In another odd twist, Alexandra was also linked to Prince Charles. Her aunt Amanda was an old flame of Charles's: one year before he proposed to Diana, the Prince of Wales had asked Amanda Knatchbull to marry him—and she turned him down.

As for William and Alexandra: "They're completely potty for each other," said a friend of Alexandra's. When William showed up to watch a hockey game at Alexandra's school, St. Mary's, "all the girls were in awe of him," said one observer. "But he only has eyes for Alexandra."

Not exactly. At the same time, William also had eyes for Emilia d'Erlanger, the Devonshire beauty he had invited on his "Royal Love Boat" cruise. In early 2001, William brought Emilia to see Prince Charles on at least two occasions—a sign to Palace-watchers that their relationship was perhaps turning serious.

As the press engaged in frenzied speculation about how he would celebrate his coming-of-age and with whom, it quickly became clear that life for William would soon be very different. The press ban protecting his privacy was about to be lifted.

In the words of one reporter, "Now all bets are off."

The Palace strategy had been to launch a pre-emptive strike, offering up packaged glimpses of William in the hopes that that would suffice. In addition to Archer's written Q&A, there were still photographs and a brief film showing Prince William playing water polo and soccer, strolling through Eton's chapel cloisters, and in the kitchen whipping up paella with chicken, rice, garlic, and beans. (Cooking was only one of William's elective courses. Aware that his father was at last giving him the Kawasaki motorcycle he had been asking for, he also signed up for a class in motorcycle maintenance.)

To underscore his desire to be treated no differently than he had in the past, William insisted that he not be called His Royal Highness or addressed as "Sir," as protocol would have dictated once he turned eighteen. All these tactics—the interview, the color photographs, the short film, the official announcement that he wanted to be "just William"—were personally approved by William, Charles, and the Queen.

For the time being, William hunkered down at Eton, studying for his "A-levels," the British equivalent of final exams and SATs. That would be the excuse he used for missing the party to celebrate a royal flush of birthdays. Scheduled to coincide with Wills's actual birth date of June 21, the affair hosted at Windsor Castle by Queen Elizabeth celebrated five milestone birthdays occurring in the year 2000. Princess Margaret was turning seventy, Princess Anne fifty, and Prince Andrew forty. But the stars of the evening were to have been the Queen Mother, celebrating her one hundredth birthday on August 4, and, of course, William.

Not only did the Queen Mother join the seven hundred guests, but so did the Duchess of York. It marked the first time Fergie had been invited to a royal function in three years. Prince Charles, sans his persona non grata mistress, pulled up behind the wheel of a sports car, still wearing his polo togs. Harry also managed to make an appearance. But, despite the fact that Windsor was just a seven-minute walk away, William did not attend. Instead he stayed hunched over his books at Manor House, studying for his art history exam the next day.

Words like "headstrong" and "stubborn" were now being used in Palace circles to describe William, who resisted all attempts by the "men in gray" to control him. He wanted nothing less for Harry, at times encouraging his younger brother to buck the system with him.

The young princes did not have to defy the Palace to skip the next high-profile event they had been asked to attend. On what would

have been Diana's thirty-ninth birthday—
July 1, 2000—a new three-million-dollar children's playground was dedicated in the
Princess's honor within sight of Kensington
Palace. The playground, where Diana used to
take her children, had originally been paid for
in 1909 by another lover of children, *Peter Pan*
creator J. M. Barrie. Now it featured a pirate
ship, rope swings, and wigwams as part of its
never-never land theme.

Diana's friends and family were not surprised
that both the Queen and Prince Charles chose
not to attend the opening of the Princess
Diana Playground—her first memorial in
London. But they were "shocked," in the
words of one, that William and Harry also failed
to show.

"Sometimes I think they just want to forget
about her," Diana's friend Wayne Sleep said
of the entire Royal Family. "It's almost as if
she never existed." Indeed, although polls
showed that an overwhelming number of her
subjects wanted a statue to be built in London
to honor Diana, the Queen resisted the idea.
Meantime, the Queen Mother attended the
unveiling of a bust in her own likeness, Prince
Charles presided over the dedication of a
plaque in honor of his uncle, Lord Mountbatten, and at the London Zoo, Queen Elizabeth II proudly unveiled a statue of a dung
beetle.

But there was no satisfactory explanation for
the absence of Diana's own sons at the dedication of her memorial. "You wonder if

they've been brainwashed," said a former member of Diana's staff. "They love their mother, obviously. But Prince Charles or the Queen must have led them to believe that it just wasn't very important. The only other possibility is that they just can't go back to Kensington Palace. Perhaps it's just too painful for them."

Only weeks after skipping his own official birthday party and the dedication of the Princess Diana memorial playground, William convinced Harry to forgo another party for the Queen Mother—this one her one hundredth birthday gala pageant—to go rock climbing in England's Lake District. "They didn't go because they didn't *want* to go," said a Palace staffer. "It's basically as simple as that."

William, who intended to major in art history, avoided both Oxford and Cambridge in favor of St. Andrew's University in Scotland. The Queen had mentioned to her grandson over tea at Windsor that a Scottish school might be a good idea. Given the rise of Scottish nationalism, such a move could only serve to strengthen the ties binding Scotland to England—and shore up the monarchy's position in the process. But Buckingham Palace was quick to deny that Her Majesty had urged William to attend St. Andrew's for political reasons. "It was a personal decision for William," said a Palace spokesman. "He was not forced into anything."

Indeed, St. Andrew's probably owed its good fortune to Andrew Gailey, William's housemaster and mentor at Eton, and a St. Andrew's alumnus. Without fanfare, Gailey had taken William on a guided tour of the university only weeks before the prince announced his decision to enroll there.

Beyond its sterling academic reputation, the Gailey connection, and the fact that neither the Windsors nor the Spencers had championed it, William had other reasons for choosing St. Andrew's. His idyllic summers at Balmoral had instilled in him an enduring love of Scotland and its people. With a student body of six thousand, St. Andrew's had a distinctive small-college feel. And, perhaps more than any other top-rated university in the United Kingdom, "St. Randy's" had a well-deserved reputation as an anything-goes party school.

With only one theater (the New Picture House) and twenty-two pubs (more per capita than any other town in Scotland), student life at St. Andrew's, observed journalist Charlotte Edwards, "is all about getting drunk." Old Etonian Crispin Dyer, a student at the university, agreed. "At St. Andrew's," Dyer said, "there's really nothing to do *except* get lashed."

One time-honored St. Andrew's activity for "freshers" (freshmen) is the Student Run, which involves consuming vast quantities of liquor at each of five pubs. As they make their way from one pub to the next, students stop to urinate through the mail slots of unfortunate homeowners. It is common practice among female freshers to write the names of their residence halls on their forearms, so that if they do pass out they will be helped home.

No sooner had William announced his decision to attend St. Andrew's than the university was flooded with applications from both sides of the Atlantic—a 44 percent increase over the previous year. Not surprisingly, 90 percent of the applicants were women. "We all know what the girls are like up here," said nineteen-year-old St. Andrew's student Gemma Duncan. "They'll be all over him. They will all try and kiss him or get an item of his clothing, or just touch him..."

They would have to wait a year. In what would be a continuing effort to broaden his horizons while testing himself physically, William flew secretly to the tiny Central American country of Belize to train with a unit of the Welsh Guards. Braving scorpions, poisonous snakes, and wild boars along with 150 soldiers, William trekked through steaming jungles and slept on a hammock covered with mosquito netting.

William was out of phone contact in Belize when his father e-mailed him the results of his final exams using an army computer link. William received an A in geography, a B in art history, and a C in biology—scores that nevertheless put him in the top 7 percent of all British students taking the tests.

As he would with all of his adventures, William found his stint with the Welsh Guards in Belize "exhilarating." Before long, he would be spending three weeks snorkeling and scuba diving on Rodriguez Island in the Indian Ocean as part of the Royal Geographical Society's marine observation program.

Staying in a forty-dollar-a-night tin-roofed lodge with no television, no telephone, and no bedroom door—only a cotton curtain hung over the doorway—the prince managed to remain relatively anonymous. Housekeeper Michelette Eduard and her sister-in-law Simone served the tall blond English boy the same breakfast every morning—eggs, ham, cheese, beans, toast, and coffee—without ever realizing who he was. "We had no idea it was Prince William," Michelette said. "Then, after people started talking about him being on the island, we realized we had been looking after him."

William's only companion on the trip was Mark ("Marco") Dyer, the former Welsh Guards officer and onetime aide to Prince Charles who had become one of William's closest aides and confidants. It was Dyer who, along with Tiggy Legge-Bourke, had organized William and Harry's African adventure a year earlier. On Rodriguez Island, Dyer motorbiked, swam, and fished with his royal friend. His most vivid memory of the trip, however, would be of William, clad in T-shirt, shorts, and sandals, patiently teaching locals the finer points of rugby.

Harry, meantime, emerged from his brother's shadow to mark his sixteenth birthday. Now ranking comfortably as the second-tallest member of the Royal Family at an even six feet, Harry was proving to be as easygoing as his brother was obstinate. "William can be quite headstrong if he's asked to do something he doesn't want to do, even by his father," a royal aide told the *Daily Telegraph*. "But Harry will generally shrug his shoulders and cheerfully get on with it."

Harry celebrated his sixteenth by making his first-ever visit to a pub frequented by the likes of Madonna and Brad Pitt, the Ifield in Chelsea. After washing down a lunch of crispy duck salad, roast beef, and bread-and-butter pudding with an alcohol-free energy drink called Red Bull, Harry complimented the owner. "It was lovely," he told Ed Bains. "I'll tell my grandmother to pop in next time she's in the area!"

In fact, Granny much preferred the company of both Harry and William to that of her own son. Prince Charles, conceded one of his closest aides, "is a world-class, wall-to-wall whinger"—the English phrase for whiner. Neither of his sons had, apparently, inherited that unfortunate trait.

Yet William was not above striking back when he felt someone he loved had been unfairly attacked. On September 29, 2000, he held what amounted to his first press conference outside Highgrove. Wearing a beige Burberry crew-neck sweater and jeans, his father at his side, William blasted a new tell-all book by Diana's senior aide P. D. Jephson.

In *Shadows of a Princess,* Jephson painted an

unflattering portrait of Mummy as an insecure, unstable, shrewd, and often ruthless manipulator. Diana, Jephson wrote of his former boss, "combined a radiant smile with a knife between the shoulder blades."

William, who claimed he was "mortified" when he read excerpts from the book in the *Sunday Times* of London, told his father he had to speak out. Harry agreed. "Of course, Harry and I are both quite upset about it," he said, eyes narrowing, "that our mother's trust has been betrayed and that even now she is still being exploited. But, um, I don't really want to say any more than that."

That he said that much seemed remarkable. So, too, was the sound of William's voice; the press embargo had worked so well that this marked the first time the public actually heard the Prince speak. His clipped, upper-class speech pattern was something of a dulcet cross between the actor Hugh Grant and his own father.

Combining the poise and confidence of a future king with an adolescent slouch and tendency to bite his lower lip, Wills went on to talk about plans for his "gap year." Prince Charles had shot down William's original proposal—to play polo in Argentina—as too "elitist." Then he planned to work as a volunteer on an ecological project in the Brazilian rain forest—until the project's director insisted he could not bring along his five bodyguards.

Now William could reveal where he would be heading: to the remote Chilean province of Patagonia, where he would spend ten weeks working alongside 110 other volunteers aged seventeen to twenty-five under the auspices of a nonprofit group called Raleigh International. Among the volunteers would be more than two dozen recovering drug addicts, juvenile offenders, and homeless youngsters who signed up through At-Risk, a program geared to helping Britain's "socially excluded" young people.

"I thought this was a way of trying to help people out," William explained, "and meeting a whole range of people from different countries, and at the same time trying to help people in the remote areas of Chile." He had organized a water polo match to raise eight thousand dollars for his trip, but reporters asked if his father had "chipped in."

"He might have helped slightly," William answered with a grin.

When the laughter of the press subsided, Charles blurted, "I chip in all the bloody time!"

As for what he planned to do after he returned from Chile, "The rest of my plans are not sorted," William said coyly. "I'm hugely disorganized."

Aware of his audience and not above politicking, William took the time to praise the press for the restraint they had shown since the death of Diana. "I just want to enjoy my gap year and hope that goes well," he said. "So far, thanks to all of you, it has gone very well." As for his treatment at Eton: "I was a bit anxious about how it was going to turn out, but thanks to everyone it really has been brilliant. The whole of Eton made a big difference with everyone not trying to sort of snap a picture every time I was walking around the streets. I hope," he added, "it just continues for Harry as well..."

Her Majesty, meanwhile, was glued to her television set at Buckingham Palace. "She was very pleased with her grandson's performance," said a Palace spokesman, "very pleased indeed." No more so than Papa. Holding the press conference was "absolutely Prince William's decision," said Prince Charles's spokeswoman Colleen Harris. "And those were his words."

Once again the press—and the public—rallied behind Diana and her boys. OUR MOTHER WAS BETRAYED, SAYS WILLIAM, screamed the front-page headline in the *Times* of London. The *Sun* blared, WILLS FURY AT TRAITOR, while WILLIAM'S FURY OVER BETRAYAL was splashed across the front page of the *Daily Mail*. "Now William could look forward rather than back," wrote Simon de Bruxelles in the *Times*. "The score was settled."

Satisfied that he had defended his mother's memory—and defended it well—William packed some last-minute personal items for the trip. The most important: a small framed photo of his mother that, like Prince Charles with his ubiquitous teddy bear, Wills carried everywhere with him.

The prince flew to Santiago on October 1,

then boarded a bus for the two-day trip to Coihaique, in southern Chile. From there they trekked to Tortel, a tiny village on the coast of Chile. He and fifteen other workers slept on the cold floor of an old nursery with a leaky roof. They shared a single working toilet. "The living conditions here," he said in a masterpiece of understatement, "aren't exactly what I'm used to. You share everything with everyone. I found it very difficult... because I am a very private person. But I learned to deal with it."

As soon as he arrived, Prince William was given the same warm welcome as every other recruit. "I told him off in the first ten minutes for being lazy," said one of his supervisors. "After that, he got on with it. You can trust him to do a job."

Over the next three and a half months, he painted houses, worked as a carpenter, chopped wood, scoured toilets, and tutored local schoolchildren. "I did Operation Raleigh not because I wanted to find myself," he explained, "but because you're actually making a difference in other people's lives. I didn't want to just sit around and get a job back in London."

Impressed with his utter lack of pretense, the other young volunteers quickly warmed to the young royal. "Even though we're from different backgrounds," said Tom Kelly, "it made me realize that everyone is human. He's been through some tough times as well."

In addition to hard labor, there was plenty of time for adventure—like tracking a rare

Heruemel deer in the Tamango National Reserve and kayaking through the majestic Patagonian fjords. At one point, William and several fellow kayakers were stranded on the beach during a freak storm. "The wind whipped up into a storm," he recalled. "The tents were flapping around so violently that we thought they were going to blow away. Everything was soaked through. It was quite demoralizing."

But there were light moments as well. As a means of teaching English to the local children, William asked each pupil to draw an animal that started with the first letter of his or her name. "My name is William," he wrote on the blackboard, using the nickname Mummy had given him. "William Wombat." The kids dissolved in giggles. From that point on—whether he was hoisting them up on his shoulders, playing patty-cake, or zipping his parka over his head and playing monster—Prince William was the children's favorite.

For William, the most memorable child in the group may have been six-year-old Alejandro Heredia, who barked orders to the prince as he rode on his shoulders. Alejandro used prods, slaps, and the occasional tug of the royal scalp to point his mount in the desired direction. "This one's the worst," Wills said of Alejandro. "So bossy! He treats me like a horse... Being with the children is so funny," he continued. "Even if they are pulling your hair out, they're still good for a laugh."

Wills also took the opportunity to make

his debut as a radio deejay, albeit for the tiny Tortel station. "Hello all you groove jets out there," William purred into the microphone. "This is 'Tortel Love' and we are in the mood for some real groovin' here…"

The prince also tried his hand in the kitchen, rising at 6:15 A.M. to make porridge for the group. The result, by his own admission, was "revolting. Ugh! This is absolutely hideous. Oh, that is foul. Urgh!" Another student took one look at the steaming concoction and asked if he wasn't "embarrassed" by it.

"Yes," William replied. "I'm so embarrassed about it, I don't know what I'm going to do. I might shoot myself this afternoon."

Raleigh staffer Marie Wright was impressed by Wills's dedication—and his endearing talent for self-deprecation. The prince, Wright said, "struck a balance between working hard, having fun, and taking on the team spirit."

Given their close proximity to one another, it was no surprise that the volunteers quickly bonded. "It didn't matter which social group you came from," At-Risk volunteer Diane Tucker recalled of her time in Patagonia. "Everyone mixed and everyone got on. There were lots of little romances, about twenty-five percent of the people who went had relationships out there."

Rumors of princely romance abounded. On more than one occasion, William's bodyguards reportedly looked the other way while he was locked in a passionate embrace with a female volunteer. During the weeks they lived in a tent city, William was seen entering a young woman's tent at night and leaving the next morning. Once he supposedly spent the night with two women—"one blonde and one brunette," said another volunteer. "There's been a lot of bed hopping going on."

One girl who caught the prince's eye was a California beauty named Sarah, who belonged to a church group doing volunteer work in the region. William and Sarah, a San Diego native, spent hours walking hand in hand or just talking in Wills's tent. They exchanged phone numbers and e-mail addresses when she left, and William confessed to one of the other volunteers that he was smitten. When the volunteer asked if he would ever consider marrying someone who wasn't English, William shrugged. "I rather like American girls," William said. "I can easily see myself marrying one. Why not?" What was he looking for in a young lady? "She's got to be gorgeous, of course. She's got to be brilliant. And she's got to have a marvelous laugh..."

Most of William's dalliances seemed to be with tall, leggy, "fit" (a British term for "attractive") blondes who sometimes bore a more than passing resemblance to Princess Diana. The Princess of Wales was also known for her explosive, window-rattling laugh.

It seemed unlikely to those who knew him that William would settle down early. He confided to one friend at Eton that his parents' turbulent marriage left him with serious doubts about the institution. "People should never go into it," he mused, "unless they are absolutely sure they've found the one for them. And they should never *think* about having children unless they are certain of this. Far too many people are parents who should never have gotten married in the first place, you know."

Meantime, William continued to earn his growing reputation among fellow volunteers as a "one-man wrecking crew among the girls." After kicking a soccer ball around with the prince, aspiring hairdresser Claire Flood, nineteen, cozied up to Wills by the campfire. After several glasses of wine, she suddenly heard herself asking the future king if he was a virgin. For all his girl-chasing, William was not above being embarrassed by a tactless remark. "He didn't answer my question," Flood said. "He just turned red!"

According to Kevin Mullen, a reformed heroin addict who was also a volunteer, William made a brazen play for his girlfriend at a party to mark the end of their stint. At the bar where the party was held, "Wills had a few drinks," Mullen said. "He was dirty-dancing with a lot of the girls and making a spectacle of himself. The girls didn't mind because I think they liked him."

It was only when Wills began bumping and grinding with Mullen's girlfriend, Sasha Hashim, that Mullen ran up to the prince and began shouting at him. "Let's just say words were exchanged," Mullen recalled. "It was nothing nasty, because he and I get along very well. But I don't care if you are the future king—you don't start messing with other people's girlfriends."

Hashim conceded that "Kevin can be very possessive and he yelled at Will. I was really embarrassed! Luckily, Will was okay about it. He knew what Kevin could be like."

William simply laughed it off. "When he tried to move in on my girl," Mullen said, "I had to lay down some rules. But Wills is good fun. He's a joker and popular with everyone."

Patricia Sandoval, a waitress at the bar, was simply delighted to see Diana's son enjoying himself. "He was so relaxed and having so much fun," Sandoval said. "His mom would have been proud."

And, given what was happening back in the U.K., very worried. Not long after he left for Chile, it was discovered that the "Real IRA"—a hard-core breakaway group from the mainstream IRA—had targeted William for assassination.

The Real IRA had already shown what it was capable of in August of 1998, when it planted a bomb in the sleepy Ulster market town of Omagh. Twenty-eight people, mostly women and children, were killed. Another two hundred were seriously injured.

Now the terrorist group was using its Internet Web page, accessible only by use of a password, to disclose details concerning security measures to protect William at St. Andrew's. The site not only told where the prince and his bodyguards would be staying—a closely guarded government secret—but it also provided the precise location of the security system being installed in William's quarters. The Real IRA Web site went on to provide precise details concerning those places on and around the St. Andrew's campus where William could be "overlooked at extremely accurate range."

As soon as authorities learned of the Web site's existence, they moved to shut it down. But that did little to quell mounting fears for William's safety. No one was more anxious than Charles, who knew all too well what the IRA and its splinter groups were capable of. The Prince of Wales's beloved great-uncle Lord Louis Mountbatten and two others (including Mountbatten's fourteen-year-old grandson) were killed when the IRA blew up the family's fishing boat in 1979.

Lining up behind the Real IRA was yet another extremist organization: the English-hating Scottish Separatist Group (SSG). The SSG Web site carried the message: "There is nil security at the Yooni [university] and you can wander in and out as you please. Anyone could shoot the fucker any time they wanted."

Equally disturbing were SSG e-mails to the IRA intercepted by Scotland Yard. "In the event that the prince is permitted to attend St. Andrew's," one read, "the SSG recognizes it is inevitable some people will turn to extreme violence against him personally." Scotland Yard's response: to dispatch undercover agents posing as undergraduates to spy on students and faculty members.

After William returned to England in December, there was yet another security scare. This time MI5, Britain's intelligence agency, conducted an electronic sweep of the St. Andrew's dormitory room where William eventually planned to stay and discovered electronic listening devices. All fingers pointed to the Real IRA—until those in charge of royal security admitted they had planted the bugs at St. Andrew's as a means of ensuring the student prince's safety.

William, incensed at this flagrant breach of his privacy, confronted Papa. Reminded of Diana's infamous "Squidgygate" tapes and how his own intimate—and hugely embarrassing—conversations with Camilla had been taped, Charles wasted no time apologizing.

Now that her uncle was President of the United States, William stepped up his steamy correspondence with *Vogue* model Lauren Bush. Wills admitted to one pal that he had a "serious crush" on Lauren, who was two years his junior. A friend of Lauren's in Texas described the e-mails as "very flirty and quite sexy and the letters quite intimate. It would be fair to say they got a bit carried away with the fun of it all." But after two years, it remained to be seen when the future king and the American beauty would actually meet, and if their e-mail relationship could be sustained person-to-person.

In another ironic turn, William made his first official public engagement on February 7, 2001, when he attended the tenth anniversary of the Press Complaints Commission. "This is Prince William's way of saying thank you to all newspapers," said a St. James's spokesman, "for respecting his privacy and Prince Harry's privacy while he was at Eton and during the first part of his gap year." In an oxymoronic turn of phrase, William also praised the Press Complaints Commission for "enforcing self-regulation." The commission did just that when it censured a British magazine called *OK!* for publishing innocuous but unauthorized photos of William in Chile taken with a telephoto lens.

But the gala evening was more than a chance for William to court the media: it would mark the first time Prince Charles, his controversial mistress, and his elder son appeared together at the same public event (Harry remained at Eton, where he was immersed in his studies). It was certainly the strangest of settings for such an event—a room crammed with 550 guests, most of whom were journalists.

The "joint" appearance still had all the earmarks of a covert operation, however. The Queen had made it clear to Charles that she did not want either William or Harry to be seen publicly with Camilla. Granny grudgingly accepted the fact that there was little she could do to keep her fifty-one-year-old son from being seen with his lover. But when it came to her grandsons, Elizabeth was unwavering in her resolve. "Prince William and Prince Harry must never be photographed with her," she declared. *"Never."*

To comply with Her Majesty's wishes,

Charles and William arrived together at Somerset House in Central London, then split up to work the room. With the explicit understanding that everything said at the party was off the record, Wills regaled guests with stories of his adventure in Chile and his current gap-year job working on a farm in southwest England. "William moved among the guests," Richard Kay observed, "sipping a glass of cold Chablis, and with each step gaining in confidence."

He was confident enough to approach Lady Victoria Hervey, the renegade aristocrat who posed topless for *GQ* magazine, and ask for her phone number and e-mail address. Six-foot-tall Lady Victoria, who was wearing skintight leather pants, with a bare midriff, had shocked London society by showing up at one affair in a blouse that exposed her breasts. Her reputation grew when she appeared at a charity ball dressed as a "naughty nurse."

"He's terrific," allowed Lady Victoria, "but I think he's too young for me... I told William to be careful, especially of older girls. I wish I was a bit younger..."

Camilla, meanwhile, arrived fifteen minutes after the princes, and entered at the opposite end of the room. There she remained without ever being in proximity of either Charles or William. Ninety minutes later, William and his father left. "It was brilliant," Wills said of the evening. Half an hour after that, informed that the princes had departed, Camilla made her exit.

As Camilla continued to insinuate herself into the lives of the princes, it seemed to many that the Windsors were going out of their way to show contempt for Diana's memory. In March 2001, both William and Harry were invited to the dedication of France's official memorial to their mother—the Diana Garden and Nature Center in Paris. Volunteers who had labored for more than a year on the center were profoundly insulted when not a single representative of the Royal Family attended the ceremony—not even William or Harry.

This time, however, William and Harry had not been made aware of the ceremony in Paris honoring their mother. When they learned that no one representing the Royal Family had been at the Paris dedication, the brothers complained bitterly to Papa. "Shouldn't *someone* have gone," William asked, "out of respect for Mummy?"

There would be other memorials to Diana. After much debate the boys approved a plan to build a fountain in her memory along the seven-mile-long Diana Memorial Walkway meandering from Westminster Abbey to Kensington Palace. The walkway was to be marked by seventy plaques featuring an English rose.

But none of these, in her sons' eyes, would be the most fitting memorial to their mother. William and Harry both told friends they wished to do something "meaningful" with their lives. "My mother was the people's princess," William said. "I wish to be the people's king."

With his brief stint as a farm worker behind

him, William now faced a new adventure. In mid-March, William left for a four-month stint mending fences, digging trenches, and tracking wildlife on game preserves in southern Africa. If anything, conditions there were even more taxing than they had been in Chile. There was no plumbing; the future king made do with a hole in the ground and, for showering, a canvas bucket slung overhead. He also learned to cope with the hyenas, monkeys, vipers, rodents, and every imaginable kind of oversized insect that invaded the camps on a regular basis. Yet the payoff was experiencing firsthand a part of the world one naturalist described as "a secret Eden." Being there, Charles once recalled of his first extended trip to Africa, was "like a wonderful dream."

Yet no journey would ever stir more emotions than the one Diana's sons made secretly every year—before the July 1 date that marked both their mother's birthday and the annual opening of Althorp to the public. They would make the trip without their father. Incredibly, in the four years since Diana's funeral he had not visited her grave a single time.

Originally, only two employees were kept on the Spencer payroll to tend Althorp's extensive gardens—men armed with sticks whose main job was to prevent cattle from poking their horns through the ground-floor windows of the manse. Now, centuries later, the stone stables had been transformed into a museum honoring the life of Diana, complete with café and gift shop. The museum's centerpiece: Diana's spectacular bridal gown. And where once only two gardeners worked the estate, there was now a small army of workers toiling to maintain one of the most extensive privately owned gardens in England.

On the day of Diana's funeral, thousands had lined the M1 highway to shower her hearse with flowers as it made the ninety-minute journey from London to Althorp—so many flowers, in fact, that the driver had to use his windshield wipers to see. Motorists traveling on the opposite direction pulled their cars off to the side of the road and clambered over the center guardrail to catch one last glimpse of her; flowers rained down from the overpasses. A placard placed over an M1 sign read, "We miss you, Queen of Hearts."

But now there were no crowds, no flowers raining down on the boys as they made their way anonymously along the same route. Without fanfare, Althorp's black iron gates—sixty feet wide and tipped with gold—swung open to welcome the princes. Ringed by miles of stone walls, the fifteen-thousand-acre estate had been a Spencer family refuge for five centuries. Earl Spencer greeted his nephews at Althorp House, the sprawling Tudor mansion filled with some of Europe's greatest art treasures, and together they walked through the formal gardens toward the ornamental lake called the Round Oval.

Wreathed with majestic oaks and pines, the Round Oval was situated a few hundred yards to the north of the manor, and seemed both part of and apart from the rest of Althorp. At its northern rim was "the Temple," a pillared, terra-cotta-colored, neoclassical shrine to the late princess. "DIANA" was carved in large letters across the edifice, bordered by the years of her birth (1961) and death (1997). Topped by a cross, the memorial had at its center a large carved marble cameo of Diana, flanked by quotations from Earl Spencer's stirring eulogy. During the summer months, hundreds of thousands would come to take snapshots and, not infrequently, be overcome with emotion.

But today no one was there—only the young princes. They were led to a small wooden boat and, at their insistence, rowed themselves to the tiny island. Just as flowers engulfed all of London in the days surrounding the Princess's funeral, Diana's island had been carpeted with roses, carnations, tulips, peonies, daisies, daffodils, lilies, and mums— bouquets left at the gates of Althorp by grieving strangers. Earl Spencer, who made the decision to have them brought here to his sister's grave site, strolled ankle-deep through a surreal tide of yellows, violets, pinks, and reds.

Now, however, only a few flowers from loved ones graced the site. There was a monument to Diana on the island—a Grecian urn designed by Edward Bulner—but it was already engulfed in wild vegetation. In striking contrast to Althorp's manicured formal gardens, Diana's final resting place was dense with ancient trees, wild vines, and thick underbrush. It was untamed, much like the lady herself. Here—away from the tumult, expectations, and incursions of the outside world—the brothers bowed their heads. The only sound was the rustling of the wind in the trees as they said a silent prayer for Mummy.

So the world watched and waited as Diana's boys grew into the men she would never know. On that journey, they would be guided first and foremost by two people: a father seeking to marry the mistress who destroyed their mother's marriage and a grandmother who, now that the furor surrounding Diana's death had dimmed, had little interest in honoring her memory.

"I think he can make the whole thing work," one of Prince Charles's closest friends said of William. "He's a much tougher character than his father and, because of Diana, he'll have the people with him. He's incredibly nice, you know." Concurred an ex-courtier: "He seems to know exactly where he is going. He is a bright boy who knows what he wants, assertive but cool at the same time. It is already very clear that he will have a purpose in life that relates to the real world as well as his birthright of the throne."

Yet nagging doubts remained. Would Diana's sons take into adulthood the lessons she taught—lessons that stressed warmth over chilly indifference, humor over implacable stuffiness, change over soul-killing stagnation? Or would the boys succumb to the deadening legacy of their Windsor forebears?

In life, Princess Diana planned to guide her sons as they carried out the revolution she had begun. In death, the global outpouring of grief that flooded London with flowers and tears threatened to drown tired old institutions—leaving in their place a people's monarch fully in tune with the times.

But with the passage of time, William and Harry were indoctrinated more and more in the ways of the Windsors, and Diana's dream began to fade. To be sure, the princes did not always participate in public ceremonies honoring their mother, preferring instead to pay tribute in more concrete ways: by rebuilding villages in the most remote, poverty-stricken regions of Chile, by being dunked thirty times for charity and laughing about it, by connecting with ordinary people the way their mother—and no other royal—could.

As what would have been Princess Diana's fortieth birthday arrived in the summer of 2001, there was something everyone could be sure of. Whether son, husband, or father—whether prince or king—William and Harry will remain one thing above all others. They will always be Diana's Boys.

Acknowledgments

W hen *The Day Diana Died* was published on the first anniversary of Diana's death, it made headlines on both sides of the Atlantic. Readers were stunned to learn that the Queen had forced Diana's sons to attend church only hours after hearing of their mother's death, but also pleasantly surprised to discover that Charles—long thought to be a cold and uncaring parent—had not only cried with his sons over Diana's death, but battled the Palace to ensure that the boys' mother would have a funeral befitting her status as the "People's Princess."

From my perspective as the author of three books on the Kennedy dynasty—*Jack and Jackie, Jackie After Jack,* and *The Day John Died*—Diana's wish that her sons handle being in the spotlight with the same grace as John Kennedy Jr. seemed especially poignant.

This marks my seventh book with the consummate professionals at William Morrow. I am blessed to have as my editor Betty Kelly, who brought the same insight and passionate commitment to *Diana's Boys* that she did to *The Day Diana Died* and *The Day John Died.* I also owe a debt of gratitude to the entire team

at Morrow and HarperCollins, particularly Jane
Friedman, Cathy Hemming, Michael Morrison,
Laurie Rippon, Lisa Gallagher, Chris Goff,
Beth Silfin, Richard Aquan, Brad Foltz, Rome
Quezada, Michele Corallo, Kim Lewis, Betty
Lew, Christine Tanigawa, Debbie Stier, and
Camille McDuffie of Goldberg-McDuffie
Communications.

Ellen Levine, incomparable literary agent
and steadfast friend for nearly twenty years,
may tire of reading these words of praise
book after book—but they are no less sin-
cere now than they were twenty books ago. Ellen
surrounds herself with the best, and once
again I owe a debt of gratitude to her tal-
ented colleagues Diana Finch and Louise
Quayle.

My parents, Jeanette and Edward Andersen,
continue to prove that theirs was indeed the
greatest generation. My daughter Kelly and
her big sister Kate, who studied political science at Oxford University while I wrote this
book, are a constant source of wonder to me.
So is Valerie, my wife of nearly thirty years—
generous of spirit and still the cleverest person
I know.

Additional thanks to Peter Archer, Dr. Frédéric
Mailliez, Richard Greene, Thierry Meresse,
Janet Jenkins, Richard Kay, Béatrice Humbert,
Jeanne Lecorcher, Rachel Whitburn, Lady
Elsa Bowker, Claude Garreck, Andrew Gailey,
Mark Butt, Delissa Needham, Alan Hamilton,

Remi Gaston-Dreyfus, Peter Allen, Penny Russell-Smith, Grigori Rassinier, Andy Radford, Michelle Lapautre, Jeanette Peterson, the Countess of Romanones, Tom Corby, Paula Dranov, Jean Chapin, Ezra Zilkha, Fred Hauptfuhrer, Patrick Demarchelier, Jessica Hogan, Rosemary McClure, Elizabeth d'Erlanger, Elizabeth Whiddett, Tom Freeman, Michael Shulman, Cathy Cesario Tardosky, Valerie Wimmer, Joy Wansley, Lawrence R. Mulligan, Mary Beth Whelan, Vivian Simon, Gered Mankowitz, Tobias Markowitz, Ray Whelan Jr., John Marion, Charles Furneaux, Dudley Freeman, Steve Stylandoudis, Betsy Loth, David McGough, Vincent Martin, Deborah Eisenman, Norman Currie, Julie Graham, Yvette Reyes, Bob Cosenza, Ian Walde, Dawn Conchie, Kevin Lamarque, Manuel Ribeiro, David Bergeron, Connie Erickson, Tamar Salibian, Gary Gunderson, Stefano Rellandini, John Stillwell, Djamilla Cochran, Alain-Philippe Feutre, James Price, Michael Crabtree, Wolfgang Rattay, Tasha Hanna, Mick Magsino, Marcel Turgot, Francis Specker, Chris Helgren, Pitié-Salpêtrière Hospital, SAMU, the Gunn Memorial Library, the New York Public Library, the Silas Bronson Library, the BBC, Channel Four Television Ltd., the Litchfield Library, Kensington Palace, the New Milford Library, Brown's Hotel, Althorp, the Lansdowne Club, the Reform Club, the London Library, the Press Association, Buckingham Gate, the Southbury Public Library, the

Brookfield Library, the Boston Public Library, the Ritz Hotel, the *Times* of London, the Woodbury Library, the Bancroft Library of the University of California at Berkeley, Archive Photos, Corbis, Globe Photos, Corbis-Sygma, AP Wide World, Rex, Retna, Sipa, Gamma Liaison, Big Pictures U.S.A., Reuters, the Associated Press, Graphictype, and Design to Printing.

Source Notes

The following chapter notes are designed to give a general view of the sources drawn upon in preparing *Diana's Boys,* but they are by no means all-inclusive. Understandably, certain key sources at Buckingham Palace as well as friends and acquaintances of the Royal Family agreed to cooperate in the writing of this book only if they were assured that their names would not be mentioned. Therefore, I have respected the wishes of those interview subjects who wished to remain anonymous and have not listed them, either here or elsewhere in the text. Obviously, there were also thousands of news reports and articles concerning William and Harry published in the fifteen years prior to their mother's fatal accident—which in itself may have generated more news coverage than any single event in modern history. These reports on the boys appeared in such publications as the *New York Times*, the *Washington Post*, the *Sunday Times* of London, the *Wall Street Journal*, the *Boston Globe*, the *Los Angeles Times*, *The New Yorker*, the *Daily Mail*, *Vanity Fair*, *Time*, *Life*, *Newsweek*, *Paris Match*, *Le Monde*, *U.S. News & World Report*, *The Times* of London, the *Guardian*, and the *Economist*, and were carried on the Associated Press, Knight-Ridder, Gannett, and Reuters wires.

Chapters 1 and 2

Interview subjects included Dr. Frédéric Mailliez, Jeanne Lecorcher, Thierry Meresse, Béatrice Humbert, Peter Archer, the Countess of Romanones, Mark Butt, Richard Kay, Claude Garreck, Josy Duclos, Remi Gaston-Dreyfus, Peter Allen, Miriam Lefort, Pierre Suu, Steve Stylandoudis, Vincent Martin, the Reverend Canon Andy Radford. Published sources included "The Princes' Final Farewell," *Sunday Times*, September 7, 1997; "Farewell, Diana," *Newsweek*, September 15, 1997; "The Nation Unites Against Tradition," *The Observer* (London), September 7, 1997; Annick Cojean, "The Final Interview," *Le Monde*, August 27, 1997; John Simpson, "Goodbye England's Rose: A Nation Says Farewell," *Sunday Telegraph*, September 7, 1997; Joe Chidley, "From the Heart,"

Macleans, September 15, 1997; "Lady Dies," *Liberation,* September 1, 1997; "Driver Was Drunk," *Le Monde,* September 3, 1997; "Charles Escorts Diana Back to a Grieving Britain," *New York Times,* September 1, 1997; Andrew Morton, *Diana: Her True Story* (New York: Simon & Schuster, 1997); Pascal Palmer, "I Gave Diana Last Rites," *The Mirror,* October 23, 1997; "Flashback to the Accident," *Liberation,* September 2, 1997; Howard Chua-Eoan, Steve Wulf, Jeffrey Kluger, Christopher Redman, and David Van Biema, "A Death in Paris: The Passing of Diana," *Time,* September 8, 1997; "Diana, Investigation of the Investigation," *Le Point,* September 13, 1997; Richard Kay and Geoffrey Levy, "Let the Flag Fly at Half-Mast," *Daily Mail,* September 4, 1997; Alan Hamilton, Andrew Pierce, and Philip Webster, "Royal Family Is 'Deeply Touched' by Public Support," *The Times,* September 4, 1997; Robert Hardman, "Princes' Last Minutes with Mother," *Daily Telegraph,* September 3, 1997; Thomas Sancton and Scott MacLeod, *Death of a Princess: The Investigation* (New York: St. Martin's Press, 1998); Marianne Macdonald, "A Rift Death Can't Heal," *The Observer* (London), September 14, 1997; "His Name Is Prince William of Wales," *The Times,* June 29, 1982; "Rejoice! A Prince Is Born," *Time,* July 5, 1982; Rita Dallas, "The Royal Christening," *Washington Post,* August 5, 1982; "They'll Never Call Him Bill," UPI, August 15, 1982.

Chapters 3 and 4

For these chapters, the author drew on conversations with Lady Elsa Bowker, Richard Greene, Penny Walker, Peter Archer, Delissa Needham, Fred Hauptfuhrer, Charles Furneaux, Alan Hamilton, Evelyn Phillips, Brad Darrach, Richard Kay, Hazel Southam, Janet Lizop, Janet Jenkins, and Mary Robertson.

Among the published sources consulted: Sue Ryan, "Here's Harry!," *Mail on Sunday,* October 14, 1984; Tony Frost, "Hello Bright Eyes," *Sunday Mirror,* October 14, 1984; David Ward, "Prince's Pride in His Sons," *The Guardian,* September 20, 1997; Wendy Berry, *The Housekeeper's Diary* (New York: Barricade Books, Inc., 1995); Jo Thomas, "The Early Education of a Future King," *New York Times,* April 13, 1986; Graham Jones and Jenny Shields, "Champagne Flows and Charles Hits a Polo Hat Trick," *Daily Telegraph,* September 17, 1984; "The Boy Who Would Be King," *People,* June 26, 1989; Nicholas Davies, *William: The Inside Story of the Man Who Will Be King* (New York: St. Martin's Press, 1998); Stephen P. Barry, *Royal Service: My Twelve Years as Valet to Prince Charles* (New York: Macmillan, 1983); "Di's Son Injured," Associated Press, June 4, 1991; Paul Harris, "Christmas Sadness," *Daily Mail,* December 24, 1992; James Hewitt, *Love and War* (London: Blake Publishing Ltd., 1999); Sarah Bradford, *Elizabeth,* (London: William Heinmann, 1996); Sally Bedell Smith, *Diana in Search of Herself* (New York: Signet, 2000); Oliver

Morgan and Alexander Hitchen, "Diana's Chilly Royal Christmas," *Sunday Express,* November 28, 1993.

Chapters 5 to 8

Information for these chapters was based in part on conversations with Richard Greene, Peter Archer, Peter Allen, Lady Elsa Bowker, Alan Hamilton, Richard Kay, Grigori Rassinier, Elizabeth d'Erlanger, Janet Jenkins, Penny Russell-Smith, Janet Lizop, Rachel Whitburn, Gared Mankowitz, Tom Corby, Natalie Symonds.

Published sources included Jane Harbidge, " 'Ultimate Betrayal' for Wills and Harry," *Evening Standard,* October 17, 1994; Gillian Harris, "Young Princes Shielded from the Public Glare," *The Times,* September 1, 1998; "Princes William and Harry: How They're Coping," *People,* December 1, 1997; Martha Duffy, "Can This Boy Save the Monarchy?" *Time,* July 22, 1996; Mike Jarvis and Dennis Rice, "Kidnapper Caught at Eton," *News of the World,* October 25, 1998; "Boys to Men," *Daily News,* December 21, 1997; David Leppard and Christopher Morgan, "Police Fears Over William's Friends," *Sunday Times,* February 27, 2000; Adam Sherwin, "Anti-Hunting Car Bombers Threaten Prince," *The Times,* October 23, 2000; Mark Fox, "Princes in Security Alert," *Sunday Express,* July 18, 1999; "Wills Threat Web Site Is Shut Down,"

Daily Express, October 16, 2000; Barbara Kantrowitz, "William: The Making of a Modern King," *Newsweek,* June 26, 2000; Tina Brown, "A Woman in Earnest," *The New Yorker,* September 15, 1997; Clive Goodman, "Diana and Dodi: The Untold Love Story," *News of the World,* December 7, 1997; "Diana, Princess of Wales 1961–1997," *The Week,* September 6, 1997; P. D. Jephson, *Shadows of a Princess* (New York: Harper-Collins, 2000); Anthony Holden, "Why Royals Must Express Remorse," *The Express,* September 3, 1997; Jerome Dupuis, "Diana: The Unpublished Report of Witnesses at the Ritz," *L'Express,* March 12, 1998; "The Two Vital Questions," *The People,* November 9, 1997; "It Was No Accident," *The Mirror,* February 12, 1998; Polly Toynbee, "Forever at Peace," *Radio Times,* September 13–19, 1997; Rosa Monckton, "Time to End False Rumors," *Newsweek,* March 2, 1998; Robert Lacey, *Majesty* (New York: Harcourt Brace Jovanovich, 1977); Richenda Miers, *Scotland's Highlands & Islands* (London: Cadogan Books, 1994); Henry Porter, "Her Last Summer," *Vanity Fair,* October 1997; Tess Rock and Natalie Symonds, "Our Diana Diaries," *Sunday Mirror,* November 16, 1997; Kate Snell, *Diana: Her Last Love* (London: Granada Media, 2000); "Diana: The Man She Really Loved," *Point de Vue, Images du Monde,* November 5–11, 1997; Rosa Monckton, "My Friend Diana," *The Guardian,* September 8, 1997; Richard Kay and Geoffrey Levy, "A Son to Be Proud Of," *Daily Mail*, May 23, 1998; Robert Jobson and Greg Swift, "Look After William and Harry," *Daily Express*, December 22, 1997; Warren Hoge, "William, a Shy Conqueror, Pursued by Groupies," *New York Times*, June 22, 1998; Daniel Waddell, "Diana's Mother Speaks of Her Concern Over Young Princes," *Daily Telegraph*, July 16, 1998; Charles Rae, "Wills and Harry Do Full Monty," *Sun*, August 1, 1998; Judy Wade, "Marking a Milestone in Charles's and Camilla's Relationship," *Hello!*, August 15, 1998; Christopher Morgan and David Leppard, "Party Girl in William's Circle Snorted Cocaine," *Sunday Times*, February 26, 2000; Richard Kay, "Wilful Will," *Daily Mail*, December 23, 1999; Robert Hardman, "Just (Call Me) William," *Daily Telegraph*, June 9, 2000; Alex O'Connell, "Prince Chases Adventure in Remotest Chile," September 30, 2000; Michelle Tauber, "Speaking His Mind," *People*, October 16, 2000; Gordon Rayner, "Harry's Rare Day in the Limelight," *Daily Mail*, March 20, 2000; Andrew Pierce and Simon de Bruxelles, "Our Mother Was Betrayed," *The Times*, September 30, 2000.

Bibliography

Allison, Ronald, and Sarah Riddell, eds., *The Royal Encyclopedia*. London: Macmillan, 1991.

Barry, Stephen P. *Royal Service: My Twelve Years as Valet to Prince Charles*. New York: Macmillan, 1983.

Berry, Wendy. *The Housekeeper's Diary*. New York: Barricade Books Inc., 1995.

Boca, Geoffrey. *Elizabeth and Philip*. New York: Henry Holt and Company, 1953.

Brander, Michael. *The Making of the Highlands*. London: Constable and Company Ltd., 1980.

Bryan, J., III, and Charles J. V. Murphy. *The Windsor Story*. New York: William Morrow, 1979.

Campbell, Lady Colin. *Diana in Private*. London: Smith Gryphon, 1993.

Cannadine, David. *The Decline and Fall of the British Aristocracy*. New Haven: Yale University Press, 1990.

Cannon, John, and Ralph Griffiths. *The Oxford Illustrated History of the British Monarchy*. Oxford and New York: Oxford University Press, 1992.

Cathcart, Helen. *The Queen Herself*. London: W. H. Allen, 1983.

———. *The Queen and Prince Philip: Forty*

Years of Happiness. London: Hodder and Stoughton, 1987.

Clarke, Mary. *Diana Once Upon a Time*. London: Sidgwick & Jackson, 1994.

Davies, Nicholas. *Diana: The Lonely Princess*. New York: Birch Lane, 1996.

———. *Queen Elizabeth II*. New York: Carol Publishing Group, 1996.

———. *William: The Inside Story of the Man Who Will Be King*. New York: St. Martin's Press, 1998.

Delderfield, Eric R. *Kings and Queens of England and Great Britain*. London: David & Charles, 1990.

Delorm, Rene. *Diana and Dodi: A Love Story*. Los Angeles: Tallfellow Press, 1998.

Dempster, Nigel, and Peter Evans. *Behind Palace Doors*. New York: Putnam, 1993.

Dimbleby, Jonathan. *The Prince of Wales: A Biography*. New York: William Morrow, 1994.

Edwards, Anne. *Diana and the Rise of the House of Spencer*. London: Hodder and Stoughton, 1999.

Ferguson, Ronald. *The Galloping Major: My Life and Singular Times*. London: Macmillan, 1994.

Fisher, Graham, and Heather Fisher. *Elizabeth: Queen & Mother*. New York: Hawthorn Books, 1964.

Foreman, J. B., ed. *Scotland's Splendour*. Glasgow: William Collins Sons & Co. Ltd., 1961.

Fox, Mary Virginia. *Princess Diana*. Hillside, N.J.: Enslow, 1986.

Graham, Caroline. *Camilla—The King's Mistress*. London: Blake, 1994.

Graham, Tim. *Diana: HRH the Princess of Wales*. New York: Summit, 1988.

———. *The Royal Year 1993*. London: Michael O'Mara, 1993.

Gregory, Martyn. *The Diana Conspiracy Exposed*. London: Virgin Publishing, 1999.

Hewitt, James. *Love and War*. London: Blake Publishing Ltd., 1999.

Hoey, Brian. *All the King's Men*. London: HarperCollins, 1992.

Holden, Anthony. *Charles*. London: Weidenfeld and Nicolson, 1988.

———. *The Tarnished Crown*. New York: Random House, 1993.

Hough, Richard. *Born Royal: The Lives and Loves of the Young Windsors*. New York: Bantam, 1988.

Hutchins, Chris, and Peter Thompson. *Sarah's Story: The Duchess Who Defied the Royal House of Windsor*. London: Smith Gryphon, 1992.

Jephson, P. D. *Shadows of a Princess*. New York: HarperCollins Publishers, 2000.

Junor, Penny. *Charles*. New York: St. Martin's Press, 1987.

Lacey, Robert. *Majesty*. New York: Harcourt Brace Jovanovich, 1977.

———. *Queen Mother*. Boston: Little, Brown, 1986.

Lathan, Caroline, and Jeannie Sakol. *The Royals*. New York: Congdon & Weed, 1987.

Maclean, Veronica. *Crowned Heads*. London: Hodder and Stoughton, 1993.

Martin, Ralph G. *Charles & Diana*. New York: Putnam, 1985.

Montgomery-Massingberd, Hugh. *Burke's Guide to the British Monarchy*. London: Burke's Peerage, 1977.

Morton, Andrew. *Diana: Her True Story*. New York: Simon & Schuster, 1997.

———. *Inside Buckingham Palace*. London: Michael O'Mara Books Ltd., 1991.

Pasternak, Anna. *Princess in Love*. London: Bloomsbury, 1994.

Pimlott, Ben. *The Queen: A Biography of Elizabeth II*. New York: John Wiley & Sons, Inc., 1996.

Sancton, Thomas, and Scott Macleod. *Death of a Princess: The Investigation*. New York: St. Martin's Press, 1998.

Sarah, the Duchess of York, with Jeff Coplon. *My Story*. New York: Simon & Schuster, 1996.

Simmons, Simone, with Susan Hill. *Diana: The Secret Years*. London: Michael O'Mara Books Ltd., 1998.

Smith, Sally Bedell. *Diana in Search of Herself*. New York: Times Books, 1999.

Snell, Kate. *Diana: Her Last Love*. London: Granada Media, 2000.

Spencer, Charles. *The Spencers: A Personal*

History of an English Family. New York: St. Martin's Press, 2000.

Spoto, Donald. *Diana: The Last Year*. New York: Harmony Books, 1997.

————. *The Decline and Fall of the House of Windsor*. New York: Simon & Schuster, 1995.

Thornton, Michael. *Royal Feud*. London: Michael Joseph, 1985.

Whitaker, James. *Diana v. Charles*. London: Signet, 1993.